Marching Across the Color Line

CRITICAL HISTORICAL ENCOUNTERS

Series Editors
James Kirby Martin
David M. Oshinsky
Randy W. Roberts

Marching Across the Color Line

....

A. Philip Randolph and Civil Rights in the World War II Era

DAVID WELKY

University of Central Arkansas

New York   Oxford

OXFORD UNIVERSITY PRESS

Oxford University Press is a department of the University of Oxford.
It furthers the University's objective of excellence in research,
scholarship, and education by publishing worldwide.

Oxford New York
Auckland   Cape Town   Dar es Salaam   Hong Kong   Karachi
Kuala Lumpur   Madrid   Melbourne   Mexico City   Nairobi
New Delhi   Shanghai   Taipei   Toronto

With offices in
Argentina   Austria   Brazil   Chile   Czech Republic   France   Greece
Guatemala   Hungary   Italy   Japan Poland   Portugal   Singapore
South Korea   Switzerland   Thailand   Turkey   Ukraine   Vietnam

For titles covered by Section 112 of the US Higher Education
Opportunity Act, please visit www.oup.com/us/he for the latest
information about pricing and alternate formats.

Published by Oxford University Press
198 Madison Avenue, New York, New York 10016
http://www.oup.com

Library of Congress Cataloging-in-Publication Data
Welky, David.
   Marching across the color line : A. Philip Randolph and Civil Rights in the World War II
era / by David Welky.
      pages cm
   Includes bibliographical references.
   ISBN 978-0-19-999830-2 (acid-free paper) 1. Randolph, A. Philip (Asa Philip), 1889-
1979. 2. Randolph, A. Philip (Asa Philip), 1889-1979—Political and social views. 3. African
Americans—Biography. 4. African American political activists—Biography. 5. African
American civil rights workers—Biography. 6. African Americans—Civil rights—History—
20th century. 7. Civil rights movements—United States—History—20th century. 8. Labor
leaders—United States—Biography. 9. Brotherhood of Sleeping Car Porters—History.
10. United States—Race relations—History—20th century. I. Title.
   E185.97.R27W45   2013
   323.092—dc23
   [B]
                                                                              2013005062

Printing number: 9 8 7 6 5 4 3 2 1

Printed in the United States of America
on acid-free paper

To RR:
Teacher, mentor, friend

Freedom is never granted; it is won. Justice is never given; it is exacted.

—*A. Philip Randolph*

CONTENTS

....

EDITORS' FOREWORD

....

The volumes in this Oxford University Press book series focus on major critical encounters in the American experience. The word *critical* refers to formative, vital, transforming events and actions that have had a major impact in shaping the ever-changing contours of life in the United States. *Encounter* indicates a confrontation or clash, often but not always contentious in character, but always full of profound historical meaning and consequence.

In this framework, the United States, it can be said, has evolved on contested ground. Conflict and debate, the clash of peoples and ideas, have marked and shaped American history. The first Europeans transported with them cultural assumptions that collided with Native American values and ideas. Africans forced into bondage and carried to America added another set of cultural beliefs that often were at odds with those of Native Americans and Europeans. Over the centuries America's diverse peoples differed on many issues, often resulting in formative conflict that in turn gave form and meaning to the American experience.

The Critical Historical Encounters series emphasizes formative episodes in America's contested history. Each volume contains two fundamental ingredients: a carefully written narrative of the encounter and the consequences, both immediate and long term, of that moment of conflict in America's contested history.

In *Marching Across the Color Line: A. Philip Randolph and Civil Rights in the World War II Era,* David Welky demonstrates that occasionally simply the threat of an action is enough to prompt sudden and meaningful changes. A. Philip Randolph dressed like a banker, spoke like a technocrat, and acted like a labor organizer. Equal parts Marxist intellectual, union leader, and African American crusader for equal rights, he was a born earth shaker, the sort of man who knew that the promise of America was brighter than its reality. With World War II on the horizon, and defense work tugging the nation out of a decade of depression, Randolph demanded a share of the jobs for black Americans. When polite meetings went nowhere, he called for immediate, direct action. Organizing the March on Washington Movement, he called for a bold protest against an administration that refused to push for true democracy and a national majority that declined to care about genuine democracy. Randolph's movement threatened to challenge America's belief in democracy at a time when democracy had never seemed more important.

On an even more fundamental level, Randolph's life during the wartime era exemplifies the dilemma of the "color line" for black Americans. How, in a country torn by racism, could African Americans be both black and American? How could they believe in democracy and equality of opportunity while living in a land that endorsed the notion of "separate but equal" and tolerated the reality of separate and grossly unequal? How could they join a war against racism abroad and ignore racism at home? Through the wartime struggles of A. Philip Randolph, Welky explores these contradictions, underscoring the power of a single person, as well as a people, to force change.

James Kirby Martin
David M. Oshinsky
Randy W. Roberts

PREFACE

A. Philip Randolph stood alone in the shadow of the Lincoln Memorial, tall and erect, immaculate in a dark suit with a white shirt and a perfectly folded pocket square. A round button pinned to his lapel read "March on Washington for Jobs and Freedom." August 28, 1963, had been one of the best days of Randolph's long life. Many opponents of the civil rights movement had predicted disaster. Florida congressman James Haley said the interracial march "could be the spark which would touch off an ugly, blood-letting riot, accompanied perhaps by killings." Washington, DC officials took these warnings seriously, bulking up the city's police presence and banning liquor sales for the first time since Prohibition. Their precautions proved unnecessary. A quarter-million Americans of all races and creeds laughed, cheered, and sang together on the National Mall without a hint of violence. Celebrities such as Marlon Brando, Paul Newman, and Jackie Robinson mingled with laborers, businessmen, ministers, and housewives. Together they turned the park into a lawn party with guests from around the United States. Enjoying temperatures in the low eighties, marchers dipped their feet in the reflecting pool and casually leaned against trees for shade. Rural Mississippians gathered with Harlemites to discuss the car rides, bus trips, hitchhiking adventures, and long walks they had undertaken to reach the capital. Their glorious day in the capital would become the high-water mark of the civil rights movement.[1]

Randolph, weary from his seventy-four years, had also endured a long road to Washington. He had spent innumerable hours over the past months brokering alliances between various civil rights groups associated with the march. He publicized the event in countless interviews, urging Americans of all backgrounds to crusade for "full economic equality" and "full civil rights." He pestered Congress to create a federal fair employment board to ensure that everyone had equal access to jobs. The septuagenarian was also upholding his duties as president of the Brotherhood of Sleeping Car Porters, a railroad union he had headed since the 1920s; serving as a vice president in the powerful AFL-CIO labor union; and leading the Negro American Labor Council. And he met these crushing obligations while mourning the passing of Lucille, his wife of fifty years, who had died in April. He was exhausted.[2]

Randolph's trickiest job might have been convincing the March on Washington's other headliners to stow their egos for the common good. The civil rights movement's titans, including Randolph deputy Bayard Rustin, the Reverend Fred Shuttlesworth, the NAACP's Roy Wilkins, and the Reverend Martin Luther King, Jr., had momentarily united for the cause. Randolph, the only man they all trusted and respected, soothed bruised feelings and kept the march alive through months of thorny negotiations. It was Randolph who stiffened backbones when President John F. Kennedy discouraged them from marching. "There *will* be a march," he informed the young president in his precise, commanding bass. Randolph had the kind of voice one would expect from a Greek god, a rumble so booming it seemed to emanate from the very bowels of the earth. The White House could not intimidate him. After all, Randolph had met with four previous presidents. JFK was still in short pants when Randolph stood in President Calvin Coolidge's office. Reverend King hadn't even been born yet.[3]

None of that mattered today. A huge grin played across Randolph's face as he joined hands with Roy Wilkins and United Auto Workers president Walter Reuther for the stroll to the Lincoln Memorial. But after mounting the marble steps, the assembled luminaries began bickering about the speaking order and the contents of each others' speeches. They retired to a guard station beneath Lincoln's chair to argue in private. Wilkins nearly punched John Lewis, an Alabama-born member of the Student Non-Violent Coordinating Committee and a future member of Congress, because Lewis's prepared text bristled with provocative references to "the masses" and "revolution." Bayard Rustin improvised out front while Randolph pleaded for calm. "I waited my entire life for this opportunity," Randolph said. "Please don't ruin it." He was fine with Lewis's incendiary words. Nevertheless, King and others fiddled with the speech while the crowd outside stewed.[4]

Randolph finally emerged to give his opening remarks. As was his tendency, he wielded hammer-like declaratives rather than soaring rhetoric. "We are not a pressure group," he told the audience. "We are not an organization or a group of organizations. We are not a mob. We are the advance guard of a massive moral revolution for jobs and freedom." Repeating arguments he had made for decades, Randolph presented economic, social, and political equality as inseparable. It was, after all, a march for jobs *and* freedom—African Americans couldn't have one without the other. He chided doubters who said mass actions like today's would spawn race riots. "Those who deplore our militancy, who exhort patience in the name of a false peace, are in fact supporting segregation and exploitation," he retorted. "They would have social peace at the expense of social and racial justice."[5]

Reverend King mounted the podium soon after to deliver a half-scripted, half-improvised sermon quickly recognized as one of the most stunning orations in American history. "I have a dream," he declared as he scanned the massive crowd, "that my four little children will one day live in a nation where they will be judged not by the color of their skin but by the content of their character." Enthusiasm swelled as he commanded Americans to let freedom ring "from the prodigious hilltops of New Hampshire ... the mighty mountains of New York ... the heightening Alleghenies of Pennsylvania ... the snow-capped Rockies of Colorado ... the curvaceous slopes of California ... Stone Mountain of Georgia ... Lookout Mountain of Tennessee ... every hill and molehill of Mississippi."[6]

Most people today imagine that King was the only speaker on that magical August day. His stirring words indeed enshrined the 1963 March on Washington as the civil rights movement's signature moment, the one episode from that long, tumultuous saga familiar to every schoolchild. Equally significant, however, is what we forget, or perhaps choose not to remember. Few recall Randolph introducing King as "the moral leader of our nation," a title Randolph himself bore a generation earlier. Nor do they know that the 1963 march rested on intellectual foundations constructed largely by Randolph. Every orator who demanded equal access to employment, housing, and economic opportunity on that warm summer afternoon parroted arguments he crafted twenty years earlier. Just like Randolph had in the 1940s, speakers demanded a federal fair employment practices committee and condemned the hypocrisy of fighting tyranny abroad, in the form of Soviet communism, while tolerating discrimination at home. King himself assailed economic inequality, observing in a little-remembered passage that "the Negro lives on a lonely island of poverty in the midst of a vast ocean of material prosperity." The civil rights movement's sit ins and street demonstrations echoed Randolph's controversial use of civil disobedience during World War II. "A. Philip Randolph, more so than any other man, has earned the right to be called the Father of the Civil Rights Movement," Bayard Rustin wrote in 1972.[7]

The sun was sliding behind the Lincoln Memorial as the last ripples of applause died down. Energized marchers left the Mall to board buses or to find their way to the train station. Randolph hung back,

A. Philip Randolph at the 1963 March on Washington, the crowning event of his long career as a civil rights activist. © *Bettmann/CORBIS*

delaying his descent to the car waiting to whisk him to a White House meeting with President Kennedy. Although too modest to claim the event as a personal victory, the man associates dubbed "the Chief" wanted to savor what he saw as the culmination of his life's work. Rustin spotted Randolph standing alone, his back to the crowd, staring at the Lincoln Memorial. As Rustin approached he saw tears streaming down Randolph's cheeks, a rare show of emotion from a stoic man. Rustin put his arm around his shoulders. "Mr. Randolph, it looks like your dream has come true," he said.[8]

Even though Randolph's ideas resounded throughout the 1963 March on Washington, modern Americans think the day reflected Martin Luther King's dream, not A. Philip Randolph's. In fact, few Americans think of Randolph at all. Yet there was a time, not so long ago in the grand scheme of things, when Randolph was one of the country's most famous people and its best known agitator for black rights. "Who the hell appointed you as guardian of all the Negroes in America?" labor leader George Meany shouted after one of Randolph's blistering attacks on discrimination.[9]

Randolph assumed many roles during his life: eager student, sidewalk socialist, soapbox preacher, radical agitator, magazine editor, prolific author, union leader, grassroots organizer, professional provocateur. More accurately, he was all these things at the same time, pursuing multiple paths toward a single destination. His great ambition was make American democracy real for all citizens, regardless of race, creed, or economic status. He fought relentlessly for fair treatment and equal opportunity. His refusal to compromise compelled him to confront presidents, generals, white racists, apathetic African Americans, and even other civil rights leaders. Randolph's outstanding traits—tenacity, honesty, stubbornness, bluntness, expansiveness—made him a polarizing figure. Some loved him, others hated him, and still others grudgingly respected him even if they despised his ideas or his methods.

Contradictions defined the man. Randolph was hardheaded and idealistic, capable of dispassionate analysis and visionary flights of fancy. He could be irritating, inspiring, aloof, and warmhearted. His arguments aroused both hope and fear. Although eager for the limelight, he closely guarded his personal life. His voluminous papers include reams of material from the dozens of boards, councils, and campaigns he worked for, but contain hardly a word about his wife, who he either doted on or ignored, depending on which biographer one reads. One researcher calls Randolph a religious man, another calls him an atheist. In sum, he was a puzzling, enigmatic figure who for many years occupied a marginal position in histories of the civil rights movement. "It's so sad," NAACP director Benjamin Hooks said when Randolph died in 1979, "because there are so many young people today for whom that name means very little."[10]

Popular memories of the crusade for equal rights center on its so-called classical era, defined as the decade stretching from the Supreme Court's 1954 *Brown v. Board of Education* decision, which declared segregation in public schools unconstitutional, and the twin legislative victories of the 1964 Civil Rights Act and 1965 Voting Rights Act. This interpretation ennobles the powerful white judges and politicians who, with prodding from King and other (rarely mentioned) black activists, moved America toward integration.

Randolph fits poorly into this conceptual framework. He simply doesn't match our picture of a civil rights leader. He was a proud socialist, a political affiliation most Americans reject, and one that opened him to spurious charges of disloyalty throughout his career. His decades as a labor organizer conjure images of sweaty men smoking cheap stogies in union halls, not of mighty moral leaders. His precise diction rarely attained oratorical heights. It featured neither ministerial cadences, like King's, nor streetwise patter, like Malcolm X's. He floated from cause to cause, forming and dissolving issue-oriented pressure groups at a head-spinning pace. His sole long-term attachment, the Brotherhood of Sleeping Car Porters, disbanded decades ago. Few modern Americans have ever been in a sleeping car, or even know what one is.

And yet, as was so often the case when he was alive, the world is coming to Randolph. Updated interpretations of African American history, and of the civil rights movement, are calling Randolph in from the fringes. Historians often speak of a "long civil rights movement" extending from the late 1930s to the 1970s. These scholars treat racism and racial injustice as national rather than Southern phenomena and argue that African Americans understood equality in economic as well as racial terms. "Freedom" demanded not just the death of

Jim Crow, but also an end to the systemic economic exploitation that trapped both blacks and working-class whites in a kind of second-class citizenship.[11]

Randolph was among the first to weave race, class, and justice into a seamless message. In doing so, he helped establish the vocabulary, methods, and goals of the long civil rights movement while developing lines of attack the next generation of leaders exploited to win equality, at least at a legislative level. Randolph's close associate E. D. Nixon recruited King to lead the 1955 Montgomery Bus Boycott that initiated the mass-protest era of the classical civil rights movement. Randolph's disciples also played crucial roles in the 1963 March on Washington and innumerable other demonstrations. King's emphasis on nonviolent resistance borrowed from Randolph's earlier struggles for economic and political justice. Malcolm X and other "black power" advocates updated Randolph's calls for economic self-sufficiency and, sometimes unwittingly, emulated the all-black activist groups he founded in the 1940s.

This book furthers our understanding of the long civil rights movement. It is not a full biography of Randolph. It is not a comprehensive history of the United States during World War II, or even of African Americans in those years. Instead, it uses A. Philip Randolph as a vehicle to discuss the major political, social, military, and economic factors impacting the drive for equal rights during the World War II era. It would be absurd to assign Randolph sole credit for liberalizing America's racial policies, but he makes an obvious center for this study. He played pivotal roles in the two critical moments that bookend this volume: President Franklin Roosevelt's 1940 executive order abolishing discrimination in the defense industry and President Harry Truman's 1948 order desegregating the military. Further, his almost ubiquitous involvement in the key civil rights topics of that moment—segregation, discrimination, economic opportunity, the distribution of political power—make him an ideal touchstone in what could otherwise be a sprawling tale.

Although the struggle for equality began the moment African slaves arrived in the New World, momentum for the civil rights movement really took off with the start of World War II. Popular understandings of the conflict revolve around simplistic notions of a Greatest

Generation winning the last Good War. There is some truth to this. The Americans who endured the Great Depression of the 1930s and reached adulthood amidst the bloodiest fight in human history made enormous sacrifices for their country, and for humanity as a whole. The present would be much bleaker had Hitler conquered Europe and Japanese militarism subjugated Asia.

But the Good War was much messier than we prefer to remember. Wartime pressures opened cracks in the United States' social foundation. Segregation, discrimination, and race riots shook the country even as movies, posters, and radio programs depicted a harmonious nation focused on winning the war. Randolph exposed the hypocrisy behind this propaganda, asking time and again how Americans could claim unity when the nation's minorities lived as second-class citizens. He prodded his countrymen to fight for true democracy at home as well as overseas, urging them to redress America's unequal portioning of freedom, jobs, equality, and justice. In doing so, Randolph came to embody one side of a larger clash between those who placed victory above all other concerns and those who saw the war as a once in a lifetime chance to dismantle racial inequities. Randolph insisted that Americans could not win liberty abroad if they accepted discrimination at home.

Most white Americans experienced World War II secondhand, as a distant conflict lived through newsreels, Hollywood films, and letters from loved ones. African Americans, in contrast, saw a firsthand, domestic component to the war. For them, victory meant defeating both foreign enemies and domestic inequality.

Randolph was a general in this fight for racial justice. He sensed that the war would forever change American business and industry. If racism shut blacks out of the transition to a new, high-tech economy, their lack of job skills might retard economic and social progress for decades to come. Randolph announced his presence on the battlefield in early 1941, eleven months before Pearl Harbor, when he threatened to march 100,000 African Americans to the Lincoln Memorial unless President Franklin Roosevelt guaranteed blacks a fair shot at jobs in the burgeoning, and almost exclusively white, defense industry. He fashioned a grassroots organization, the March on Washington Committee, later known as the March on Washington Movement, to back up his threat. A tense standoff ended when FDR signed a landmark executive order forbidding discrimination in defense plants. Roosevelt created a new federal agency, the President's Committee on Fair Employment Practices, to enforce the mandate. With a stroke of the pen, Roosevelt opened opportunities for economic advancement to millions of nonwhites.

The 1941 showdown made Randolph a hero among African Americans and initiated a period of intense civil rights activity. Randolph became a persistent thorn in the side of anyone hoping to ignore or perpetuate racial divisions. He denounced the nefarious poll tax, a tool Southern states used to curtail African Americans' voting rights. He decried lynching. He demanded the integration of the armed forces. He organized dozens of protests for equality. More generally, he asked Americans to acknowledge the essential dignity and value of every human being. His actions fostered a spirit of self-worth among blacks while convincing some whites to accept minorities as true Americans. Although his message of racial advancement frightened many, it meshed well with the larger thrust of a war against totalitarian brutality, the Nazis' ghastly treatment of minorities, and the notion that might, in the form of the largest armies and most powerful weapons, made right.

Wartime agitation, combined with political, economic, and military needs, produced significant gains for African Americans. The postwar desire for normalcy imperiled this progress. Peacetime therefore opened a new front in Randolph's war for equality. Another fight for democracy, a cold war pitting the United States against Soviet-style communism, provided the backdrop for renewed efforts to guarantee first-class citizenship for all Americans. Randolph undertook a long and ultimately futile campaign to save the fair employment commission, which he saw as the best way to ensure that blacks had a fair shot at decent jobs. At the same time he launched a controversial program of massive, nonviolent demonstrations intended to push the federal government to integrate the armed forces. His actions contributed to President Truman's landmark 1948 order to desegregate the military, a move that helped resolve a key issue lingering from the wartime civil rights movement.

Randolph's shadow still looms over America. His impact resonates every time an African American applies for a job or serves in uniform. It affects every interracial couple out on a date and every black family moving into what was once a "white" neighborhood. If such things appear too common to merit much thought, we should remember that a few decades ago many Americans thought these notions imperiled the social bedrock. Not just African Americans benefit from Randolph's legacy. Every white person who enjoys a relationship with a black friend, or coworker, or neighbor, or lover, or comrade-in-arms, or who joins a union, or gets a fair chance at a job despite being part of an ethnic or religious minority, owes something to a figure once deemed the most dangerous black man in America.

For all that, in many ways Randolph's dream still eludes us. We often imagine "civil rights" in terms of racial integration, equal access to the ballot box, and color blindness, or the idea that race does not matter. Randolph viewed civil rights from a very different perspective. To him, the phrase implied economic as well as political and social reform. Randolph certainly opposed segregation and wanted to guarantee all citizens' right to vote. Achieving real democracy, however, could not happen until the United States revolutionized its economic system. He believed that powerful interests—politicians, plantation owners, big businessmen— kept the working class divided and weak by encouraging poor whites to demonize African Americans. Race and class were therefore intertwined. Working-class whites and blacks needed to recognize their common plight and, operating through interracial labor unions, fight for better wages, better treatment, and better futures. Only then, when the voices of employees rang as loud as the voices of employers, could the United States truly call itself a democracy. This, in turn, required an activist federal government committed to economic planning, job training programs, protecting the right to organize, and ensuring equal access to jobs. African Americans would fall farther behind whites unless all these factors clicked into place. They could not have pride unless they had jobs, and they could never win equality without first having self-respect.

In contrast to today's emphasis on creating a postracial society, where one's race is irrelevant, race mattered to Randolph. In the 1940s, a time when many light-skinned African Americans considered themselves superior to their darker neighbors, and when African Americans spent lavishly on hair-straightening and skin-lightening products, Randolph spoke in blunt terms of a "black" struggle for freedom. Respectable African Americans shied away from "black," instead preferring the word "Negro," which they believed conveyed more dignity.

Randolph's use of "black" forced them to acknowledge that skin color made a difference. It challenged them to turn their most defining characteristic, one that had been used against them for centuries, into a source of pride.

Randolph serves as a useful filter through which to view America's struggle for equality between 1940 and 1948 because he either introduced, popularized, or employed ideas that resonated throughout the long civil rights movement. Through him, we see the stirrings of a revolution destined to reshape the world. From his perspective, it remains an incomplete revolution, with dreams yet unrealized and goals beyond our grasp, confined to some far-off place where the better angels of our nature hold sway.

ACKNOWLEDGMENTS

I accumulated numerous debts while writing this book, none of which can ever be adequately repaid. The good people at Oxford did a marvelous job throughout the research, writing, and editing process. Many thanks to Brian Wheel for his input, and to Christian Holdener, Theresa Horton, and Karen Omer for their hard work. I am also indebted to the outstanding staffs at the Franklin D. Roosevelt Presidential Library, the Harry S. Truman Presidential Library, and the Chicago Historical Society. The interlibrary loan department at the University of Central Arkansas's Torreyson Library did their usual outstanding job.

Aram Goudsouzian, Matt Harper, Story Matkin-Rawn, and Randy Roberts, all extraordinarily talented scholars, read and critiqued earlier drafts of this book, as did Johnson A. Adefila, Tonia M. Compton, Ingrid Dineen-Wimberly, Nishani Frazier, Claudrena Harold, Mary Linehan, Marko Maunula, Thomas J. Noer, Tobin Miller Shearer, and John G. Turner. I appreciate all their suggestions. Thanks also to Jack Pointer for putting me up, and for putting up with me, in Chicago.

Most important, I want to thank my wonderful wife Ali, who listened patiently whenever I babbled on about A. Philip Randolph, and our two children, Jude and Kate, who tolerated daddy's absences and, at times, feigned an interest in the book he was writing.

CHAPTER 1

....

The Hour and the Man

A. Philip Randolph was a well-known figure in black America by 1940. For him, strolling down the streets of Harlem, or of Chicago's Black Belt, was like walking through a room full of friends. Tall, barrel chested, and elegantly dressed, he cut a distinctive figure on the bustling sidewalks. Well-wishers stopped to shake his hand, offer words of support, solicit advice, or share their woes. He represented black integrity, black success, and black militancy.

Yet who A. Philip Randolph was depended on where A. Philip Randolph was. Tailored suits and cultured speech counted for little whenever his work carried him to Manhattan, Chicago's Loop, or other predominantly white areas. In those places he was just another Negro, another colored man. Few whites had ever heard his name. "I am an invisible man," Ralph Ellison wrote in his searing 1947 novel *Invisible Man*. "I am a man of substance, of flesh and bone, fiber and liquids—and I might even be said to possess a mind." And yet, Ellison continued, "I am invisible ... simply because people refuse to see me." Randolph experienced the same feeling whenever Northern whites looked through rather than at him, dismissing him without a second thought simply because of his skin color. Randolph faced worse when he crossed the Mason-Dixon line. In Dixie, Randolph was nothing more than a well-dressed member of an inferior race. Most Southern whites would have been horrified to learn who he was and what he stood for. Some would have advocated violence against a man who despised the racial hierarchy and segregation they saw as essential threads in their social fabric.[1]

1

"We are creatures of history," Randolph once said, "for every historical epoch has its roots in a preceding epoch." He believed African Americans' current difficulties originated in decisions made decades or even centuries earlier. Similarly, their future prospects depended on what he and his contemporaries did as the United States contemplated its role in a second World War.[2]

Randolph had seen much in the fifty years preceding 1940. Like a single leaf on a mighty oak, he had played a small part in the great movements that defined African Americans in the nation's final year of peace. His story paralleled black America's. To make sense of wartime transformations, it is necessary to understand what life was like for African Americans, and to come to terms with one of the most important black leaders of the wartime era.

"Half the time I feel like I'm on the outside of the world peeping in through a knot-hole in the fence," remarked Bigger Thomas, the twenty-year-old protagonist of Richard Wright's 1940 novel *Native Son.* Thomas expressed the frustrations of millions of African Americans at a moment when the United States hovered between peace and war. Adolf Hitler's armies overran Poland several months before Wright's novel appeared. Asia had been in flames since Japan invaded China in 1937. American politicians and newspapers touted national unity for the sake of self-preservation. This call left many black Americans unmoved. For them, white America was something akin to a foreign land, a mysterious realm on the other side of the invisible lines separating white neighborhoods from black neighborhoods, white jobs from black jobs, white businesses from black businesses, and white schools from black schools. "White folks and black folks is strangers," Thomas comments. "We don't know what each other is thinking." Life as an African American meant being part of "a separate nation, stunted, stripped, and held captive *within* this nation."[3]

"Did you ever hope for anything, Bigger?" asks Boris Max, a white lawyer who befriends him. "What for?" Thomas replies. "I couldn't get it. I'm black." Being black in 1940 meant narrowing one's options. It meant recognizing that you and your family were unlikely to live the American Dream. On average, African Americans lived ten years less than whites. Black unemployment ran about twice the rate for whites. Black families earned about one third of what white families made.

Around 5 percent of black men worked in the professions, compared to one third of white men. Two thirds of employed African Americans held unskilled or service jobs, as opposed to just one fifth of employed whites. Unions, churches, social clubs, fraternal organizations, restaurants, hotels, universities, and professional sports teams all practiced racial discrimination. "I reckon we the only things in this city that can't go where we want to go and do what we want to do," Thomas concluded.[4]

Racism pervaded the country. Early twentieth-century researchers used dubious methods to "prove" blacks' inherent inferiority. William Calhoun, a North Carolinian, wrote that African Americans were "a fungus growth that the white man will totally destroy" in his 1902 book *The Caucasian and the Negro in the United States.* "Scientific racists" like Calhoun claimed the Negro race was born with "sluggish blood ... beastly sexual passions," and brains "as simple as those of the primates." High mortality rates did not reflect poor nutrition, substandard housing, and brutal working conditions, but rather an inability to adapt to the cooler climate outside of Africa. It was only a matter of time before stronger races shoved aside their darker cousins. "His innate nature, like his hair or wool and color, can never be changed by either education or man," Calhoun concluded. Much of the general public continued to accept these arguments long after advancements in biology and sociology discredited them among scientists.[5]

Popular culture reinforced these resilient racial assumptions. Although early twentieth-century hit songs such as "Coon, Coon, Coon" and "All Coons Look Alike to Me" lost favor by 1940, movies and radio shows consistently portrayed African Americans as slothful, foolish, and servile. In 1940 black leaders decried an attempted re-release of the notorious 1915 film *Birth of a Nation*, objecting to scenes where freed slaves appeared as rapists and the Ku Klux Klan heroically defended white rights. Theaters were still screening the previous year's blockbuster, *Gone With the Wind*, with its images of happy darkies and comic mammies. *Amos 'n' Andy* ruled the airwaves as radio listeners tuned in five nights a week to hear two white men adopt stereotyped black accents for a comedic tour of life in the ghetto.

Three quarters of the nation's 12 million African Americans lived in the South in 1940. Southern politics were essentially negative, focused on preserving the racial and economic status quo rather than on improving the overall quality of life. Businessmen who paid whites more than blacks to do the same job argued that blacks were inefficient workers who required fewer material comforts than whites. Employers claimed low wages actually benefited blacks because they discouraged whites from pursuing unskilled jobs, the kind of work that best suited African Americans' limited capabilities. American concepts of equality and democracy did not apply to African Americans; a 1940 Mississippi law forbade all-black schools from using textbooks containing references to voting, elections, or civic responsibilities. Poll taxes, property requirements, and other restrictions limited the black voting rate in the South to about 5 percent. Fewer than one in two hundred voting-age African Americans living in Alabama, Louisiana, Mississippi, and South Carolina participated in the 1940 election.

World War I, fought more than twenty years earlier, initiated a massive demographic shift. Defense contractors needed vast numbers of unskilled laborers. Crippling labor shortages meant that even African Americans could get hired. Hundreds of thousands of blacks walked, drove, or rode the rails out of Southern fields and servants' quarters for a better life above the Mason-Dixon line. Black newspapers offered glowing reports of life in the North. Migrants wrote letters promising their friends and families more freedom, higher wages, and better schools than they could find in the South. "I am fed up with Jim Crow laws," Langston Hughes wrote in his 1949 poem "One Way Ticket." "I pick up my life, and take it away, on a one way ticket—gone up North."

The black populations of New York City, Chicago, and Los Angeles more than doubled between 1920 and 1930. Detroit's tripled. Realtors shoved these newcomers into substandard, overpriced "black belts." No black neighborhood was more famous than Harlem, the noisy, dangerous, exciting, vibrant district on the northern end of New York City's Manhattan Island. "Harlem! Harlem," exclaimed Jake, the lead character in Claude McKay's 1928 novel *Home to Harlem*. "Where else could I have all this life but Harlem? Good old Harlem! Chocolate Harlem! Sweet Harlem." Langston Hughes remembered his arrival in similar terms. "I came out onto the [subway] platform with two heavy bags and looked around," he wrote. He stood with jaw agape as the city passed before his eyes. "Hundreds of colored people! I wanted to shake hands with them, speak to them," he exulted. "I stood there, dropped my bags, took a deep breath and felt happy again."[6]

Harlem was the center of the African American universe by 1920, a mecca stretching north from 130th to 145th Street and east from 5th to 8th Avenue. Black fraternal groups such as the Odd Fellows, the Elks, and the Pythians had outposts there, as did most black churches, both established and transitory. Reverend Adam Clayton Powell, Sr., ministered to 10,000 congregants from his pulpit in the Tudor and Gothic style Abyssinian Baptist Church at 138th and 7th. On the other end of the social spectrum, the Reverend Madame V.D.S. Armistead charged a quarter to summon spirits at her Holy Star Spiritual Church, housed in the second floor of a tenement building (she promised visitors a better experience if they also bought a ten-cent bottle of Prosperity Oil). Street vendors and drugstores sold roots, herbs, and powders with alleged magical properties. Some buyers relied on High John the Conqueror, a root either worn as an amulet or incorporated into good luck potions and vitality elixirs. Others swore by Black Herman the Magician's folk remedies.

Life in 1920s Harlem occurred in public. Funeral processions and fraternal parades clogged the streets. Preachers, cranks, and political theorists—including a transplant from Florida named A. Philip Randolph—mounted soapboxes on Lenox Avenue and 7th Avenue to compete for audiences. None outshone Marcus Garvey, the Jamaican-born head of the Universal Negro Improvement Association (UNIA). Garvey, who dubbed himself the president-general of Africa, promoted black nationalism and a back-to-Africa movement. Fueled by Garvey's bewitching speeches and his fiery editorials in the weekly newspaper *Negro World*, the UNIA grew into the era's largest black activist group. Its parades became the stuff of legends. Tens of thousands of uniformed devotees filed past Harlem landmarks, accompanied by the UNIA marching band. Garvey rode in a limousine at the head of the column, resplendent in an admiral's hat and epaulets.

Harlem's reputation for loose morals drew curious whites with a taste for exotic nightlife. *Collier's* magazine called it "a garish pleasure ground ... a national synonym for naughtiness—of savage and sordid pleasure." Hollywood and Broadway stars mingled with truck drivers and shoeshine boys in Lenox Avenue's famous Savoy Ballroom, where revelers defied gravity as they performed the latest steps, or invented new ones, while Duke Ellington, Count Basie, Benny Goodman, and other ace musicians hammered out beats. Insiders knew that Pod's

and Jerry's boasted the best stride piano in town, Tillie's Chicken
Shack served the best comfort food, and the Lenox Club offered the
best floor for dancing away the wee hours of the morning. There was
also the Cotton Club, where African Americans lined up on Sunday
nights to watch celebrities arrive. Two beefy doormen kept black
people from entering the palace; whites only was the rule for the
Cotton Club, Connie's Inn, Small's Paradise, and other top entertainment venues, although blacks could work as waiters.[7]

It often seemed that Harlem was a world unto its own, discon-
nected from the metropolis around it. Living there meant learning a
new language. "Kill me" meant "I want a good time," a "lead sheet" was
a topcoat, light-skinned blacks were "high yallers," and the Savoy Ballroom was "the track." Apathetic policemen ignored Harlem's many
gambling, prostitution, and bootlegging rings. Drugstores, cigar stores,
and delicatessens served as fronts for speakeasies. Street gangs men-
aced solid citizens. Union Jacks flew from the windows of the district's
sizable West Indian enclave. American-born blacks mocked the ambitious, business-oriented Caribbean immigrants as "Black Jews."

Harlem had its refined side. Black intellectuals gathered around
town to discuss history, sociology, and economics. Painters and poets
crafted works of genius in overpriced apartments. The 135th Street
branch of the New York Public Library doubled as the cultural heart
of the Harlem Renaissance, a movement dedicated to showcasing
black achievements in art, literature, and poetry. Its meeting rooms
hosted gifted writers who debated current events and offered insights
into their craft. Celebrated black thinkers such as W. E. B. DuBois,
James Weldon Johnson, and Arthur Schomburg shared their wisdom
in public lectures there.

Langston Hughes commented that ordinary African Americans
"hadn't heard of the Negro Renaissance. And if they had, it hadn't raised
their wages any." Harlem's poverty became obvious to anyone who ventured beyond Strivers Row's tree-lined boulevards and Sugar Hill's fine
brownstones. Enormous demand for housing pushed rents to astronomical levels. Landlords subdivided buildings into microscopic units
and neglected needed repairs. "The State would not allow cows to live in
some of these apartments used by colored people," the chair of a city
housing reform committee reported. Harlem had few parks or play-
grounds despite having New York City's highest population density.

Inhabitants referred to Harlem's understaffed hospital, where patients slept on floors or benches, as "the morgue" or "the butcher shop."[8]

The Great Depression of the 1930s made a bad situation worse. Overcrowding intensified as migrants poured in from the rural South and the West Indies. Finding a job, a tricky proposition in good times, became harder. The whites who owned most area businesses inflated prices while hiring few African Americans. "It was the white man's world, entirely the white man's world," one resident complained. Most employed Harlemites had to commute to jobs downtown or in the Bronx rather than work close to home. The unemployed dodged rent collectors; stood in breadlines; and rubbed the Tree of Hope, a straggling elm outside 7th Avenue's Lafayette Theater, for good luck, at least until the city cut it down in 1934, leaving the hopeful to rub the stump instead. Nearly everyone played the numbers, trying to pick a daily three-digit combination that paid off at 600 to 1.[9]

Many Depression-era blacks found established civil rights groups such as the National Association for the Advancement of Colored People (NAACP) and the National Urban League too conservative for their tastes. They yearned for charismatic leaders who spoke directly to the marginalized masses. Although Marcus Garvey flamed out in the mid 1920s, street speakers from Garveyite spinoffs such as the Ethiopian Pacific Movement and the Moorish Science Temple drew large audiences with antiwhite harangues. In Chicago, Elijah Muhammad of the Lost-Found Nation of Islam attracted thousands of supporters with promises that black people would one day wrest control from the white devils who had enslaved them. The Communist Party, whose doctrine endorsed racial equality, organized cells in black neighborhoods. Randolph and other black socialists also gained considerable followings.

Rural blacks had their own problems. Plunging farm prices forced struggling sharecroppers deep into debt. Rural ministers and school-teachers accepted wages in food rather than cash. Deteriorating conditions hastened the ongoing exodus from agricultural regions. More than 600,000 African Americans deserted the South for Northern cities during the 1930s. Southern cities also swelled with rural immigrants seeking jobs and opportunities. Most found neither, as employers hired whites for the dirty, low-paying positions traditionally reserved for blacks. Armed mobs enforced this new order. In Atlanta, a group called the Black Shirts rallied under the standard: "No Jobs for Niggers Until Every White Man Has a Job!"[10]

Despite their Depression-fueled woes, in 1932 two thirds of black voters continued a half-century long bond with the Republicans, the party of Lincoln and emancipation, by voting for the incumbent president, Herbert Hoover. Although Hoover had done little for African Americans, his Democratic challenger, New York governor Franklin Roosevelt, showed even less interest in them. Twenty years earlier, while assistant secretary of the navy, Roosevelt had remained silent when President Woodrow Wilson segregated the fleet. During his presidential run he courted white Southerners, a vital element of the Democratic coalition, by calling himself an adopted son of Georgia—a reference to his long stays at the polio rehabilitation center in Warm Springs. In another slap at African Americans, he named a Texan, Speaker of the House John Nance Garner, as his vice-presidential candidate.

Once in office, Roosevelt's advisors urged him to steer clear of civil rights for fear of ruffling Southern Democratic feathers. "It is not the purpose of this administration to impair Southern industry by refusing to recognize traditional [wage] differentials," FDR snapped when liberals squawked about clauses in the 1933 National Industrial Recovery Act allowing employers to pay blacks less than whites. The new Agricultural Adjustment Administration issued checks to white planters while leaving sharecroppers to fend for themselves. White Southerners who administered New Deal relief programs in their region ignored Washington's nondiscrimination rules with impunity. They disproportionately denied benefits to African Americans and gave them smaller relief payments. Locals in charge of New Deal employment offices trained blacks only for menial jobs. Roosevelt, whose electoral majority rested on white Southern support, kept silent about these injustices.[11]

"The Negro worker has good reason to feel that his government has betrayed him under the New Deal," one 1935 conference of African Americans concluded. FDR had not campaigned as a friend to blacks, but his emphasis on the so-called forgotten man, and his support for Jews, Catholics, and other minorities raised black expectations of dramatic change. Roosevelt's expansion of federal power convinced many African Americans that Washington could abolish inequality if politicians mustered the will to do so.

African Americans' appeals for action sharpened as the 1936 election neared. Roosevelt knew his personal popularity had put black votes in play for the first time since Reconstruction. He signaled his friendliness through a series of symbolic gestures. For example, he invited members of the black press and a handful of African American delegates to the 1936 Democratic convention. This move, insignificant though it was, aroused considerable wrath. South Carolina senator and convention delegate Ellison "Cotton Ed" Smith fled his seat when a black minister rose to give an invocation. "By God, he's as black as melted midnight!" the senator shouted. "Get outta my way. This mongrel meeting ain't no place for a white man!"[12]

Controversial though they were, Roosevelt's token acts paid off handsomely. The president won a remarkable 76 percent of black voters in 1936. "Let Jesus lead you and Roosevelt feed you," one black preacher told his congregation. With African Americans flocking to the Democratic party, and with what everyone assumed was his last election behind him, FDR grew more accommodating on black issues. He posed for photographs with black visitors, publicly criticized lynching, appointed William Hastie as the first black federal judge, and created a civil rights section in the Justice Department.[13]

Roosevelt maintained an artful vagueness when it came to African Americans. At times, especially when speaking with Southerners, he displayed an easy confidence in white supremacy. Yet he appeared comfortable with blacks (as, to be fair, he did with pretty much everyone). In 1917, while on an inspection tour of Haiti, he had danced with black women while white Marine officers grumbled their disapproval. He was kind and generous to black employees without being condescending. Roosevelt was neither crusader nor race-baiter. He was a politician above all else, unwilling to do anything that jeopardized his larger agenda. Much as he disapproved of blatant racism, he knew he could not win an election without support from the white Southerners who comprised the conservative wing of the Democratic party.[14]

Cautious though he was, FDR did more than any previous president to bring African Americans into the halls of power. Every Friday evening a loose coalition of federal appointees dubbed the "Black Cabinet" gathered at the home of Mary McLeod Bethune, the National Youth Administration's Director of Negro Affairs, for snacks, drinks, and political banter. They discussed government agencies' treatment of minorities, drafted antidiscrimination clauses to insert into pending legislation, and laid plans to pressure administrators into expanding access to federal jobs or integrating federal facilities. African American leaders from outside of government often joined these gatherings, making Bethune's group a key link between the president's inner circle and black activists.

First Lady Eleanor Roosevelt had an even greater impact on FDR's thinking. Her thoughts on race had evolved since her days as a young bride, when she called black servants darkies and pickaninnies. Her travels around the country awakened her to America's vast inequalities. Her compassionate heart led her to push Franklin to do something about them. Eleanor built close relationships with prominent African Americans. They knew a note to her was more likely to reach the president's desk than one addressed directly to FDR. "No individual in my lifetime has created as much trouble," one white Southerner complained. "She preaches and practices social equality." Phony rumors about Eleanor Clubs, clandestine organizations dedicated to upending racial hierarchies, swept the South. Allegedly, black women indicated their membership by wearing a feather in their hat. The size and color of the feather showed their rank in the organization.[15]

Eleanor touched off a furor when she attended a 1938 conference on Southern poverty in Birmingham, Alabama. Black and white delegates mingled in defiance of the city's racial code until public safety commissioner Eugene "Bull" Connor, who became infamous in the 1960s for abusing civil rights protestors, arrived to enforce segregation ordinances. Participants had retreated to separate sides of the auditorium by the time Eleanor arrived. Taking a quick glance around, she walked to the black side of the room. A chagrined policeman asked the first lady to sit with the whites. Eleanor instead dragged her chair to the line running down the center aisle and sat down with one foot on either side. She feigned innocence when asked about the incident. "I would not presume to tell the people of Alabama what they should do," she smiled in response to a reporter's question. Eleanor made more headlines in 1939 when she resigned from the Daughters of the American Revolution after the group denied black contralto Marian Anderson permission to sing in Constitution Hall. Eleanor's influence cleared the way for Anderson to perform instead from the steps of the Lincoln Memorial.[16]

Walter White, the NAACP's dapper, shrewd, high-strung executive secretary, was the most persistent black voice in Eleanor's ear, although few strangers saw him as black. "Now Walter White/Is mighty light," Langston Hughes joked in his "Ballad of Walter White." Blond haired and blue eyed, White was a "voluntary negro" who could pass as white but chose not to. He grew up among Atlanta's black elite, the son of college-educated and socially respectable parents. After graduating from Atlanta University, he spent a brief, unhappy time selling life insurance before becoming a charter member of the NAACP's Atlanta branch. His networking and public speaking skills soon earned him a spot at the national office in New York. White's ambiguous racial status made him a perfect candidate for dangerous trips into the South to investigate lynchings and race riots. These undercover journeys required White to adopt a split persona, becoming black or white depending on whom he was talking to.[17]

Walter White, executive secretary of the NAACP. *Library of Congress, Prints and Photographs Collection, LC-USZ62-110593*

White was a tireless worker who placed extraordinary demands on his body. He consumed prodigious quantities of scotch. Acquaintances rarely saw him without a cigarette dangling from his mouth. An unrelenting advocate for African Americans, he was also a relentless self-promoter who cultivated famous people who could elevate both the race and his own public profile. He first turned his charms on Eleanor Roosevelt when they met at a 1934 dinner. Captivated, she became a reliable source of information and political clout. Her husband's confidants disliked the pushy White. Stephen Early, the president's secretary, called him "one of the worst and most contentious of troublemakers."[18]

White's influence in Washington exceeded his appeal on the street. He lived in "the White House of Harlem," a sumptuous, thirteenth-floor apartment at 409 Edgecombe Avenue, the ritzy Sugar Hill district's most prestigious address. There he entertained out-of-town guests and an African American A-list of friends from the building, including W. E. B. DuBois, painter Aaron Douglas, poet William Stanley Braithwaite, future Supreme Court justice Thurgood Marshall, and NAACP assistant secretary Roy Wilkins.

White's urbane lifestyle epitomized the NAACP's struggle to connect with working-class African Americans. At heart, White was a politician who preferred dignified negotiations to rabble rousing, and incremental change to revolution. Rather than antagonize the Roosevelt administration with crowd-pleasing stubbornness, he cut deals with it, accepting small victories that steadily advanced the race. The NAACP quietly lobbied congressmen to pass antilynching legislation and invested heavily in legal challenges to segregation.

White's younger colleagues, along with such old lions as W. E. B. DuBois, urged him to immerse the NAACP in more economic justice issues that could grow its membership beyond its traditional middle- and upper-class base. White found their arguments compelling but hesitated to spread his organization too thin. He also worried that expanding the NAACP's agenda might alienate deep-pocketed white liberal donors. Moreover, a well-publicized campaign to uplift the black working class could provoke charges of communism.

This ideological dispute plagued the NAACP well into the war years. As of 1940, however, most poor, rural, uneducated, and politically radical African Americans held aloof from it. This underserved constituency instead looked to the Communist Party, the left-wing

National Negro Congress, Garveyite splinter groups, and church-based organizations for guidance. As of 1940, none of them had emerged as the dominant voice of the African American masses. There was still room for someone to mobilize the black grassroots.[19]

Two events in Harlem suggested possible futures for the growing multitudes of African Americans who were tired of mistreatment and impatient for reform. The first occurred on a gorgeous afternoon in March 1935. An employee of Kress Five and Ten Store, across the street from Harlem's famous Apollo Theater, nabbed a young Puerto Rican stealing a ten-cent pocketknife. The boy bit the clerk's thumb, hoping to escape his grasp. "I'm going to take you down to the basement and beat the hell out of you," the wounded man shouted. A crowd gathered outside, drawn by the commotion. Rumors spread that the clerk had killed the shoplifter, who became black in the retelling. The arrival of an ambulance seemed to confirm the mob's suspicions. The would-be thief had actually escaped through a basement door.[20]

This trivial case of a white man, in a white-owned store, threatening a boy who committed a minor offense unleashed Harlem's pent-up economic and social frustrations. Street speakers leapt atop soapboxes to demand retribution. Barbershops, pool rooms, and bars hummed with talk of revenge. African Americans poured into the streets as night fell, looting, smashing windows, and attacking policemen. Lenox Avenue resembled a war zone. Three people lay dead and more than two hundred were wounded before the uprising exhausted itself.

New York City mayor Fiorello LaGuardia appointed an interracial panel to figure out what had happened. The district attorney blamed communists. LaGuardia's commission offered a more thoughtful interpretation. No one planned the riot, it argued. Rather, it was a spontaneous expression of longstanding "resentments against racial discrimination and poverty in the midst of plenty." Filth, overcrowding, unemployment, underfunded schools, poor city services, an artificially inflated cost of living, and suspicion of white authorities had pushed Harlem to the brink of explosion. The slightest nudge was enough to tip it into chaos. With no end to the Depression in sight and little momentum for the reforms needed to alleviate racial tensions, the threat of additional riots haunted American cities long after Harlem returned to normal.[21]

A second, more constructive path forward took the form of an economic justice movement centered around a Harlem preacher with a megawatt smile and a knack for getting his name in the papers. As a boy, Adam Clayton Powell, Jr. had watched Marcus Garvey's parades from the rooftop of his father's pastorate, the Abyssinian Baptist Church. Powell, who could have passed as white, grew into a proud black man who marched to the beat of racial pride. He had a big body, and knew how to use it. Swaddled in his signature white, double-breasted suit, he looked as comfortable gliding down the church aisle as he did sauntering down 125th Street. Awestruck female parishioners called him "Mr. Jesus."[22]

Powell inherited his father's post, one of black America's premier pulpits, in 1937. From this perch he launched an economic fairness drive that merged his altruism with his gift for showing up at the exact moment the press arrived. The preacher targeted white-owned stores along 125th Street that refused to hire blacks, or hired only light-skinned blacks. Why, he asked, could black people live next door to a store, and shop in that store, but not work in that store? Managers who smiled as they took your money changed their tune when you asked for an application. "No jobs," they muttered as they showed you their backs. White Irishmen drove the buses that took Harlemites to work. Utility companies would not hire blacks.

"Mass action is the most powerful force on earth," Powell declared. To prove it, he dispatched a flying force of picketers called the People's Committee whenever discrimination reared its ugly head. Scores of shops felt the committee's wrath during the late 1930s. Committee members invaded businesses to conduct floor-by-floor searches for black employees. Mr. Jesus himself appeared at moments of maximum press attention.[23]

Powell's street-pleasing tactics and charismatic leadership proved effective. Stores granted the committee's demands rather than infuriate black customers. Metropolitan Life Insurance Company caved in. Electricity provider Con Edison did too, after Harlem exchanged lights for candles and started paying its bills in pennies. "Jobs-for-Negroes" campaigns cropped up in Chicago, Baltimore, and other cities. Soapbox agitators incited crowds with chants of "Don't buy where you can't work." City by city, block by block, African Americans were winning economic justice, and doing it without support from established black organizations or Washington New Dealers.[24]

Multiple paths lay before them, all of them proven effective to some degree. Franklin Roosevelt's New Deal was losing steam by 1940, but the administration still seemed amenable to civil rights if the political calculus proved favorable. Walter White's methodical, legalistic approach paid off when the Supreme Court ruled in the 1938 *Gaines* case that the University of Missouri could not deny admission to its law school based on an applicant's race. The verdict represented the first chink in a formerly unbroken wall of segregated public education. Violence, as seen in the 1935 riot, had not brought lasting change, but it alerted public officials to the frustration seething in black neighborhoods. And Adam Clayton Powell was trying to achieve economic equality one office building at a time.

For all that, much about being an African American remained unchanged from previous years, or even decades. Discrimination was an everyday occurrence. Segregation was a basic fact of life. Jobs remained scarce, and housing substandard. Restrictive voting laws made a mockery of democracy. The threat of lynching lurked everywhere.

"The time has come for the Negro to close ranks," Powell decreed. Black America wanted action rather than words. Revolution was in the air in 1940. The opening shots of World War II, a conflict grounded in concepts of race and racial superiority, promised to further disrupt black–white relations. This dynamic, fluid moment offered unique opportunities for a motivated, articulate African American possessing street credibility, political savvy, and experience organizing on a national scale.[25]

A half-century before Adam Clayton Powell began his economic justice campaign, another minister, James Randolph, offered his sons Asa Philip and James, Jr. a deceptively simple piece of advice: "Speak the whole word." On the surface this motto was a lesson in elocution, a reminder that clear enunciation conveyed a sense of gravitas. On a deeper level, the elder Randolph was telling his sons to stand up for truth no matter the consequences. Speaking the whole word meant telling people what they needed to hear, not what they wanted to hear.[26]

Speaking the whole word in Crescent City, Florida, where Asa Philip Randolph was born in 1889, could get an African American into serious trouble. The Randolphs lived in a world where race dictated destiny. They could work in the lush orange groves surrounding the town but were unlikely to ever own one. Housing and schooling were segregated. Blacks were expected to keep their heads down, speak only when spoken to, and defer to whites.

James Randolph was an itinerant African Methodist Episcopal preacher who espoused the church's message of social justice and uplifting the oppressed. He was a passionate speaker, if not a particularly eloquent one, who spent much of his time traveling between outposts on his circuit. Largely self-educated, he was too unpolished to rise in the church hierarchy or to capture a plum position with an upscale AME congregation.

Reverend Randolph accepted his modest lot in life but harbored great ambitions for his sons. His desire to expand their horizons motivated him to assume leadership of a tiny congregation in Jacksonville, Florida, a bustling port city with a small black middle class. Not that the Randolphs were middle class. They occupied a nondescript house in a poor section of town. Their white picket fence was missing half its slats. James supplemented his meager income with numerous side ventures, none of them lucrative. He ran a meat market, mended clothes, sold wood, and raised chickens without much success. "There were no business brains in our household," Asa later commented. James's wife Elizabeth acted as the family disciplinarian, whipping the boys for playing in the streets or neglecting their chores. Neither whisky nor playing cards crossed her doorstep. She enforced the children's Bible study and ensured that no swear word crossed their lips. "I have never used profanity in a single instance," her younger son noted decades later. "I wouldn't know how."[27]

It was a strict home, but a loving one. Elizabeth smiled on James Jr. and Asa's every accomplishment. Reverend Randolph boosted his kids' self-respect by introducing them to important African Americans passing through town. "I want to present to you my two sons, two of the finest boys in the country," he told visiting dignitaries. Asa, named for a rigidly moral Old Testament king, grew up on tales of black heroes Frederick Douglass, Harriet Tubman, Nat Turner, and AME founder Richard Allen. His father encouraged all kinds of learning; copies of Shakespeare, Dickens, and Darwin sat alongside the *Christian Recorder*, the *AME Review*, and the radical political journal *Voice of the Negro*. Asa's frequent church visits reinforced Elizabeth's insistence on order and James's teachings on self-empowerment.

He preferred muscular sermons to the "blessed are the meek" variety, especially when they incorporated uplifting music. "Before I'd be a slave/I'd be buried in my grave," he sang, "And go home to my God/ And be free."[28]

A born mingler, young Asa did his best to play baseball, shoot marbles, fly kites, wrestle, and run without dirtying the suits his mother so carefully tailored for him. Persistent reminders of his second-class status haunted his youth. Everyday life meant being sent to the back of the line at a newspaper stand. It meant cowering indoors when rumors of a lynching swept through town. It meant dropping your eyes when a white man insulted your father. James advised his boys to quietly resist segregation. He forbade them to patronize the public library's segregated reading room. They walked rather than ride segregated streetcars. Asa understood the futility of these individual protests but wondered what would happen if others followed the Randolphs' example. Numbers, he concluded at an early age, brought strength.

James and Elizabeth had a good marriage based on a shared sense of morality and racial uplift. The reverend loved reading his boys black newspapers, Bible stories, and tales of Africa, pausing occasionally to fiddle with his pipe, light a cheap cigar, or stress the importance of precise enunciation. No one ever accused the Randolphs of loose living. They embodied learning, rational argument, and self-esteem.[29]

Asa carried those lessons to the Cookman Institute, a local Methodist school whose curriculum emphasized classical education and proper morals. The tall, wiry fourteen-year-old excelled in both areas, acing his classes and avoiding trouble. He was also the star catcher and first baseman on the school's baseball team. Classmates thought he could have played professional baseball, although not in the all-white major leagues.

Asa's true passion was the theater. His booming voice seemed a natural for the stage, but his father disapproved. Nor could James afford to send Asa to a black college, such as Howard or Fisk, to train as a lawyer or a teacher. Brilliant and impatient, Asa spent several listless years driving a delivery wagon, collecting life insurance premiums, clerking in a grocery store, and performing manual labor. In his free hours he gave public readings, sang in a barbershop quartet, and appeared in amateur stage productions. He politely yet firmly rejected his father's entreaties to preach. Jesus appealed to him as a political figure, an advocate for the downtrodden who advocated social change through nonviolence. Spirituality was a different matter. Randolph never felt the call. He considered himself an agnostic who admired the AME's social consciousness but doubted the existence of God.[30]

The North, not the Holy Spirit, called Randolph. It offered excitement and opportunity. Just as important, it was where Asa's hero, author and historian W. E. B. DuBois, lived. "The problem of the Twentieth Century is the problem of the color line," DuBois wrote in his most famous work, 1903's *The Souls of Black Folk*. DuBois challenged African Americans to press for full political, social, and cultural equality. He chided his great rival, Tuskegee Institute president Booker T. Washington, for urging blacks to focus on learning a trade and proving that they could take care of themselves. DuBois thought Washington worried more about pleasing whites than advancing blacks. Washington's message might have made sense to the generation transitioning from slavery to freedom, but Dubois thought present-day African Americans needed to train their minds as well as their hands. To become complete men—and DuBois spoke primarily of men—African Americans needed university educations. They needed to enter the professions. They needed to dismantle barriers to advancement.[31]

DuBois's bluntness, so reminiscent of James Randolph, entranced the ambitious Asa. In 1911 he hopped a steamer bound for New York, one drop in the flood of African Americans leaving the South. He washed dishes in the galley to pay for his trip. It was a supremely confident twenty-two-year-old who stepped from the gangplank into the big city. Dark skinned, slender, and six foot two inches tall, he cut an imposing figure. His commanding voice and piercing brown eyes magnified his allure. Despite his poverty, he maintained a fastidious appearance, affecting rakish derbies, smart overcoats, and polished shoes.

Randolph, now calling himself "Phil," shared a $1.50-a-week Harlem apartment with a friend from Jacksonville. He haunted the New York Public Library and pursued a stage career. Within months he was broke. He took a go-nowhere job as a switchboard operator in an apartment building, the first of many short-lived positions, while dabbling in various church-based youth groups, favoring those with theater clubs.

A. Philip Randolph soon after his arrival in Harlem, circa 1911. *Library of Congress, Prints and Photographs Collection, LC-USZ62-97538*

Bored and directionless, Randolph enrolled in some public speaking courses at City College. The price was right, as the school did not charge tuition. "The only kind of college *I* will ever be able to afford," he joked. He soon discovered that City College was a hotbed of radicalism. The charged atmosphere thrilled him. He devoured socialist texts and attended lectures by intellectuals and labor leaders. Although he never graduated, his time at City College left a permanent imprint. His exposure to leftist thought led him to see connections between racism and economic inequality, between color and class. The perpetual scramble to survive in competitive capitalism's ruthless economic environment encouraged whites to denigrate their black peers to better their own chances of success. A divided working class could not resist plutocrats bent on keeping wages low.[32]

By 1914 Randolph fancied himself a devoted socialist tasked with articulating the desires of the industrial proletariat. His sincerity helped ensure his poverty. He lost his porter job at Consolidated Gas Company for trying to organize a union, then got fired from a waiter position for doing the same thing. Randolph was content to tread water, promoting the cause while living hand to mouth. "We were having a great time," he remembered. "We didn't think of the future, of establishing a home, getting ahead, or things of that sort. Those things weren't as important as creating unrest among the Negroes."[33]

Randolph's affair with Lucille Green ended his carefree youth. A thirty-one-year-old widow with light skin, silver hair, and a quick smile, Green owned a prosperous hair salon. Randolph fell in love the first time he saw her. On first glance the two made an odd couple. Lucille was a socialite whose fair complexion confirmed her status among the color-conscious Harlem elite. Phil, a head taller and considerably thinner than Lucille, was a dark-skinned drifter without pedigree or fortune, a dreamer without prospects or purpose beyond rousing the

Lucille Green Randolph. *Library of Congress, Prints and Photographs Collection, LC-USZ62-97536*

working class. But they shared interests in socialism and Shakespeare. Both were generous with their money and valued loyalty. Phil found Lucille elegant and witty. Lucille liked Phil's seriousness, dignity, and good looks. After a brief courtship, they married in 1914. The newly-weds called each other "Buddy," and would for almost fifty years.

Lucille's income kept Randolph afloat financially. Soon after his marriage he joined a new friend, an acquaintance of Lucille's named Chandler Owen, on Harlem's soapbox circuit. Like Phil and Lucille, Phil and Chandler were a study in contrasts. Randolph was tall, proper, and abstemious, whereas Owen was short, chunky, and uninhibited. They never played cards or drank together, but they made a good speaking team whose economic and racial critiques became the talk of the streets. The Harlem intelligentsia dubbed them Lenin and Trotsky. Their fiery sermons also drew interest from police officers, who dispersed their listeners with billy clubs whenever too many gawkers stopped to listen. Randolph discovered a clever way to pacify the cops, most of them Irish. Whenever he saw them coming, he shifted oratorical gears and started blasting British imperialism in Ireland. Randolph resumed his original lecture once the officers passed out of earshot, nodding with approval.

A chance encounter with William White, president of the Head-waiters and Sidewaiters Society of Greater New York, advanced their fortunes. White had heard their sidewalk speeches. Impressed, he invited them to edit a monthly magazine for his membership. Randolph and Owen leapt at the chance. White not only promised them editorial freedom, but also free office space and equipment. The duo commandeered a large, sunny room overlooking Lenox Avenue. They hammered out the new *Hotel Messenger* magazine while lounging in soft leather chairs and sharing an enormous desk. Their office became a gathering place for radicals seeking conversation. Randolph, feeling expansive in his new digs, changed his name yet again, referring to himself as "A. Philip Randolph" instead of plain old "Asa" or "Phil."

The *Hotel Messenger* folded in August 1917, after just eight issues. Randolph and Owen aroused White's wrath when they published an exposé detailing how headwaiters extorted money from the subordinate sidewaiters. Outraged, and looking to stay in the headwaiters' good graces, White canned them.

The unrepentant editors rented space next door to start a new magazine called the *Messenger*. They hoped to create an elegant, readable journal that brought radicalism to the masses. Although they never gained a large circulation, they crafted one of the period's most impressive publications, a socialist organ committed to racial self-empowerment. Each issue commanded readers to shed their dependence on whites. African Americans should never settle for anything less than complete equality. "Patriotism has no appeal to us; justice has," Randolph and Owen declared. "Party has no weight with us; principle has. Loyalty is meaningless; it depends on what one is loyal to."[34]

Congress voted to enter World War I in April 1917, seven months before the *Messenger* appeared. Like most socialists, Randolph saw the conflict as an imperialistic grab for resources rather than a noble crusade to make the world safe for democracy. "Our aim is to appeal to reason, to lift our pens above the cringing demagogy of the times," he wrote in the *Messenger*'s inaugural issue.[35]

These were fighting words to a nation whipped into a nationalistic frenzy by wartime propaganda. Randolph and Owen, having captured the bull's attention, spent the next several months waving red flags in front of it. A string of features blasted the war as a corrupt money-making venture for capitalists who employed patriotic rhetoric to strangle the labor movement. They saved their strongest venom for black leaders, including Randolph's hero, W. E. B. DuBois, who told followers to support the war without first demanding their rights. "Lynching, Jim Crow, segregation, discrimination in the armed forces and out, disfranchisement of millions of black souls in the South— all these things make your cry of making the world safe for democracy a sham, a mockery, a rape on decency and a travesty on common justice," they wrote in an open letter to President Woodrow Wilson. After reading this and other *Messenger* editorials, Attorney General A. Mitchell Palmer branded Randolph and Owen "the most dangerous Negroes in the United States."[36]

At an August 1918 mass meeting in Cleveland, Randolph and Owen advised a predominantly African American crowd to refuse induction into the military until the United States stopped discriminating against its citizens. Undercover federal agents yanked Randolph from the platform, grabbed Owen, and deposited them in prison for violating the Sedition Act, a draconian new law that outlawed criticism of the government or the war. The law carried a maximum penalty of twenty years in prison.

Two days later, bailiffs herded Randolph and Owen from their cell to a courtroom. The judge, after leafing through some confiscated copies of the *Messenger*, eyed them as if they had just fallen from the sky. "You really wrote this magazine?" he asked. "What do you know about socialism?" A bewildered look crossed his face as the defendants detailed their knowledge of Karl Marx and other leftists. "Don't you know that you are opposing your own government and that you are subject to imprisonment for treason?" the judge continued. We value human dignity more than the law, Randolph and Owen replied. The magistrate's expression wavered between anger and confusion. He concluded that devious white radicals had filled the two black men's heads with wild ideas. "I *ought* to throw you in jail," he said, "but take my advice and get out of town. If we catch you here again, you won't be so lucky."[37]

Randolph picked a new battle once peace came in November 1918. His target this time was Marcus Garvey, the showboating head of the UNIA. When Garvey first arrived in Harlem, Randolph descended from his soapbox to give the Jamaican a place to speak. The two collaborated until Garvey's disdain for socialism and his dealings with the Ku Klux Klan, which like Garvey advocated racial separation, tore them apart. Although Randolph never admitted it, he envied the interloper whose star had so quickly soared above his own.

Garvey inflated the quarrel into a blood feud when he told an audience that Randolph's arrogance might cost him a limb. Randolph called the FBI's New York City office soon after. An agent dispatched to the *Messenger*'s offices found a brown paper package containing a white man's hand. Inside was a letter signed "K.K.K." "We have been watching your writings in all your papers for quite a while but we want you to understand before we act," it read. "Let me see your name in your nigger improvement association as a member, paid up too, in about a week from now. ... If you can't unite with your own race we will find out what's the matter with you all." Randolph published the letter in the *Messenger*'s next issue as proof of Garvey's close ties to the Klan. Garvey dismissed the incident as a publicity stunt. Authorities never determined who the hand belonged to.[38]

Randolph was one of Harlem's leading radicals by 1925, when Garvey began a five-year prison term for mail fraud. The *Messenger*'s two-room headquarters became an outpost of the Harlem Renaissance. Fellow intellectuals treated it as an extension of their own homes. They orbited Randolph like planets around a sun, soliciting his opinions on social, economic, racial, and historical questions while dodging an aster-oid field of files and back issues cluttering the third-floor office. Randolph, with his penetrating insights, even temper, and quick laugh, served as both enlightener and moderator of a combative bunch. "His deep drawl poured oil over the stormy waters of dispute that inevitably arose among these intellectual *prima donnas*," a compatriot remembered.[39]

But all was not well. The *Messenger* was losing money, its circula-tion stagnant at 5,000. Randolph's unconventional politics drove cus-tomers from Lucille's salon. His attempts to mobilize the masses went nowhere. He and Owen unionized several groups of black workers only to see those organizations quickly collapse. Owen abandoned Harlem for Chicago in 1923 to become a newspaper editorialist and manage public relations for local politicians. Randolph absorbed an-other blow when his father died of heart and kidney troubles in 1924. Randolph was a middle-aged man with a sputtering career. His radical vision of a just society foundered beneath a wave of postwar conserva-tism that nurtured not just the revived Klan, but also antipathy toward labor unions and political radicals. "It was a dark period for us," he later remembered.[40]

Yet he enjoyed his life, being a man of boundless determination and few material needs. Every Sunday he and Lucille welcomed a handful of intimates for breakfast at their West 142nd Street apart-ment. Conversations ranged from current events to literature, from Garvey's latest misadventure to Harlem's newest gossip. The gang hit the streets at noon, dressed to the nines as they promenaded down 7th Avenue. Even Randolph, the aspiring voice of the masses, joined the weekly ritual of seeing and being seen, losing himself in the flurry of fur coats, knee-length dresses, swinging canes, gaiters, boutonnieres, monocles, and lorgnettes sweeping down the sidewalk. Still a theater fan, he sometimes dragged friends to the back balcony of the segregated Alhambra Theater to catch a vaudeville show.

Randolph was meandering down 7th Avenue one day in early 1925 when he bumped into Ashley Totten, a forty-year-old native of the Virgin Islands. Tall, wiry, and tough as a steel rail, Totten was a

Pullman sleeping car porter, part of an army of black service workers who catered to white train passengers' every need. Totten was also one of the *Messenger's* few regular readers. He had heard Randolph speak from many a soapbox. Doffing his out-of-season Panama hat, Totten began lecturing Randolph about the porters' problems.

Pullman cars represented the height of luxury. With their fold-out beds, lush carpeting, and upholstered seats, they transformed the grind of long-distance travel into a joy. Relaxation for some demanded backbreaking labor from others. Pullman porters, who earned $67.50 per month, started preparing a train for departure hours before they punched the time clock. They often worked double shifts without a break. Company spies, known as "spotters," scrutinized cars for dusty windowsills. Porters slept, when they found time to sleep, atop tables or on piles of baggage. As a final insult, they had to purchase their own cleaning supplies. "They had us constantly on our knees," one former porter remembered. Porters' need to supplement their income with tips forced them to grovel before white customers, who condescendingly called them "George," a reference to company founder George Pullman.[41]

Totten persuaded Randolph to address a clandestine meeting of porters considering unionizing. Randolph had never been on a Pullman car, but he knew how to reach workingmen. His fiery talk convinced Totten's colleagues to ask this erudite man with the unidentifiable accent—Was it Harvard? Was it Oxford?—to help them form a union. Randolph accepted. His other ventures were going nowhere anyway. An August 1925 meeting of five hundred porters and an unknown number of company informants in Harlem's Elks Hall voted to install Randolph at the head of the new Brotherhood of Sleeping Car Porters and Maids, later shortened to the Brotherhood of Sleeping Car Porters (BSCP). Randolph insisted on "Brotherhood" because the word implied deep common interests. He converted the *Messenger* into a porters' mouthpiece, running a series of articles detailing how the Pullman Company dehumanized thousands of "Georges."

Randolph embarked on a nationwide recruiting tour, preaching the gospel of unionism to every porter he met. He promised better wages, shorter days, and improved working conditions if they threw in with the Brotherhood. Dubious employees hesitated to risk their jobs just because a lanky newcomer with big ideas and ten-cent words asked them to.

He did win over Milton P. Webster, a gruff, cigar-chewing man who appeared to be carved from a six-foot-four-inch block of black granite. The Chicago-based Webster had spent twenty years with Pullman before the company fired him for talking union. Area porters still saw him as their leader. Webster's initial doubts about Randolph evaporated when he heard him address a meeting. Webster soon assumed the loyal lieutenant role Chandler Owen had recently vacated. They made an effective speaking team, with Webster employing a combination of charm and blunt words to soften audiences for Randolph's logical, thoughtful appeals. Together they drew thousands of porters into the Brotherhood.

Randolph's activities aroused controversy among African Americans. Articles in the black press alleged Klan involvement in the labor movement, criticized porters who upended social conventions by demanding equal pay with whites, and fretted about alienating a major employer of black workers. Randolph suspected that Pullman was bribing newspaper editors. Indeed, large Pullman Company ads proliferated in African American papers at the very moment he began organizing, even though few blacks ever rode in the expensive cars.

Pullman's opposition went well beyond buying off the press. The company fired employees with BSCP connections. It set up a rival union, then granted minor improvements to its contract to show porters that they didn't need the BSCP. At one point Pullman sent Randolph a blank check, not-so-subtly inviting him to take the money and run. Randolph held firm. By late 1926 he had enrolled a majority of porters in the BSCP, although many of them were behind on membership dues. Still, the company showed no interest in recognizing the union as a legitimate bargaining entity.

The BSCP was shaping up as another one of Randolph's failures. Union coffers were running dry. Porters grumbled about sticking out their necks for nothing. Personal tragedy accompanied professional futility. Randolph's mother, Elizabeth, died in March 1926. Randolph got the news while on a West Coast organizing tour. "I didn't have a nickel to get back to New York," he lamented. "My wife and my brother had to take care of the funeral." Desperate for a breakthrough, he looked for some way to upset the status quo. In April 1928 he called a strike vote. More than 6,000 porters voted in favor. Just seventeen disapproved. The move energized the demoralized porters, sometimes to dangerous levels.

Ashley Totten wanted to stockpile weapons to prevent strikebreakers from infiltrating rail yards in the event of a walkout.[42]

Randolph knew the wealthy Pullman Company could outlast a strike. His real goal was to force the company to recognize the Brotherhood in order to avoid negative publicity. To his dismay, the company held firm, daring the BSCP to exhaust its scarce resources on a futile act. Making matters worse, diphtheria killed Randolph's brother James, who was just thirty-eight years old, as the confrontation heated up.

Randolph turned to American Federation of Labor (AFL) President William Green for advice. From a chair in Green's Washington, DC, office, Randolph laid out the situation. Pullman had already quartered strikebreakers near rail yards. It had extra policemen ready to spring into action in case of a strike.

"How about your men?" Green asked. "Will they walk off the job if the Brotherhood calls a strike?"

"I don't know," Randolph replied. "I get the feeling that they never really believed it would come to such a drastic step."

Green sat silent for a moment. He leaned forward. In a soft, sympathetic voice, he said, "Phil, I'm afraid a strike would fail."[43]

Green was right. Randolph slinked back to New York and cancelled the upcoming strike. Membership in the Brotherhood cratered. Overdue utility bills piled up. Landlords demanded rent checks on their meeting halls. Randolph folded the *Messenger* after years of red ink. His suits, always a point of pride, grew thin and ragged. The Great Depression hit soon after the strike fiasco, driving masses of African Americans from their jobs and causing those who still had jobs to cling to them with all their strength. Pullman, feeling the pinch, laid off hundreds of porters.

Randolph spent years rebuilding the shattered Brotherhood. He rallied his few remaining troops to believe in themselves and their cause. He lobbied progressive black churches, as well as white churches that preached the social gospel, for moral and financial support. He also turned to the AFL. If Randolph could persuade the giant labor organization to accept the Brotherhood as an affiliated union, he could gain access to its considerable resources, including a strike fund capable of carrying porters through a walkout. The AFL also offered desperately needed legitimacy and political clout.

The AFL had rejected an earlier Brotherhood application for membership. William Green endorsed a second try largely because he respected Randolph. Even with Green's support, the limping Brotherhood faced an uphill climb. Other AFL unions claimed the right to organize porters into segregated auxiliary units. Randolph rejected this plan outright. Years dragged past without a resolution. The national economy sank, the trains ran, the porters stretched themselves thinner, and the Brotherhood scrambled to survive. The Chief often hit the road with nothing but the clothes on his back. "The hope that this movement would become the center and rallying point of Negro labor as a whole is now dead," one Brotherhood organizer lamented.[44]

The BSCP's fortunes improved when Franklin Roosevelt assumed the presidency. Section 7(a) of the 1933 National Industrial Recovery Act, an attempt to revitalize slumping factories, guaranteed workers' collective bargaining rights. The Emergency Transportation Act, passed the same year, outlawed company unions, a weapon Pullman had long exploited to sap support from the Brotherhood. The new laws invigorated the labor movement and inspired Randolph to make one final push for recognition. Finally, in 1935, the AFL accepted the Brotherhood's application, giving Randolph a major victory after a decade of defeats.

He still needed to negotiate a contract with Pullman, which opposed the insurgents in every way possible. "There is no occasion for a conference with you," the company replied to one of Randolph's many requests for a meeting. Pullman executives challenged Roosevelt's pro-labor laws in court. Two years passed while the case wound its way through the legal system. The Supreme Court upheld the New Deal acts in April 1937, closing off Pullman's last option for ignoring the Brotherhood. It signed a deal with the union in August, twelve years to the day after the secret gathering in Elks Hall. Porters gained nearly $2 million a year in additional wages, had their work hours cut by a third, and saw their monthly travel requirement lowered from 11,000 miles to 7,000 miles. From Randolph's perspective, a small group of working-class African Americans, with help from an activist federal government, had won a measure of economic justice.[45]

The Brotherhood's triumph confirmed Randolph as black America's foremost advocate for the working class. One admirer called him "free from scheming or duplicity, honest to the point of being almost naïve." Unique among black leaders, he was neither teacher, nor preacher, nor politician. "He might use a lot of ten-cylinder words, but the layman was crazy about him, because he was so different," remarked musician Noble Sissle. "He had a little beat-up office, a raggedy desk and a few chairs. ... He might have sounded like a Yale or Harvard graduate with his talk, but there was a ring of sincerity to it and brotherly love to it, and you were proud to have someone like that to talk to you."[46]

After defeating Pullman, Randolph turned toward national issues. He appreciated President Roosevelt's pro-union gestures and recognized the progress African Americans had made under his administration. Yet he chafed at the incremental gains made at a time rich with revolutionary possibilities. The New Deal "did not change in the least any essential aspect of the profit system," Randolph asserted in 1936. It never challenged segregation and discrimination, the great ramparts separating millions of minorities from the American Dream. With the country in a progressive mood, he sought new ways to transform his interest in the intersection of race and labor, blackness and the working class, into tangible results.[47]

Randolph turned fifty in April 1939. The world was tumbling toward war. Japan had gobbled up large chunks of China since invading it two years earlier. In Europe, Adolf Hitler had negotiated nearly bloodless takeovers of Austria and Czechoslovakia and was bullying Poland. Americans still stinging from the slaughter of World War I hid behind a series of Neutrality Acts designed to isolate the country from a fight.

Randolph viewed Hitler's rise with horror. Despite his innate pacifism, he understood that there was no place for dark-skinned peoples in an Axis-dominated world. In case of war, however, he planned to extract concessions for blacks before committing to the cause. In a sense, his whole life had prepared him for this moment. His father's teachings, combined with his readings of the Bible and of history, convinced him that nonviolent resistance could change the world. His studies of socialist texts and his experience in the labor movement demonstrated the need for mass organization and racial self-empowerment. "The task of realizing full citizenship for the Negro people is largely in the hands of the Negro people themselves," he wrote in 1937. "Freedom is never given; it is won. And the Negro people must win their freedom. They must achieve justice. This involves struggle, continuous struggle."[48]

A. Philip Randolph was spoiling for a fight. His war would be about more than national boundaries or control of resources, about more than who ruled what patch of land or who traded with whom. Randolph was preparing to fight a war for equality, a war to ensure every person's right to basic human dignity. Before it was over, A. Philip Randolph's war would help redefine America and Americanism, pointing the country toward a future when all Americans, regardless of their economic status or the color of their skin, enjoyed equality and justice.

CHAPTER 2

....

We Want True Democracy

Africa Americans' frustration swelled as World War II deepened. Adolf Hitler's September 1939 invasion of Poland ended years of negotiations and saber-rattling. France and Great Britain declared war on Germany but could not halt the *Wehrmacht*'s momentum. In spring 1940, as Adam Clayton Powell's People's Committee infiltrated office buildings to search for black employees, Hitler sent his armies crashing into Norway, Denmark, Belgium, Luxembourg, and the Netherlands. A British force sent to halt the tide narrowly avoided capture when a ragtag fleet of yachts and fishing boats rescued it from the encircled French port of Dunkirk. German tanks rolled into Paris on June 14. Western Europe had collapsed in just six weeks. Britain now stood alone against Hitler. Few thought it would stand for long.

Franklin Roosevelt had been president of the United States for seven eventful years. He had entered the White House at the bottom of the Great Depression, when national unemployment rates topped 30 percent and an epidemic of bank failures left many predicting the death of capitalism. Roosevelt's New Deal prevented a total financial breakdown while restoring hope for the future. Despite the president's best efforts, unemployment remained high throughout the 1930s.

The outbreak of World War II forced another burden onto Roosevelt's shoulders. FDR despised Hitler. He believed victory for Germany and its Axis partner, Benito Mussolini's Fascist Italy, would spell disaster for the United States. Americans faced isolation in a hostile world should totalitarian empires control Europe, and should autocratic Japan, which joined the Axis in September 1940, control Asia. The United States would have to militarize to survive. Roosevelt feared this overwhelming need for security would sweep away freedom, democracy, and equality. A. Philip Randolph and some other African Americans might have questioned whether those principles existed in the first place.

Twenty-five years earlier, when World War I broke out, President Woodrow Wilson advised Americans to "remain impartial in thought as well as in action." Roosevelt offered more hardnosed advice. "Even a neutral cannot be asked to close his mind or his conscience," he told radio listeners two days after Germany entered Poland. Roosevelt wanted to keep the United States out of war. He also wanted to assist anti-Axis nations in any way possible.[1]

Current law limited FDR's options. Neutrality Acts passed in 1935 and strengthened in subsequent years forbade arms sales to belligerents and prohibited American ships from entering war zones. A vocal isolationist movement watched for evidence that FDR was inching the country toward the fight. The president tried to thread a political needle, aiding anti-Hitler forces while forestalling warmongering charges. In 1939 he persuaded Congress to repeal the arms embargo, clearing the way to send a trickle of weapons to Great Britain and France, at least until the Nazis occupied it.

Germany's spring 1940 *blitzkrieg* pushed Roosevelt into more dramatic measures. He began branding isolationists as either naïve or disloyal and warned Americans to beware German spies sowing dissention with "false slogans and emotional appeals." FDR pressed Congress for supplemental defense appropriations. "The Atlantic and Pacific oceans were reasonably adequate defensive barriers when fleets under sail could move at an average speed of five miles per hour," he said, "but the new element—air navigation—steps up the speed of possible attack to two hundred, to three hundred miles an hour.... So-called impregnable fortifications no longer exist." Roosevelt asked industrialists for at least 50,000 airplanes over the next year, a fivefold increase over their current production capacity.[2]

The president knew his request represented the start of a much larger campaign to revitalize American defense. He did not yet understand that putting the nation on a wartime footing had galvanized black resentment of discrimination and other social ills while elevating black hopes that a new era was dawning. Over the next several years, African Americans would revolutionize their relationship with the military, industry, and America itself.

Randolph cast a cynical eye on the growing war scare. Although he loathed Hitler, he saw little reason to support the Allies. "England and France have stolen the land and labor of black men in Africa, brown and yellow men in India and China, and with arrogance and pomp, abused and insulted those helpless peoples until they are well-nigh stung to revolt," he fumed. Viewing global events through the lens of racial liberation, Randolph saw neither the Axis nor the Allies championing liberty for nonwhites. "The only rational conclusion," he decided, "seems to be that the Negro and the other darker races must look to themselves for freedom."[3]

Randolph's disaffection coursed through black America. "It is not a war between dictatorship and democracy," the *Pittsburgh Courier* insisted. "If this total war destroys white civilization, there are hundreds of millions of people in Africa and Asia who will not mourn." The only war news generating much interest in black neighborhoods came from Ethiopia, the African kingdom Italy invaded in 1935.[4]

African Americans had volunteered in great numbers for earlier wars. They did so not just out of patriotism, but also because military service offered a path to respectability. Strong black battlefield performances could persuade white America to lift barriers to social and economic equality. How could the nation discriminate against valiant warriors who sacrificed for their nation's good?[5]

Past experience, however, left blacks deeply suspicious of the military. In 1775 General George Washington barred black recruits from the Continental Army, then reversed his order when the army failed to reach its enrollment targets. About 5,000 African Americans served in the Continental Army, most of them in racially segregated units, and none as officers.

Washington's move established a precedent for exhausting white reserves before enlisting significant numbers of blacks. In the Civil War, President Lincoln delayed recruiting African Americans for fear of outraging white Northerners. It took Union defeats at Fredericksburg and Vicksburg to change his mind. By war's end African Americans accounted for roughly 10 percent of the Union army. The War Department recognized their service by establishing six all-black regiments, later reduced to four, in the peacetime army. Known as Buffalo Soldiers, these highly disciplined units, under the supervision of white officers, protected remote western settlements from Indian attack. They were among the first regiments deployed to Cuba when the Spanish-American War broke out in 1898. Black soldiers stormed the San Juan heights as part of the charge that immortalized Colonel Teddy Roosevelt and his Rough Riders.[6]

Returning black soldiers found the doors of opportunity tightly closed. Good jobs and decent housing remained off limits. White mobs regularly attacked uniformed black veterans. *Plessy v. Ferguson*, the 1896 Supreme Court decision legitimizing racial segregation, remained in full force. Participation in the 1899-1902 Philippine War, a brutal guerrilla conflict that squashed native opposition to American annexation of the Pacific archipelago, did nothing to improve black fortunes. Frequent clashes between black and white units shattered hopes that patriotism would someday translate into equality.[7]

A 1906 incident in Brownsville, Texas, reinforced these doubts. White civilians reacted with horror when three companies of the 24th Infantry settled into Fort Brown that summer. They taunted the black soldiers, shoved them off sidewalks, and barred them from local saloons. One day a rumor flew through town that a GI had dragged a white woman by her hair down a street. That evening shots rang out in a white neighborhood near the camp. A bartender lay dead and a police officer wounded. Suspicion fell on the soldiers even though their officers had counted them all present and confined them to quarters as soon as the shooting began. Following an inconclusive investigation, President Theodore Roosevelt dishonorably discharged all 167 soldiers in the three companies.

In 1917, when the United States entered World War I, most black leaders urged cooperation. W. E. B. DuBois, Randolph's hero and the era's preeminent black intellectual, thought the conflict could advance civil rights if African Americans proved their patriotism. "Let us, while this war lasts, forget our special grievances and close our ranks shoulder to shoulder with our white fellow citizens and the allied nations that are fighting for democracy," he wrote. More than 400,000 African Americans took his advice, exchanging civilian garb for khakis. Army brass had no intention of making them the white soldiers' equals. Secretary of War Newton Baker approved a plan to train black recruits primarily for service roles. About 90 percent of African American doughboys performed unskilled or semiskilled tasks. Black troops left their segregated training camps with sketchy understandings of formation marching and rifle work. Some officers leased them to civilians needing manual labor, then pocketed the profits. Sentries barred them from recreational facilities, doctors gave them cursory medical care, and white recruits refused to salute them.[8]

The first U.S. troop convoy sailed for France in June 1917. On board were several hundred black stevedores, but no black combat soldiers. The army sent the Buffalo Soldiers to the American Southwest, Hawaii, and the Philippines instead of Europe. Eventually some 200,000 black troops reached France. Only about one quarter of those served on the front lines. Not surprisingly, the inexperienced, illtrained, poorly equipped, largely uneducated men performed unevenly. "Poor Negroes! They are hopelessly inferior," concluded Alabama-born general Robert Lee Bullard, whose 1st Army included black units. Army brass focused on the negative; a postwar assessment found black soldiers to be "jolly, docile, tractable, and lively," but also "stubborn, sullen and unruly."[9]

The military carried racial prejudices across the Atlantic. American officers asked their French counterparts not to shake hands, eat, or talk with black soldiers. Too much familiarity might inspire thoughts of equality. Nor should the French praise black soldiers in front of whites. The Army, convinced that African Americans' uniforms clothed potential rapists, warned French women to keep their distance. In a final insult, military leaders excluded black units from the enormous postwar victory parade down Paris's Champs-Élysées.

"This war is an End, and, also, a Beginning," W. E. B. DuBois argued. "Never again will darker people of the world occupy just the place they have before." The War Department saw matters in a different light. It kept only enough black soldiers to fill the same four segregated regiments that existed before the conflict. Washington assigned one unit to serve as orderlies at West Point Military Academy. Another went to Fort Benning, Georgia, to drive trucks, cook, collect garbage, and work as stablehands.[10]

Whites, particularly in the South, clung to prewar racial customs. Howling mobs stripped the uniforms from African American veterans exiting troop trains. Members of the recently revived Ku Klux Klan rode in defense of white womanhood. Lynchings, considered an effective way to discourage uppity blacks, became more frequent and brutal. Lynchers burned many of their victims alive. Race riots struck Northern cities, where white residents resented blacks' intrusions into "their" jobs and "their" neighborhoods. A 1919 riot in Chicago, one of twenty-five that year, killed thirty-eight people, twenty-five of them black, and injured 537.

Woodrow Wilson's promise of a war to make the world safe for democracy rang false to African Americans. A generation later, in 1940, they again heard platitudes about liberty and democracy wherever they went. Superman, the great hero of the fledgling comic book industry, smashed foreign conspiracies and protected defense plants from antidemocratic foes. Influential radio commentators such as Edward R. Murrow praised the plucky Brits for gumming up the Nazi war machine. Warner Bros. released a series of short films, including "Give Me Liberty," "The Declaration of Independence," "The Bill of Rights," "Lincoln in the White House," and "Old Hickory," extolling the sacrifices made in defense of freedom. Feature-length movies promoted national unity. "Every day, more and more are joining us," an army major remarked in *The Fighting 69th*, one of several pictures about World War I released in 1940. "They're not coming here as easterners or southerners, or Alaskans or New Englanders," he continued. "Those men are coming here as Americans, to form an organization that represents every part and section of our country.... We're all one nation now, one team. An all-American team pulling together, and known as the United States Army."

"Whose army is it?" inquired the *Pittsburgh Courier*, the country's most popular black newspaper. African Americans scoffed at defending democracy when the all-American team boasted so few black faces. The July 1940 cover of *Crisis*, the NAACP's monthly magazine, showed a B-17 Flying Fortress roaring over an aircraft manufacturing plant. Emblazoned across the photograph were the words "FOR WHITES ONLY." "Negro Americans may not build them, repair them, or fly them, but they must help pay for them," the caption declared.[11]

Two months later, Jehu Jasper, a reporter for the *Baltimore Afro-American*, caught a bus into Washington after his shift ended. Disembarking at Union Station, he traversed the length of the National Mall. Passing the White House on his right, he entered the century-old Winder Building, a five-story wall of limestone that housed a grab bag of federal agencies. A Marine recruiting office occupied the first floor, and Jasper wanted to volunteer. The young African American admired the service's first-into-the-fight mentality. He knew even before he opened the door that rejection awaited him inside. The Marines did not accept black recruits.

Jasper was an ideal physical specimen, a three-sport athlete in high school with 20/20 vision and excellent hearing. The expanding military should have welcomed him. He entered the Marine office and approached a sergeant. "I want to enlist," he said.

"In what?" the sergeant asked.

"I'd like to enlist in the Marine Corps," Jasper explained.

"You can't enlist in here," replied the sergeant. "We don't have any place for you."

Following a brief, futile exchange, Jasper walked six blocks to Marine Headquarters. An officer there informed him that the Marines did not accept Negroes, spun on his heel, and walked away. Out of options, the reporter went home to write up his tale of woe.[12]

Congress was at that moment debating a bill to initiate a peace-time draft. Although the measure enjoyed overwhelming support, progress had stalled while the Senate debated an amendment to forbid discrimination and segregation in the military. White Southerners joined the War Department in denouncing the proposal. "I hope for heaven's sake they won't mix the white and colored troops together in the same units for then we shall certainly have trouble," Secretary of the Navy Frank Knox wrote in his diary. Like many congressmen, Secretary Knox believed African Americans lacked leadership skills and thought equal treatment would ruin morale. A 1940 navy board study endorsed his fears. "The enlistment of Negroes (other than as mess attendants) leads to disruptive and undermining conditions," it concluded. This moment of crisis was no time for risky experiments in social engineering.[13]

Passed in mid September, the Selective Service Act included a toothless antidiscrimination clause. "No Negro, because of race, shall be excluded from enlistment in the Army for service with colored military units," it read. In other words, the military could not prevent black recruits from joining segregated regiments simply because they were black. Of the 500,000 men in the Army when President Roosevelt signed the bill, 4,700 of them, less than 1 percent, were black.

The Army had just five black officers: Colonel Benjamin Davis, Sr.; his son, Lieutenant Benjamin Davis, Jr.; and three chaplains. No African Americans served in the Army's medical, dental, veterinary, signal, field artillery, or coastal artillery branches. There were no black pilots in the Army Air Corps, and none enrolled in flying cadet programs.[14]

The Navy had an even shoddier record. All of its 4,600 African Americans served as mess attendants. Their uniforms closely resembled waiters' outfits, and they lived in segregated quarters both on base and on ships. There were no black midshipmen at the United States Naval Academy. As Congress was debating the conscription bill, fifteen frustrated messmen from the *U.S.S. Philadelphia* penned an open letter to the *Pittsburgh Courier*. "We sincerely hope to discourage any other colored boys who might have planned to join the Navy and make the same mistake we did," they wrote. "All they would become is seagoing bell hops, chambermaids and dishwashers." Outraged officers tossed the authors into the brig, then dishonorably discharged them.[15]

America's defense contractors also kept blacks on the sidelines, maintaining discriminatory hiring practices even as they strained to fill escalating orders for planes, tanks, and ships. Of the nation's 100,000 aircraft industry workers, just 240 were black. Steel mills and shipyards funneled the few blacks they did hire into unskilled positions. Businessmen made no secret of their bigotry. "The Negro will be considered only as janitors and in other similar capacities," North American Aviation's company spokesman said. "Regardless of their training as aircraft workers, we will not employ them." Many unions accepted this exclusionary policy for fear that introducing black workers might disrupt labor unity. Defense plants also kept Jews, Mexican Americans, and other minorities outside their gates.[16]

"We want democracy to survive," argued NAACP executive secretary Walter White at the group's 1940 national conference, "but we want true democracy and not the spurious hypocritical brand which has been handed out to us in the past." White was one of many African Americans voicing their outrage. A. Philip Randolph's Brotherhood of Sleeping Car Porters (BSCP) passed a resolution urging the Roosevelt administration to dismantle discrimination. Black newspapers ran stories about closed factory doors and mistreated African American soldiers. The *Pittsburgh Courier* formed a Committee for the Participation of Negroes in the National Defense to pressure the federal government to act. Michigan state senator Charles Diggs electrified blacks when he called for nation-wide protest marches.[17]

All this talk changed nothing. Neither industry nor the military seemed interested in African Americans' services. Washington offered grand rhetoric about preserving democracy without doing anything to make it a reality at home. Black activists requested meetings with the president, hoping to convince him to equalize opportunities. Roosevelt's subordinates intercepted their missives before they reached the president's desk. African Americans watched as the military buildup lifted white workers out of the decade-long economic depression. They saw themselves being left behind again, shut out of a great movement that would forever change their country's economic, social, and cultural pathways. They had no clear leader and no consistent program.

Randolph saw opportunity amidst the anger. America's nightmarish post-WWI racial climate had informed his early years as a radical magazine editor. His long struggle to unionize the porters had given him a firsthand look at racial and class inequalities. He had observed the NAACP's unwillingness to court the black masses and noted radicals' inability to unite them. Now, well into middle age but still bursting with energy, he decided to seize the mantle of leadership. The world was marching to war, and Randolph was determined to be part of the parade. No one in power wanted to challenge the racial status quo. But for Randolph that was the whole point of the war. There was no use saving democracy so long as democracy applied only to whites.

Franklin Roosevelt opened his eyes at 8:00 A.M. on September 27, 1940. Lying in his old-fashioned mahogany bed, he looked around at the clutter that seemed to follow wherever he went. Roosevelt was an exceptional compartmentalizer who warehoused issues in the deep recesses of his mind until the exact moment he needed them. His room, however, betrayed a man better at collecting items than storing them. Pictures, most of them with nautical themes, covered the walls. Most hung slightly askew. Books and papers overflowed his nightstand.[18]

Roosevelt used his tremendous upper-body strength, a compensation for his withered legs, paralyzed for nearly twenty years, to maneuver himself to where he could reach a button by his bed. He pressed it, and a valet entered the room, carried him to the bathroom, and returned him to bed. FDR tossed an old blue cape over his ratty pajamas. Another servant brought his breakfast and the daily press. The president ate his soft-boiled eggs, buttered toast, and orange juice while reading the newspapers strewn around him. He tucked a Camel cigarette, the first of forty for the day, into his ivory cigarette holder and lit it with a sigh. Aides dropped off reports while a body man bathed, dressed, and shaved the president. Treasury Secretary Henry Morgenthau stopped by to discuss the latest economic data.

At 10:30 a valet lifted FDR into his customized wheelchair, really just an armless kitchen chair retrofitted with small wheels and an ashtray. He rolled the president across the hall to the elevator. A Secret Serviceman trailed with an armload of baskets stuffed with the day's paperwork. The doors, paneled with oak boards cut from Boston's Old South Church, opened on the ground floor. Roosevelt's man pushed him down the sunny outdoor colonnade, then swung right to enter the president's oval-shaped office. FDR hoisted himself into the chair behind his desk, where he became a virtual prisoner for the rest of the day.

By presidential standards he had a light Friday, with nothing scheduled after lunch. Ambassador William Bullitt, recently returned from Nazi-occupied France, stuck his head in for a quick word just as an usher waved in a gaggle of reporters for the 683rd press conference of FDR's presidency. Roosevelt flicked a switch on his desk lamp as they entered, activating a microphone concealed within the shade. A recording device in a padlocked compartment under the floor clicked into action.

Roosevelt turned in his usual brilliant performance. He mocked his enemies, regaled reporters with stories, and twisted their questions to suit his agenda. An usher showed them out after ten minutes of banter. Roosevelt forgot to turn off his brand-new eavesdropping system. The tape rolled as he leaned back in his chair, lit another cigarette, and contemplated the three black men waiting to discuss African Americans' role in the defense effort with him. He had met two of them, T. Arnold Hill of the Urban League and Walter White of the NAACP. He figured he could appease them without much difficulty. The third, A. Philip Randolph, was a stranger, although Roosevelt knew his reputation for stubbornness and incorruptibility. FDR thought Randolph might be tricky, but felt sure he could handle him.

Randolph awoke that morning in a cheap, segregated hotel in Washington's Black Belt. After donning his suit—no one could remember ever seeing him without a suit—he stepped into the crisp autumn morning to meet White and Hill for some premeeting strategizing at the local NAACP office. At Hill's suggestion, they hammered out a one-and-a-half-page proposal to revolutionize the defense establishment's use of African Americans. Their memo demanded more black officers, the immediate training of black pilots, a desegregated Army, additional opportunities for blacks in the Navy, and more African American defense workers.[19]

Designing their blueprint was easy. Convincing Roosevelt to embrace it would be far more difficult. The president had avoided meetings with African American groups since the war crisis began. Today's sit-down was happening only because of Eleanor's intervention. Mary McLeod Bethune, a member of FDR's "Black Cabinet" and Eleanor's close friend, had spent months passing the first lady information about discrimination in the military. Yet Eleanor did not fully grasp the situation until she accepted Randolph's invitation to address a Brotherhood of Sleeping Car Porters' convention in Harlem. Right before taking the stage, she listened as Randolph and White described the military's treatment of African Americans and informed her that FDR had ignored repeated requests for a conference. Finally convinced, she promised to do what she could.

A crowd of 2,000 porters stomped and cheered when Bethune introduced Eleanor as the "personification of democracy." They went wild when the first lady pledged her "faith, cooperation, and energy" to the cause of racial justice. Later that evening, Eleanor dictated a note to her husband from her Greenwich Village apartment. "There is a growing feeling amongst the colored people ... [that] they should be allowed to participate in any training that is going on, in the aviation, army, navy," it read. "This is going to be very bad politically besides being intrinsically wrong and I think you should ask that a meeting be held."[20]

Two days later, Eleanor, still in New York, took a call from Stephen Early, FDR's press secretary. Early was furious about the first lady's end run around the president's schedulers, who had shielded Roosevelt from African Americans bearing petitions. Not only had FDR accepted Eleanor's suggestion to meet the black leaders, Early said, he had also followed her recommendation to invite the secretaries of war and the navy. This was an important matter, Eleanor replied, and Franklin needed to make sure the secretaries treated it as such. She returned to the capital a few days later with a gift from Walter White to the president: a clutch of newspaper clippings about military segregation and discrimination.

As much as FDR disliked discrimination, his about-face stemmed from political rather than moral calculations. The election was just five weeks away, and the president, running for an unprecedented third term, needed the black vote. African Americans had renounced their Republican loyalties in 1936. It was unclear whether their defection represented a short-term electoral hiccup or a long-term realignment. Roosevelt wanted to keep black Northerners in the Democratic column. He needed to at least make a show of hearing their concerns.

Roosevelt also needed white Southern votes. Electoral victory therefore required delicate political maneuvering. Democrats inserted a vague civil rights plank into their 1940 platform, hoping to satisfy African Americans and Northern liberals without repelling Southern conservatives. Republicans sensed an opportunity to recapture Northern states they lost in 1932 and 1936. Their platform demanded an end to discrimination in the military and endorsed a federal antilynching law. Their candidate, Indiana businessman Wendell Willkie, blasted the president's record on race as he plied the campaign trail. Willkie's pro-civil rights stance won over black editorialists who had supported Roosevelt in previous elections.

Roosevelt received mixed signals from the black community. Influential black papers, including the reliably Democratic *Baltimore Afro-American*, endorsed Willkie. On the other hand, BSCP delegates gave Ashley Totten a rowdy standing ovation when he remarked that "President Roosevelt is without doubt the greatest man that has ever slept in the White House." FDR spent cabinet meetings pondering whether black defections might tip the electoral balance in New York, New Jersey, Ohio, and other heavily urban states. With the elections fast approaching, his meeting with Randolph, White, and Hill loomed as a possible make-or-break moment for his candidacy.[21]

Confidence mingled with nervousness as Randolph waited with White and Hill outside the president's office. Randolph maintained an external aura of calm dignity, smoothing his dark suit and adjusting his already perfect pocket square. He had recently called Wendell Willkie "one of the best white friends the Negro people have ever had," but was willing to give Roosevelt a chance to satisfy African Americans' demands. Randolph knew that FDR's need to court black voters gave him unprecedented political leverage.[22]

Randolph had visited the White House once before. In 1925 he joined a delegation headed by black newspaperman W. Monroe Trotter to meet Calvin Coolidge. Randolph stood mute while Trotter pleaded for federal protection from lynching. Coolidge fidgeted behind his desk, offering no response. "He just sat there, listening, betraying no emotion whatever," Randolph recalled. As the group was leaving, the president broke his silence to ask Trotter how things were back in Boston, where Coolidge had lived during his term as governor of Massachusetts. "All right, all right, Mr. President," Trotter replied. At least Coolidge hadn't been hostile, Randolph thought as he exited the room.[23]

This time would be different. Randolph would speak, and the president would listen. He strode into the Oval Office with White and Hill. They perched on a sofa across from Navy Secretary Frank Knox. Secretary of War Henry Stimson was nowhere to be seen. Thinking the whole thing ludicrous, he dispatched Assistant Secretary Robert Patterson in his place. Randolph glanced around the room, taking in the nautical prints and Hudson River valley landscapes surrounding him. A riot of paperweights, lighters, salt and pepper shakers, toy donkeys, and other knickknacks covered the president's oversized desk. Wire in-baskets overflowed with papers. Roosevelt leaned back in his chair, his big head cocked and his eyes dancing from left to right, taking the measure of the men before him. His cigarette holder stood at attention. A welcoming smile played across his face. What lay behind that smile was anybody's guess; Roosevelt's face was both extraordinarily expressive and utterly detached from his true thoughts.

Randolph saw himself as the president's ally on foreign affairs. Like FDR, he opposed direct American involvement in the war. "It would be the graveyard of our civil liberties," he believed. Yet a Nazi victory was unthinkable. "If Hitler wins," Randolph wrote in an editorial for the Committee to Defend America by Aiding the Allies, "the black tides of reaction, tyranny and despotism, the cult of force, mass murder and espionage will not only sweep away the last vestige of humanity in Europe, but will threaten our American system of democracy and liberty." Even though Britain had an abysmal record on race in its colonies, it still stood on the side of democracy against fascism.[24]

Randolph now aimed to win over the president on domestic policy. But Walter White, who knew Roosevelt best, considered himself the delegation's spokesman and tried to seize the initiative. "The Negro people … feel that they're not wanted in the various armed forces of the country," he said as FDR's secret recording unit whirred, "and they feel they have earned the right to participate … , [but] they're feeling that they are being shunted aside."[25]

Roosevelt shifted into stall mode, hoping to run out the clock by spinning yarns and charming his guests into submission. Randolph refused to play along. He frequently interrupted FDR's ramblings, violating White House etiquette. The contrast between the two men's conversational styles was stark. FDR bobbed and weaved, speaking in almost random puffs of verbiage that somehow congealed into a cloud of rhetoric. Randolph, his deep voice betraying no emotion, responded in sentences so perfectly formed that he could have been reading from a book. His tenacity forced Roosevelt to come to the point. The president assured his guests that the military would open new branches to African Americans soon. Patterson chimed in, noting that the regular Army was planning to call up hundreds of black reserve officers.

Randolph wanted more. "Mr. President, it would mean a great deal to the morale of the Negro people if you could make some announcement on the role that Negroes will play in the armed forces of the nation." "Yeah, yeah, yeah, yeah," the president stammered, promising to mention African Americans in a future speech. At least my administration has enrolled some black soldiers into combat units, Roosevelt retorted. "That's a start," Randolph allowed. "Hell, you and I know it's a step ahead," Roosevelt replied in a conspiratorial voice, as if to suggest that more steps were coming. FDR observed that all-black units serving next to all-white units might get mixed together under the stress of war, allowing the forces to "back into" integration. Patterson seconded his hypothesis.

Randolph, feeling emboldened, asked Secretary Knox about integrating the Navy. "We have a factor in the Navy that is not so in the Army," Knox replied, "and that is that these men live aboard ship. And in our history we don't take Negroes into a ship's company." This was not technically true, as blacks had filled many roles aboard vessels until President Woodrow Wilson segregated the fleet in the 1910s. "If you could have a northern ship and a southern ship it would be different,"

Roosevelt laughed, "but you can't *do* that." He promised to discuss military discrimination with his cabinet and assured his guests that they would meet again. White handed over their memo as a smiling Roosevelt waved them goodbye. They left in high spirits, convinced they had bested the cagey president. It took them a while to realize they had never discussed discrimination in the defense industry.

Secretary Knox stayed behind as FDR prepared for his next meeting. "I forgot to mention we are training a certain number of musicians on board ship, the ship's band," Roosevelt mused. Knox nodded in agreement. "Now, there's no reason why we shouldn't have a colored band on some of these ships, because they're darn good at it," Roosevelt continued, unconsciously replacing the "Negro" he had used a few minutes ago with more derogatory title.

"You know," he concluded, "at worst it will increase the *opportunity*. That's what we're after."

Knox threatened to resign if the president integrated the Navy.

"I sent Patterson to this meeting, because I really had so much else to do," Secretary of War Stimson wrote in his diary that night. "According to him it was a rather amusing affair—the President's gymnastics as to politics. I saw the same thing happen 23 years ago when Woodrow Wilson yielded to the same sort of demands and appointed colored officers to several of the divisions that went over to France, and the poor fellows made perfect fools of themselves.... Leadership is not embedded in the Negro race yet.... Colored troops do very well under white officers but every time we try to lift them a little beyond where they can go, disaster and confusion follow.... I hope for heaven's sake they won't mix the white and colored troops together in the same units for then we shall certainly have trouble."[26]

Randolph took FDR's vague assurances at face value, failing to recognize his role as a pawn in a political chess match. Deferring to the White House's wishes, Randolph and White kept mum about the substance of their visit. As days passed without comment, they began to wonder whether the president's sympathy actually meant anything. White pressed Roosevelt's people for some public comment about their meeting. None came. Sensing the momentum slipping away, he banged out a press release describing the Oval Office conversation. "While very little was definitely promised so far as action against these barriers is concerned," it stated, "we believe definite progress was made."[27]

White's optimistic statement invited the president to publicly denounce racial prejudice. Roosevelt declined this offer. It took the White House two weeks to acknowledge that the meeting occurred. On October 9, Press Secretary Stephen Early gathered reporters around his desk for an informal press conference. Twirling his horn-rimmed glasses in his right hand, his pipe in easy reach, Early ran down the president's appointments for the day in his gentle Virginia drawl. He then reminded the scribes of FDR's recent sit-down with "Walter White and, I think, two other Negro leaders." "As a result of that conference," he continued, "the War Department has drafted a statement of policy with regard to Negroes in national defense." He then distributed copies of the statement. Nobody bothered to ask about the meeting or about a memo that read in part: "The policy of the War Department is not to intermingle colored and white enlisted personnel in the same regimental organizations."[28]

Early was a loyal member of the president's inner circle, known for his intimate familiarity with FDR's thinking. Journalists therefore took his words to mean that FDR's black visitors had okayed an order reaffirming military segregation. African American newspapers reacted with outrage. "Race 'Leaders' Demand Jim-Crow Army Units" screamed the *Chicago Defender*. Randolph and White immediately telegraphed the president. White called Early's statement "one of the most unexpected blows the Negro has received from the hands of one supposed to be a friend." Roosevelt's secretaries withheld the missives from the president, hoping to resolve the flap without involving the boss.[29]

"It is manifest that once more the President has surrendered abjectly and completely to the most bitter anti-Negro forces of the country," Walter White vented in a letter to New York City mayor Fiorello LaGuardia. He rumbled about staging mass meetings around the country to protest the administration's indifference toward racial justice. Early waited nine days before trying to defuse the crisis. In a personal letter to White, whom Early saw as the instigator of the backlash, the press secretary blamed the media for misinterpreting his statement. The White House had no responsibility for setting the facts straight, he claimed. Assistant Secretary Patterson invited White, Randolph, and Hill to meet with him. White was interested, but Randolph rejected the proposal.[30]

A White House Run- Around Conference

Cartoon from the *Baltimore Afro-American*, 12 October 1940. Black newspapers ridiculed Randolph, White, and Hill when they appeared to endorse segregation in a 1940 White House meeting with President Roosevelt. *Courtesy of the* Afro-American *Newspapers Archives and Research Center*

White, with Randolph's support, insisted on a clarification from FDR himself. The administration had a "moral obligation" to correct the misunderstanding, he told Early. With the election drawing close, Roosevelt called a ceasefire in the battle of semantics. He ordered Early to apologize for his poor choice of words and sent White, Randolph, and Hill letters affirming that African Americans would some day serve in all branches of the military. He promised to ask the Army to call up black reserve officers and said black GIs would receive an equal shot at officers' commissions. "Rest assured," FDR concluded, "that further developments of policy will be forthcoming to insure that Negroes are given fair treatment on a non-discriminatory basis."[31]

Roosevelt tempered his apology, which contained precious few specifics and no timetable, with a separate statement to the press. "As to the policy of the War Department regarding the intermingling of

White and Colored personnel," he wrote, "the thought in my mind ... was that in the present dangerous crisis ... we dare not confuse the issue of prompt preparedness with a new social experiment, however important and desirable it may be." Caught between two crucial voting blocs, the president was aiming to play the middle, promising African Americans that change was coming while promising the South that the status quo would remain intact.[32]

Wendell Willkie pounced on his squirming opponent. Republicans had no hope of carrying the South, which had voted Democratic ever since Southern "redeemers" toppled Republican-led state governments during the Reconstruction era. To win the 1940 election, Willkie needed to sweep the North, and black voters might just provide his margin of victory. His campaign took out full-page ads in black newspapers touting his antidiscrimination positions and guaranteeing African Americans a voice in his administration. The Republican candidate attracted 10,000 admirers to a rally at Harlem's Golden Gate Ballroom. He captured an endorsement from the most popular black man in America, heavyweight champion Joe Louis.

"The Negroes are taking advantage of this period just before [the] election to try to get everything they can in the way of recognition from the Army," Secretary of War Henry Stimson groused. Indeed, the intense pressure African Americans placed on the White House, along with the botched handling of the September 27 conference, forced the president to endorse several measures aimed at securing the black vote. Roosevelt answered African Americans' demand for a voice on Selective Service, the agency charged with overseeing the draft, by appointing YMCA executive director Campbell Johnson as an executive assistant to the director. He quieted calls for a black assistant secretary of war when he named Judge William Hastie as Secretary Stimson's civilian aide. Hastie, a graduate of Harvard Law and a former dean of Howard University's law school, planned on using the position to expose discrimination and to open opportunities for blacks. Aware of the military's innate conservatism, he doubted his efforts would produce much tangible change. Stimson opposed Hastie's appointment, complaining that he might next have to deal with "a colored Admiral." The secretary kept Hastie at arm's length, ordering him to submit recommendations through

Assistant Secretary Patterson instead of going directly to him. Hastie, hamstrung though he was, became a hero within the black community.[33]

African Americans celebrated again when Roosevelt promoted sixty-two-year-old colonel Benjamin Davis to become the United States' first black brigadier general. It was a blatantly political move; only two weeks earlier the Army had elevated one hundred white colonels with less service time over Davis's head. The Army did not know what to do with its new general, who had enlisted during the Spanish-American War and whose last posting was with the New York National Guard's all-black 369th Coast Artillery. For the moment it kept him as a general with no command so as not to place him above white officers. He eventually accepted a desk job in Washington.

No race crusader could have advanced so far in the Army. The light-skinned, bespectacled Davis was a get-along officer. Black soldiers would mock the general during the war because his well-publicized inspection tours never managed to uncover any anti-black prejudice. "A military figure-head," one GI grumbled. "The name of B. O. Davis, Sr., was synonymous with 'yes-sirism' and 'Uncle Tomism,'" protested another. His promotion nevertheless touched off a firestorm of criticism. "Without deprecating the negro race," an Illinois couple telegrammed the White House, "it is incomprehensible to normal Americans for you to appoint a member of the red, yellow, or black race to the high rank of Brigadier General." A correspondent from West Virginia asked the president, "Are you crazy appointing a nigger as general in the United States Army?" *Time* magazine, understanding Davis's symbolic importance to black voters, suggested retiring him after the election.[34]

"We asked Mr. Roosevelt to change the rules of the game and he counters by giving us some new uniforms," the *Baltimore Afro-American*'s pre-election issue complained. Black leaders' appeals produced token victories over military discrimination and none against segregation, yet White and others acted as if they had won major concessions. Such bravado reflected their need to produce results to maintain their standing and their fundraising clout. At the same time they could not risk alienating their followers, most of whom remained loyal to the president. Roosevelt garnered two thirds of the black vote in 1940.[35]

"We want no favors," thundered Reverend D. A. Holmes to a crowd of 5,000 cheering Kansas Citians, "but under almighty God, there is not going to be any national defense unless the Negro has a part in it." Even black Americans who voted for Roosevelt condemned the administration's unwillingness to make politically risky moves on their behalf. African American newspapers fulminated against the lack of defense jobs at a time when the military buildup suffered from severe labor shortages. Segregation and inequality permeated the armed forces. Blacks offered to do their fair share only to be told that their country did not want them.[36]

Frustrated as they were, African Americans could not unite behind a leader or a plan. Randolph aspired to fill that void. Smarting from his encounter with FDR, he felt the time for letters and meetings had passed. His experience with the labor movement had convinced him that individuals could not win change alone, and that leaders must mobilize their supporters to action. Randolph was searching for a dramatic gesture capable of mobilizing the black community behind a single agenda.

Inspiration came during a December 1940 train ride with his trusted lieutenant Milton P. Webster. They departed from Washington, DC, planning to visit BSCP chapters throughout the South. The longtime friends discussed inequalities in the defense program as their train chugged through the Virginia hills. Webster fell uncharacteristically silent, his ample chin tucked into his expansive chest. Being in the South always unnerved Webster. They were in former slave territory now. Randolph stared out the window of their segregated coach. Virginians had once owned his ancestors.[37]

"You know, Web," Randolph finally said, "calling on the president and holding those conferences are not going to get us anywhere."

Webster looked up, waiting for the Chief to work his methodical way to a conclusion.

"We are going to have to do something about it," Randolph continued, as if prompting his companion to speak.

Webster held his tongue. He reclined in his seat and watched the countryside roll by. He did not know what Randolph had decided, but obviously he had decided something. All he could do now was act as an audience for the speech Randolph was composing in his head.

Milton P. Webster, Randolph's longtime associate and a vocal civil rights advocate. *Library of Congress, Prints and Photographs Collection, LC-USZ62-97539*

"I think we ought to get 10,000 Negroes to march on Washington in protest, march down Pennsylvania Avenue," Randolph mused. "What do you think of that?"

It was a good idea, Webster chuckled, but where did Randolph plan on finding 10,000 African Americans willing to stage such a protest?

"I think we can get them," Randolph concluded.

Silence again enshrouded them as the train rattled south. They had fought many battles together, but none involving so many soldiers, and none with such high stakes.

Randolph and Webster soon discovered how difficult it would be to convince thousands of African Americans to march for their rights. They stopped first in Savannah, Georgia, a city where blacks learned at a young age that caution was key to survival. A decent turnout nevertheless awaited the fiery labor leaders. Enthusiasm turned to horror once

Randolph started talking about raising a black army to invade the capital. "It scared everyone to death," Webster remembered. "The head colored man in Savannah opened up the meeting and introduced me, and ran off the platform to the last seat in the last row. And when I looked up there a second time, he was gone." Similar reactions awaited them in Jacksonville, Tampa, and Miami.[38]

The idea of marching on Washington to air grievances originated with Ohio businessman Jacob Coxey. In 1894, during a terrible economic depression, he paraded a ragtag band of five hundred protesters down Pennsylvania Avenue to demand public works jobs. Critics mocked "Coxey's Army" as "bums and blackmailers." Connecticut senator Joseph Hawley worried that "it may become a habit to make pilgrimages annually to Washington and endeavor to dominate Congress by the physical presence of the people." Authorities sentenced Coxey to twenty days in prison for walking on the grass outside the Capitol. His supporters disbanded soon after.[39]

Women's suffragists staged an enormous demonstration in the capital in 1913, and many more in the following years. Onlookers, most of them men, tripped, pushed, and otherwise harassed the 5,000 marchers. Henry Stimson, who served as secretary of war under both William Howard Taft and, twenty years later, Franklin Roosevelt, dispatched a cavalry unit to control the crowd. In 1932, World War I veterans descended on Washington to demand early payment of a cash bonus promised for their military service. With the Great Depression in its third year, many war heroes saw the bonus, which the government was supposed to pay in 1945, as their last hope against starvation. President Herbert Hoover rebuffed their appeals. After several fruitless attempts to talk the Bonus Army into leaving, Hoover assigned a military detachment to clear its encampments. General Douglas MacArthur expelled the demonstrators with what many considered excessive force. Troops wielded fixed bayonets, fired nonlethal poison gas, and razed the protesters' camps. Front-page photos of soldiers brutalizing ex-soldiers drove the final nail into Hoover's political coffin.

Franklin Roosevelt learned from his predecessor's mistake. When another delegation of veterans came to Washington in 1933, the new president provided tents and food and sent Eleanor to listen to their stories. His tolerance flashed a green light to other groups seeking a platform. Subsequent years saw pacifists, communists, disaffected relief workers, and anti–New Dealers march down Washington's streets. None had much effect on the president, who did a masterful job of accommodating their needs, hearing their demands, and sending them on their way with a friendly pat on the back.

Randolph could be confident that Roosevelt would not use force to disperse a march. He had no idea whether he could actually muster a 10,000-person army. Black newspapers ignored his initial calls to march. White newspapers hadn't mentioned him in years, if ever. Organizations such as the NAACP and the Urban League adopted a wait-and-see attitude. Grassroots mobilization of the black masses was beyond their experience and out of their comfort zone. Their leaders preferred more dignified activities aimed at wooing well-connected white liberals. On a more practical level, boosting Randolph's fortunes might diminish their own membership rolls and fundraising capacities.

In January 1941 Randolph wrote a press release that finally grabbed some attention. White editors tossed it into the trash. Black editors plastered it across their front pages. It opened with a full-throated roar against the status quo. "Negroes are not getting anywhere with National Defense," Randolph wrote. "The whole National Defense setup reeks and stinks with race prejudice, hatred, and discrimination. It is obvious to anyone who is not deaf, dumb and blind that the south, with its attitude that the Negro is inferior, worthless, and just simply doesn't count, is in the saddle. ... The north, east and west are also to blame, because they wink, connive at and acquiesce in this practice of discriminating against Negroes."[40]

Polite requests and august delegations were useless. The administration, beholden to white Southerners who dominated congressional committees and military leadership, pacified African Americans with empty promises. Randolph's political analysis reflected his socialist and labor roots. Government reform came not in response to moral wrongs, but rather to intense pressure from motivated social groups. And, Randolph declared in a slap at conservative black organizations, "power and pressure do not reside in the few, the intelligentsia, they lie in and flow from the masses." Power is unleashed whenever the masses coalesce behind "a definite purpose."

Randolph wanted to invest the masses with purpose. "I suggest that 10,000 Negroes march on Washington, DC ... with the slogan

WE LOYAL NEGRO-AMERICAN CITIZENS DEMAND THE RIGHT TO WORK AND FIGHT FOR OUR COUNTRY," he declared. He envisioned an all-black force. "Such a pilgrimage ... would wake up and shock Official Washington as it has never been shocked before," Randolph explained, because "nobody expects 10,000 Negroes to get together and march anywhere for anything at any time. Negroes are supposed not to have sufficient iron in their blood for this type of struggle."

His statement built to an aggressive conclusion. "If Negroes are going to get anything out of this National Defense," he asserted, "WE MUST FIGHT FOR IT AND FIGHT FOR IT WITH GLOVES OFF."

Randolph's appeal struck several familiar chords. His insistence on an all-black march recalled Marcus Garvey's boisterous parades from the 1920s. His class-based vision pitting the masses against the elite connected with socialists, communists, and laborites. His emphasis on economic justice associated the march with a major New Deal priority. It also tied Randolph's nascent movement to the Four Freedoms speech President Roosevelt had delivered ten days earlier. In it FDR outlined the fundamental rights of all men: The freedom of speech and worship, and freedom from want and fear. Randolph's release gloried in the power of free speech and offered a plan to free African Americans from want and fear. Finally, his call echoed Mohandas K. Gandhi's nonviolent, mass liberation movement in the British colony of India. It was a breathtaking vision almost completely bereft of details. Those would come later, Randolph reasoned. For now, he just wanted to arouse interest in his vision.

His announcement diverged from his previous agenda in one crucial way. An all-black march might echo Marcus Garvey while demonstrating African Americans' determination to stand on their own two feet, but it undermined Randolph's earlier efforts to promote an interracial, working-class brotherhood committed to economic justice for all. His exclusionary proviso also distanced him from moderate organizations, such as the NAACP, that benefited from close ties with white liberals. In the heat of the moment he seems to have given little thought to the matter. When questioned about the decision, he claimed a black-only march would prevent communists from hijacking the event. Subsequent events would prove it a fateful move.

Randolph focused on turning his idea into reality. He harbored private doubts about his plan, which resembled his toothless 1928 bluster about staging a walkout against the Pullman Company. But he saw no other way to strike a blow for African American rights. As he explained to author Roi Ottley, "the administration leaders in Washington will never give the Negro justice until they see masses—ten, twenty, fifty thousand Negroes on the White House lawn."[41]

CHAPTER 3

One Hundred Thousand, Mister President

N ew Deal dollars had remade Washington, DC. Construction
crews erected imposing new buildings to shelter the federal
government's growing army of bureaucrats. Laborers on the
National Mall removed fifty-year-old trees and covered Victorian-era
walking paths to create the unbroken expanse of green that A. Philip
Randolph hoped to fill with protesting blacks. Reminders of the United
States' long struggle for freedom ringed the Mall. Monuments to Washington and Lincoln, the presidents most responsible for creating and preserving the republic, stood at each end. Statues of Union generals—James
Garfield, Ulysses S. Grant, and George Meade—dotted the perimeter.

Despite the renovations and the many reminders of the war that
brought emancipation, Washington's 200,000 black residents felt excluded from the remodeled city. "Is Jim-Crow in Washington?" Randolph
asked. "What a question! Is water wet? Is fire hot? ... Washington is
not only the capital of the nation. It is the capital of Dixie. ... There,
crackerocracy is in the saddle. Ku Klux Klanism runs riot."[1]

Randolph exaggerated, but not much. Many black Americans despised the capital city. It was a place where schools segregated them,
cabbies and landlords overcharged them, restaurants (including those in
the Senate, House of Representatives, and many government buildings)
denied them seats, and stores refused to sell to them. Boxing promoters
never put more than two bouts pitting black versus white on a card. "It
was a hate-drenched city," photographer Gordon Parks recalled.[2]

Privation and discrimination existed within blocks of the White
House. Thousands of destitute African Americans crammed into

dirt-floor shacks in areas known as Pig Alley and Goat Alley. Blacks in the District suffered from astronomical rates of tuberculosis, infant mortality, and venereal disease. A young railroad worker named Malcolm Little, who later renamed himself Malcolm X, recoiled when he remembered his early 1940s arrival in town. "I had seen a lot," he wrote in his *Autobiography*, "but never such a dense concentration of stumblebums, pushers, hookers, public crap-shooters, even little kids running around at midnight begging for pennies, half-naked and barefooted."[3]

Washington's small but proud black middle class, barred from respectable white neighborhoods, lodged in crumbling red brick homes. College graduates hauled freight, mopped floors, and cooked for white families. A lucky few worked as mail carriers. These relatively affluent Washingtonians segregated themselves from the rabble beneath them. As in Harlem and other heavily black areas, light-skinned African American elites often shunned those of darker complexion. Black churches and other institutions also divided according to economic status and skin tone.

Cosmopolitan black Northerners such as Randolph imagined Washington as the gateway to the South, the place where the trains changed. African Americans coming from New York rode integrated cars, sharing the same dining and lounge services as whites, until they reached the capital's Union Station. Porters then directed black riders to the older, less-desirable cars right behind the engine and advised them that the dining car was off limits. White riders could enjoy their trip on the Robert E. Lee line to Birmingham, Alabama, or on the Orange Blossom to Randolph's old stomping grounds in Jacksonville, Florida, without ever seeing a black face, except for their porter's.

The district's racial codes made Randolph's January 1941 call to march even riskier. The labor leader was not just proposing the largest-ever gathering of black protesters, he was volunteering to lead an army into enemy territory. But that was exactly the point. "Washington is the head and front and nerve center of the world," Randolph observed, the preeminent symbol of discrimination in a nation preaching equality. African Americans could not gain self-respect, much less the respect of others, until they transformed the capital into an oasis of liberty.[4]

Randolph's summons raised more questions than it answered. He did not know how 10,000 African Americans would get to Washington, where they would eat, or where they would sleep. Nor was he sure what they would do once they got there, if anyone showed up at all. He had time to resolve those issues. For now the most important thing was the stand itself. The time for conferences and requests had passed. It was time for action, for shouting, for demands. The war in Europe had ground to a standstill while Hitler, already master of Austria, Poland, Denmark, Norway, Holland, Belgium, and France, geared up to attack the Soviet Union. In America, still at peace with the world, Randolph had declared war on racial inequality.

Randolph's audacious call resonated because of the context surrounding it. He launched his strike at a time of mounting African American frustration. "I hear you talking about freedom/For the Finn, the Jew, and the Czechoslovak—But you never seem to mention us folks who're black!" Langston Hughes wrote in his 1941 poem "Message to the President." A cacophony of angry voices competed for leadership of the black community. Sign-wielding demonstrators in a dozen cities marched for justice. Black preachers thundered against oppression. Radical splinter movements advised young men to register as conscientious objectors rather than serve in a segregated army. Walter White's NAACP promoted National Defense Day, a collection of rallies, speeches, and musical performances condemning discrimination in the defense effort. African American newspapermen howled at one outrage after another. In Chicago, a black audience booed when the narrator of the propaganda film "Eyes of the Navy" claimed the service welcomed "every race and creed."[5]

"I am afraid that Washington does not realize the steadily growing resentment," White told a friend in the administration. African Americans heard Franklin Roosevelt denounce Nazi racial philosophies while watching labor-starved corporations import white workers from hundreds of miles away rather than hire local blacks. They criticized the administration for accepting industrialists' false claims that African Americans did not apply for positions, and for allowing the United States Employment Service (USES), the federal agency responsible for matching applicants with potential defense employers, to honor "white only" requests from employers. USES placed 8,769 workers in aircraft industry jobs between January and March of 1941. Just thirteen of them were black. Over that same period the United States

Office of Education gave the state of Tennessee $230,000 to train whites for defense jobs, and just $2,000 for blacks. "Nothing short of disgraceful," huffed the *Philadelphia Tribune*. "Unquestionably un-American," concurred the *New York Amsterdam News*.[6]

African Americans faced similar insults when they enlisted. Secretary of the Navy Knox epitomized the armed forces' shoulder-shrug attitude when he told the all-black National Medical Association (the American Medical Association barred blacks from membership) that "putting Negroes in the Navy would be like putting them in hell. The relationships on shipboard are such that white and colored just cannot be mixed." One attendee shot back, "Mr. Secretary, we have lived in hell so long we have become acquainted. ... Put us in hell and we will work our way out."[7]

Racial lines hardened as African American inductees entered military camps. Fort Dix, New Jersey, provided its 20,000 white recruits with the latest equipment and ample space for drilling and mock battles. Fort Dix's 381 black soldiers lacked weapons and marched on a tiny plot of swampy land. Officers restricted black trainees to separate entertainment facilities. Yet camp leaders insisted that they neither discriminated against nor segregated African Americans.

Southern camps were even worse. In March 1941 searchers discovered the body of Private Felix Hall dangling from a tree branch on the grounds of Fort Benning, Georgia. Hall was wearing his uniform when he died. His hands and feet were bound with rope. Post authorities somehow concluded that Hall's death was probably a suicide. A cursory follow-up investigation never located the parties responsible for the lynching.

"We must recognize clearly that we are forced to fight on two fronts," asserted political scientist and future Nobel Peace Prize winner Ralph Bunche. "We must struggle to win our share of the blessings of life in a democratic society, and we must join with the rest of the nation in a wholehearted fight to preserve the democratic ideals of this society. It is only when the latter fight is won that the former can ever again have real meaning."[8]

Randolph agreed that victory overseas meant nothing without equal rights at home. Other black leaders concurred but devoted few resources to an equality-in-defense campaign. The NAACP had long focused on attacking segregation through the courts. Each case absorbed several years and a wealth of intellectual talent. The National Urban League emphasized improving access to health care and other social services. Political and military issues lay outside its realm. Neither organization had much experience mobilizing working-class blacks. Randolph, with his background in grassroots organizing, wanted to fill this gap.

Randolph spent the spring of 1941 mired in contract negotiations with the Pullman Company. He also mounted an unsuccessful bid to organize black locomotive firemen, the men responsible for regulating an engine's coal and water levels. These responsibilities kept him from spending much time on the march. Although he promised an event that would "startle the country," the country didn't seem to be paying attention. No one in the Roosevelt administration noticed him. The black press ignored him. The *Chicago Defender*, one of the few papers to follow up on his initial call, commented that convincing even 2,000 African Americans to march would be "the miracle of the century."[9]

Randolph penned an article entitled "Let the Negro Masses Speak" for the March 1941 issue of *Black Worker*, the BSCP's official organ. "Negroes have a stake in National Defense," it opened. "It is a big stake. It is a vital and important stake. But are we getting our stake?" he asked. "No. Nobody cares anything about us. We are being pushed around."

He maintained this militant tone throughout the piece. A string of staccato jabs at discrimination punctuated his argument. "Let the Negro masses speak!" he demanded. "We are not saboteurs. We are not traitors. We are Americans. We are patriots. We are fighting for the right to work! We are fighting for the right to live! ... Indeed, we would rather die on our feet fighting for Negroes' rights than live on our knees as half-men; as semi-citizens, begging for a pittance."

In a stirring conclusion, Randolph again commanded 10,000 black Americans to march on Washington. "Let them swarm from every hamlet, village and town," he declared, using words similar to those Martin Luther King, Jr. intoned from the steps of the Lincoln Memorial over twenty years later. "From the highways and byways, out of the churches, lodges, homes, schools, mills, mines, factories and fields. Let them come in automobiles, buses, trains, trucks, and on feet. Let them come though the winds blow and the rains beat against them."

Almost as an afterthought, Randolph reiterated his most controversial stipulation. "We call not upon our white friends to march with us," he said. "There are some things Negroes must do alone. This is our fight and we must see it through." Randolph claimed no ill will toward anyone who cherished equality. It was time for ordinary blacks to help themselves. Freedom required self-respect, and self-respect could come only when African Americans could achieve their goals without white support.[10]

"Let the Negro Masses Speak!" got Randolph back on the front pages, or at least on the front pages of black newspapers. The *Washington Afro-American*, an enthusiastic supporter, agreed that "white America is so busy with its own business that it doesn't know about ours." African Americans deserved "a decent, manly squawk in the nation's capital."[11]

With the wind shifting in his favor, Randolph began assembling a coalition. He turned first to Walter White, who treated the NAACP like his own personal fiefdom. White's endorsement would give Randolph access to the organization's nationwide network of chapters and its 100,000 members. Randolph broached the subject in a letter written a few days after "Let the Negro Masses Speak!" appeared. "Something drastic has got to be done to shake official Washington and the white industrialists ... to the realization of the fact that Negroes mean business about getting their rights," he said.[12]

White worried his friend had gone too far. White often appeased the NAACP's more militant members with talk of mass action but preferred to act as a lobbyist who pressed the flesh and cut backstage deals with white powerbrokers. At the moment he was quietly urging senators to convene public hearings on discrimination in defense. His organization relied on white philanthropists likely to oppose an all-black movement. Backing Randolph could cost white donors and political influence. Ignoring him might put him out of touch with the black masses, and on the wrong side of history.

White's subordinates counseled him to shun a potential competitor. Randolph assured him that the march was a one-time event, not the start of a permanent, rival organization. White opted for a middle course. He ordered local chapters to cooperate with what came to be known as the March on Washington Movement (MOWM). On the other hand, the NAACP's official publication, *The Crisis*, printed no news about MOWM. White and his lieutenants tried to neuter MOWM's radical message over the next several weeks. NAACP representatives at MOWM meetings emphasized the need for a positive, nonpartisan agenda that alienated as few people as possible. They excluded leftists from the organizing committee and pleaded without success to allow whites to join.[13]

Randolph's immense prestige, along with the fear of being left out, brought other groups on board. Lester Granger of the National Urban League, the country's second most important black organization, joined up, as did numerous church and civic groups. Members of the Brotherhood of Sleeping Car Porters carried their leader's message along the rails. Except for Randolph's porters, these groups contributed little actual work or money; the NAACP chipped in a few hundred dollars before pleading poverty. White mailed a personal check for ten dollars.[14]

As the weather warmed, MOWM remained just one of several groups agitating for similar goals. One spring weekend saw no fewer than four African American reform committees rally in the capital. Marjorie McKenzie, a *Pittsburgh Courier* correspondent on the scene, grew disheartened as she visited one meeting after another. There was the Chicago Council of Negro Organizations, a body no one had heard of. A few blocks away, the Colored Fireman's Conference drew two hundred delegates to a conference on discrimination. That topped the National Lawyers Guild, where a crowd of fifty heard Lester Granger speak about the defense effort. A gathering of the communist-influenced National Negro Conference devolved into pointless bickering over doctrine. Everyone wanted the same things, yet no one knew how to get them. McKenzie called black leadership "a hydra-headed monster that is incapable of serving us well in this emergency." She could have added that her own paper's brainchild, the Committee on Participation of Negroes in the National Defense Program, had been no more successful than the other heads of the beast.[15]

African Americans were fired up to the point of explosion. Grim statistics paraded across the front pages of their newspapers: 142 black employees out of 29,215 workers in New York City-area defense plants; fifty-six factories with defense contracts in St. Louis, averaging three black employees apiece; over half of defense employers telling the federal government they would not hire African Americans.

Blacks were through with symbolic gestures. In April 1941, Sidney Hillman, a former union leader turned codirector of the Office of Production Management, the federal agency responsible for mobilizing the economy, distributed an official memorandum urging defense contractors to "examine their employment and training policies at once to determine whether or not these policies make ample provision for the full utilization of available and competent Negro workers." Black newspapers flayed the other codirector, former General Motors head William Knudsen, for not signing the note. Hillman meant well but, as the *Chicago Defender* explained, his letter was "a theatrical stunt intended only for the gallery." It offered no enforcement mechanism or concrete actions toward ending employment discrimination. Want ads seeking "white American citizens" remained common.[16]

Randolph demanded action. His widely reprinted editorial, "Why F. D. Won't End Defense Jim Crow," urged Roosevelt to sign an executive order guaranteeing equal access to defense jobs. Randolph accused the president of catering to the "die-hard Southern anti-colored politicians" who ran Congress and the Democratic party. Only mass pressure could move him to make blacks equal citizens. African Americans needed to fight, nonviolently, for their rights.[17]

Randolph promised to issue details about the march soon. He had accelerated his preparations for the event, although he was still splitting time between MOWM and the BSCP. He spent most of May touring the South, recruiting for both organizations. A single stump speech suited both ends, as Randolph exhorted crowds to solve their economic problems through mass action rather than white charity. He usually had a new MOWM chapter in place by the time he boarded a train for his next destination. Locals sprouted like seeds from fertile soil, taking root in Washington, Baltimore, Richmond, Atlanta, Savannah, Jacksonville, and Tampa. More shoots arose as he swung north through Memphis, Kansas City, St. Louis, Chicago, St. Paul, Milwaukee, New York, Newark, and Philadelphia. In a matter of weeks he constructed what the NAACP and other organizations had never managed: a national network of ordinary African Americans dedicated to winning equality on their own rather than by relying on white benefactors.

Randolph preached empowerment in churches, union halls, fraternal chapter rooms, hairdressing salons, pool rooms, saloons, and anyplace else with receptive black ears. MOWM posters dotted urban America. Supporters distributed pamphlets outside movie theaters in black districts. Saturdays became "Button Days," as young women in Chicago, Harlem, Washington, and other cities sold ten-cent pins reading "Negroes March for Jobs in National Defense" from street corners. Soapbox speakers delivered three-minute speeches extolling MOWM. Chapters gathered in churches, YMCAs, and private dwellings to plan local demonstrations and fundraising programs.

For all the noise MOWM made, it hung from a slender thread. Buttons sat in warehouses, ordered but not paid for. Randolph spent as much time soliciting contributions as he did planning or recruiting. Fragile as MOWM was, word of the impending march broke through. Momentum built on itself as black papers vied to catch the surging wave of support. MOWM chapter meetings suddenly became newsworthy events. Randolph's latest militant pronouncements merited front-page coverage. By late May, when he announced July 1 as the date of the march, the black community was in an uproar.

Randolph made every African American, no matter how humble, responsible for social change. "We call upon you to fight for jobs in National Defense," he implored in another widely reprinted editorial. "We call upon you to struggle for the integration of Negroes into the armed forces. ... We call upon you to demonstrate for the abolition of Jim-Crowism in all Government departments and defense employment." Randolph presented the crisis through an all-American, taxation-without-representation lens. African Americans supported the defense effort with billions in taxes while enjoying few benefits from it. A mass drive for self-liberation would force President Roosevelt to abolish discrimination in the government, the military, and the defense industry. "Of course, the task is not easy," he continued. African Americans needed a new mindset. They needed to exchange defeatism for confidence, and subservience for independence.

Randolph deflected potential critics by situating the MOWM within the broader sweep of American history. He cited an array of black Americans who had fought for freedom—Crispus Attucks, Denmark Vesey, Nat Turner, Harriet Tubman, Frederick Douglass—and observed that Abraham Lincoln issued the Emancipation Proclamation at an earlier moment of crisis. Now Franklin Roosevelt had a chance to further Lincoln's legacy. With a stroke of the pen he could banish the "stigma, humiliation and insult of discrimination and Jim-Crowism." Or he could endure thousands of angry black marchers in the capital, along with satellite demonstrations at city halls across the nation.[18]

Bombastic pronouncements aside, Randolph harbored secret doubts as to whether his plan would work. In private conversations he mentioned postponing the march if omens bore ill. He worried about raising enough money and garnering enough publicity. Washington's notoriously racist police department might touch off a riot. The city lacked the restaurants and hotels needed to care for marchers. Black communists might hijack MOWM for their own ideological purposes.[19]

The march had important detractors. "Nothing is going to be accomplished by the crackpot proposal," the *Pittsburgh Courier* remarked. The paper lumped Randolph in with a long line of "publicity hounds, job hunters, and addlepates" who sweet-talked the masses into foolish acts. *Courier* editor Ira F. Lewis admired Randolph's accomplishments for black workers but resented his failure to acknowledge the *Courier's* Committee on Participation of Negroes in the National Defense Program. Lewis neglected to share that tidbit when he asked readers, "Can a parade tell [government officials] anything they do not already know?"[20]

The answer might have surprised Lewis. Randolph, in a cheeky publicity stunt, invited Franklin and Eleanor Roosevelt to address marchers from the Lincoln Memorial. During the monument's 1922 dedication, African Americans stood in a roped-off section across the street. Now, less than twenty years later, a black man was summoning the president to come visit him there. Randolph also asked Office of Production Management codirector William Knudsen to explain why he had refused to sign Sidney Hillman's letter asking defense companies not to discriminate. None of the recipients had heard of MOWM, not even the first lady. Their ignorance proved what Randolph had suspected all along. Although vaguely aware of African Americans' troubles, the administration did not fully comprehend their fury. Officials knew discrimination existed but underestimated its pervasiveness. Roosevelt believed he had done more for blacks than any president since Lincoln. He was too wrapped up in the war crisis to see that more was not enough. Events in Europe and Asia had inspired demands for equality now.[21]

"I am not certain as to the best method of procedure," Assistant Secretary of War Robert Patterson told one of the president's secretaries after reading Randolph's invitation to the Roosevelts. Patterson knew Randolph was a sincere man who favored cold logic over hyperbolic bluster. He spent several days mulling the civil rights leader's threat, or request, or promise, or whatever it was, but still could not fathom what he was up to. Patterson believed the War Department had done all it could to promote equality. It had appointed a black general, Benjamin Davis. It was implementing FDR's promise to place black units in every branch of the service. It was planning a school to train black pilots. It had urged defense contractors to examine their racial policies. What more did Randolph want? Was this call to march really about integrating the armed forces? If so, that was impossible. Morale would plummet, the South would rebel, and hostility to the president's foreign policy would rise.[22]

Anxiety spread around the White House. Roosevelt mused about requiring defense contractors to hire some fixed percentage of black workers—a form of what would later be known as affirmative action. FDR told subordinates to share his disapproval of the march with their African American contacts. Writing the script for supposedly spontaneous encounters, he advised them to say they heard the president remark, "I can imagine nothing that will stir up race hatred and slow up progress more than a march of that kind."[23]

The administration enlisted Eleanor Roosevelt to reinforce the whispering campaign. A passionate, well-timed appeal from her might convince Randolph to halt his mad crusade. "I have talked over your letter with the President," Eleanor told Randolph in a note intended for public consumption, "and I feel very strongly that your group is making a very grave mistake at the present time to allow this march to take place. I am afraid it will set back the progress which is being made, in the Army at least, towards better opportunities and less segregation." The first lady worried that a mass demonstration would stiffen congressional resistance to further progress on civil rights. "You know that I am deeply concerned about the rights of Negro people," she concluded, "but I think one must face situations as they are and not as one wishes them to be." Now was not the time to rock the boat.[24]

Randolph stuck to his guns. He could feel the excitement around him. He believed his proposal had aroused African Americans like nothing since Emancipation. Events were running in his favor, and he had no intention of backing down unless the president took decisive action. Failure to win defense jobs early in this unprecedented military buildup would set African Americans back for years, perhaps decades, to come. Training for defense employment opened access to the high-tech, high-skilled jobs of the future. Without it, black workers would remain trapped in low-skill, low-wage positions.

The war, Randolph, and a lingering illness dragged down the usually upbeat Roosevelt. He summoned Aubrey Williams, the white head of the National Youth Administration and a prominent administration link to African Americans. Williams found FDR sagging in his desk chair, rubbing his eyes with exhaustion. "Aubrey," the president said, "I want you to go to New York and get White and Randolph to call off the march. ... Get the missus and Fiorello ... and get it stopped."[25]

"Fiorello" was New York City mayor Fiorello LaGuardia. Known as the "Little Flower," LaGuardia was a five-foot-two-inch mountain of energy. His jolly rotundity enclosed a feisty crusader for minority rights. New Yorkers of all stripes viewed "Hizzoner" as one of their own. He was the son of a lapsed Catholic father and a Jewish mother, but was brought up Episcopalian. In the 1920s Spanish Harlem, an Italian-Puerto Rican neighborhood a short walk from MOWM headquarters, elected him to Congress. He spoke English, Italian, Yiddish, German, Hungarian, and Serbo-Croatian with a nasal twang that swelled to a screech when he got excited. Diminutive though he was, LaGuardia had an imperial, almost authoritarian presence. His driver zipped him around town in a customized green and white coupe with a light on the roof reading "Mayor." Five white stars—one more than a full general—adorned the vehicle. A two-way radio phone kept him abreast of emergencies, and a pistol in the glove compartment protected him during encounters with hostile constituents.

LaGuardia considered Randolph a friend and had long supported his union work. In 1933, just before winning his first term as mayor, he paid his own way to Chicago to address a BSCP convention. Considering their prior history and LaGuardia's pull in Washington, Randolph gladly accepted the mayor's request to visit City Hall on June 13. With Walter White at his side, he journeyed to lower Manhattan for the 10 A.M. conference. The imposing, French Renaissance style building, a 130-year-old pile of pillars, cupolas, and arched windows, stood about seven miles and one world away from MOWM's Harlem headquarters. The duo got a surprise when they found

Eleanor Roosevelt sitting in the mayor's office. "Franklin asked me to talk to you about the March on Washington," she said as they sat down. "I suppose I need not tell you that the White House is stirred up about it. There is great fear that someone will be killed or injured if such a march takes place."[26]

Randolph took the offensive. He detailed black America's grievances and described the widespread support for the march. He then turned to LaGuardia, ensconced behind a large, low-built walnut desk that maximized what little height he had. "We're going to march on City Hall on June 27th," he told the mayor. LaGuardia looked shocked. "What for, what have I done?" he squeaked. "To ask you to memorialize the president requesting him to issue an executive order to end this shameful practice," Randolph replied.

With LaGuardia reeling, Eleanor appealed to Randolph's practical side. Segregated Washington could not support large numbers of black visitors. Where will your marchers stay, the first lady asked, and where will they eat? Randolph settled in his chair. He thought for a moment, then replied, "Why, they'll go to the hotels and restaurants, register and order dinner."

Randolph was now proposing an assault on segregation as well as discrimination. Eleanor increased the pressure. A march "would tend to make Negroes lose the friends they now have," she observed. The first lady counted herself among those friends. Still Randolph held firm. Finally, with the clock nearing eleven, she gave in. "You know I agree with you," she sighed. "I am ashamed that it is necessary to have a march. I came to bring you the president's feelings on the matter and, I might add, also my own. I hope that you will give it serious consideration." She then extended an olive branch. "Time is getting short," she continued, "and I think the president will invite you to come to Washington to talk about it." Randolph's stubbornness had paid off. He could take his case to the White House.

The president felt terrible. A nagging fever and persistent sore throat had confined him to the White House residence for the past several days. Schedulers trimmed his appointments to a bare minimum. Already in a foul mood, he had no desire to see Randolph and White again. LaGuardia and Eleanor, however, believed a conference was the only way to stop the march. They convinced FDR to meet the black leaders on June 18, five days after the New York City meeting. In the meantime the White House urged Randolph to cancel his demonstration as a sign of good faith. Sensing the administration's fear, Randolph refused. African Americans were too worked up for him to stop the protest without first winning an executive order barring discrimination in the defense effort.

Some of Roosevelt's advisors thought Randolph was bluffing. Even Walter White wondered whether his friend could pull off a significant march. But the mood on the street was electric. Randolph seemed to be in every black church at once, raising money and signing up recruits. BSCP members carried his message to every railroad stop in America. A federation of black women's groups organized a conference in Washington to coincide with the march. Volunteers prepared banners reading "Let Negroes Serve Democracy Now" and "No Color Line on the Assembly Line." Randolph and White coordinated schedules to allow anyone attending the NAACP's convention in Houston to reach the capital by train in time to march. MOWM spent thousands of dollars chartering buses and trains. Black newspapers printed schedules and rate tables.

World War I veterans would lead the march, followed by high school cadets and Boy Scouts. A slow, solemn cadence of muffled drums would accompany the walk from the Capitol to the National Mall. Randolph announced that black singers Marian Anderson, Roland Hayes, and Dorothy Maynor would perform at the Lincoln Memorial.[27]

The march was going to happen, even if no one had any idea how many people to expect. Estimates ranged from 2,000 to 100,000. Washington's police department braced for possible incidents. Southern congressmen spread fears of crazed blacks rioting in the streets. "I think that those who are engaged today in an effort to break down racial barriers, the natural barriers which God Almighty set up, are engaged in a disservice to the civilization of which they are a part," Representative Malcolm Tarver of Georgia argued.[28]

Roosevelt groped for a way out. A march might heighten racial tensions and polarize Democrats at a time when he needed both national and party unity. Still hoping to win a cancellation through half measures, he sent a public letter on discrimination to Office of Production Management directors William Knudsen and Sidney

Hillman. "This situation is a matter of grave importance," he wrote, "and immediate steps must be taken to deal with it. ... No nation combating the increasing threat of totalitarianism can afford arbitrarily to exclude large segments of its population from its defense industries. Even more important is it for us to strengthen our unity and morale by refuting at home the very theories which we are fighting abroad." Randolph agreed with those sentiments. But the president's tepid conclusion disappointed him. "I shall expect the Office of Production Management to take immediate steps to facilitate the full utilization of our productive man-power," Roosevelt wrote.[29]

FDR's message marked the first time the president had publicly commented on discrimination in defense. Yet the White House did its best to downplay the announcement. An ailing Roosevelt stayed upstairs in the residence, leaving Press Secretary Stephen Early to distribute the memo. "[It] really boils down to one thing—the colored issue," Early said as he handed reporters the sheet before disappearing down the hall.[30]

"The president is a shrewd politician," Randolph told a group of MOWM staffers. "The Solid South is legislating Negro affairs in Washington. We won't accept a promise. His promises are political. We should take the position to act if an executive order is not issued." Some protestors would show up even if the march was canceled, White added, and retreating might leave the field open to communists eager to bend a demonstration to their own ends.[31]

Although the communist party was anathema to most Americans, many African Americans hailed it as a militant advocate for racial equality and economic justice. Randolph, a socialist who rejected communist doctrine, condemned the party. Communists nevertheless sniffed around MOWM. The party spent several months hoping the movement would disintegrate, leaving the hated Randolph looking foolish. It partially reversed itself in early June, endorsing MOWM's militancy while deriding Randolph as a misguided tool of capitalists. American communists mocked MOWM for thinking an executive order could right longstanding wrongs. "Jim Crowism does not depend for its existence on the lack of executive orders abolishing it," one communist publication insisted. "Jim Crowism exists because it serves the interests of the capitalist ruling class to keep the working class divided ... along racial lines."[32]

Randolph, overburdened with his MOWM and BSCP duties, did his best to stamp out the red menace. These radicals aimed to "distort and twist the march to serve the propaganda interests of the Soviet-Communist clique," he explained. They had no place in MOWM. At stake was his claim to represent an all-American movement that embodied the New Deal's emphasis on economic fairness. An association with communists would bring cadres of dedicated activists into MOWM while discrediting it among mainstream Americans. The price was too high for Randolph to pay.[33]

"I haven't got any news for you," Stephen Early told the reporters gathered for their morning briefing. The president, still recovering from the flu, had a light day today. Mayor LaGuardia was in the White House, as was Hollywood executive Darryl F. Zanuck. "Nothing exciting," Early said. FDR did have a 2 P.M. conference with Secretary of War Henry Stimson, Secretary of the Navy Knox, Sidney Hillman, William Knudsen, Walter White, and A. Philip Randolph to discuss "Negro discrimination in defense works."

"Who are the last two?" a reporter asked.

"Walter White is the President of the Society for the Advancement of Colored People," Early replied.

"The last fellow's name is what, Steve?" another asked.

"A. Philip Randolph," Early said. "He is coming in with White." The journalists had no follow-up questions.[34]

Roosevelt lay in bed, surrounded by newspapers. Color was seeping back into his face, but his clothes still hung loose on his frame. Every page he turned revealed new problems demanding his attention. A machinists' strike in West Coast shipyards. Fighting in North Africa. German troops massing in occupied Norway, perhaps preparing to invade the Soviet Union. Bottlenecks in defense production. At least the sun was shining. It promised to be a beautiful day outside. Not that he could enjoy it while imprisoned behind his desk, but he preferred good weather to the furious thunderstorms that had rumbled through town the past few days.[35]

FDR had a pretty good sense of how his 2 P.M. appointment would play out. Eleanor had already forwarded a list of MOWM's demands. Randolph's insistence on an executive order abolishing segregation and discrimination in the armed forces was a nonstarter.

The military rejected the idea when Roosevelt ran it past his department heads, and the president wasn't about to infuriate Southern congressmen anyway. MOWM's call for an executive order barring discrimination among defense contractors seemed more reasonable. A nondiscrimination order for the defense industry would anger the South less than desegregating the military. Roosevelt could make a compelling case that events had forced him to permit African Americans this favor. Granting this concession would enable Randolph to declare victory and cancel the march, sparing the president a political embarrassment and preventing a possible riot.[36]

Of course, Randolph could not know the president had essentially predetermined the outcome of their meeting. FDR needed his adversary to reach the desired conclusion on his own, perhaps with a few nudges in the right direction.

"How are you, Phil?" the president beamed as Randolph and White joined Stimson, Knox, Knudsen, Hillman, LaGuardia, Aubrey Williams, and Social Security Board member Anna Rosenberg in seats around the room. "Which class were you in at Harvard?"[37]

"I never went to Harvard, Mr. President," Randolph replied in his aristocratic tone.

"I was sure you did," Roosevelt countered. "Anyway, you and I share a kinship in our great interest in human and social justice."

"That's right, Mr. President."

Looking to kill some time, FDR launched into a meandering monologue. Randolph waited politely. Then, when Roosevelt drew a breath, he interjected, "Mr. President, we want specifically to talk to you about the problems of jobs for Negroes in the defense industry."

"Mr. President," White added, "we have been getting the runaround everywhere we have gone seeking to get some consideration for Negroes in national defense."

"We are trying to do all we can. You must be patient," FDR replied.

Randolph was having none of it. With White chipping in from time to time, he recited a laundry list of injustices. Segregation and discrimination, besides being un-American, hindered production. Southern officers made life hell for black recruits. African Americans could not get jobs because they lacked essential training, and could not get training because training programs refused black applicants.

"Well, Phil," the president sighed, "what do you want me to do?" Roosevelt rolled his head, fidgeting with his cigarette, conveying weakness with the skill of a poker shark sucking in an opponent while holding aces.

"Mr. President," Randolph said, "we want you to do something that will enable Negro workers to get work in these plants."

Randolph had pointed the conversation precisely where FDR wanted it to go. The president seized on the topic. He offered to personally ask executives to modify their hiring practices, knowing full well his guests would find this insufficient.

"We want you to do more than that," Randolph said.

"What do you mean?" FDR asked, as if he did not know what was coming.

"Mr. President, we want you to issue an executive order making it mandatory that Negroes be permitted to work in these plants."

Roosevelt recoiled in mock horror. "Well, Phil, you know I can't do that. … In any event, I couldn't do anything unless you called off this march of yours."

FDR had Randolph right where he wanted him. The civil rights leader himself had fashioned the outlines of a quid pro quo: one executive order for one cancelled march.

Randolph looked at FDR. He had the president on the defensive. It was time to press home his advantage.

"How many people do you plan to bring?" Roosevelt asked.

"We expect to have 100,000 people there," Randolph rumbled, locking eyes with the president.

FDR eased back in his chair, looking for all the world like a fighter on the ropes. He turned to White. "Walter," he said, "how many people will *really* march?"

White met his gaze. "One hundred thousand, Mr. President," he answered.

"You can't bring 100,000 Negroes to Washington!" Roosevelt exclaimed. "Somebody might get killed!"

FDR fumbled to end the discussion. His houseguest, Crown Princess Juliana of the Netherlands, was waiting for him, he said. It was a plausible enough story to clear the room. Roosevelt asked the conferees to carry on without him. He offered some guidance as they rose from their seats. "Now, I believe that much of the trouble Negro workers have encountered on the question of securing employment in national defense arises from the fact that there is no place for them to come to present their grievances," he said. He proposed a new federal board, possibly created by executive order, to consider cases of employment discrimination—the solution in his mind when his manservant rolled him to the elevator that morning.

With a nod from the president, the assembly relocated next door to the Cabinet Room. Arranging themselves around the long, polished black table, they admired the rose garden through the windows before returning to the business at hand. A sour mood settled over the conference. Stimson, who described the meeting as "one of those rather harassing interruptions," made his annoyance clear to all. Secretary Knox slumped in his chair. "I don't believe that it is well for Negroes and whites to be compelled to live together on the same ship," he muttered. Hillman and Knudsen were a tad more accommodating. Both agreed to support whatever FDR decided, although neither saw much need for a new agency to enforce nondiscrimination. They all wanted the march stopped, but none of them offered Randolph a reason to stop it.[38]

After two bruising hours of debate, LaGuardia, who had huddled with Roosevelt earlier, guided the combatants toward a rough agreement. He joined Randolph and White in endorsing a nondiscrimination order backed by a new federal bureau to investigate violations. The mayor offered to chair a subcommittee to draft the order. Randolph accepted. As he left to catch a train back to New York for a few days of march planning before heading to Houston for the NAACP convention, Randolph reminded the assembly that he would halt the march only after Roosevelt signed an acceptable order. He parted ways with White, who boarded a train for Houston.

None of the White House reporters asked Press Secretary Early about the meeting. The *Washington Post* mentioned "a complaint hearing of Negroes" without explanation. White Washingtonians had no idea that a black tide was headed their way. Randolph played possum with the black press, refusing to discuss the conference. "The march will go on," he declared.[39]

"Who the hell is this guy Randolph? What the hell has he got over the President of the United States?" White House lawyer Joe Rauh exclaimed.[40] Rauh's agony began a few days earlier with a phone call from his boss, special presidential assistant Wayne Coy. "Get your ass over here," Coy shouted, "we got a problem." Rauh ran the ten blocks between their offices. "Some guy named Randolph is going to march on Washington unless we put out a fair employment practices order," Coy told the panting young attorney. "Do you know how to write an executive order?"

"Sure," Rauh replied. "Any idiot can write an executive order, but what do you want me to say?"

"All I know is the President says you got to stop Randolph from marching. ... We got defense factories goin' up all over this goddamn country, but no blacks are being hired. Go down to the Budget Bureau and work something out."

As Rauh left Coy shouted, "Hey, Joe, if we're doing this don't forget the Poles!" Roosevelt had recently taken criticism from Poles claiming discrimination in Buffalo, New York, so Rauh wrote an order encompassing not just race, but also ethnicity.[41]

Rauh handed over a draft the next morning. LaGuardia liked it, but Randolph, who listened while someone read it to him over the phone, rejected it as too weak. Rauh returned to the drawing board as the factions clashed over the final wording. Undersecretary of War Patterson and Undersecretary of the Navy James Forrestal urged FDR to merely ask contractors to uphold a nondiscrimination policy "so far as practical and consistent with the expeditious performance of the work." In New York and elsewhere, the African Americans preparing to descend on the capital demanded much stronger language. Randolph, driving home his advantage, again invited Eleanor Roosevelt to address marchers on July 1.[42]

Rauh, who years later became Randolph's lawyer, incorporated LaGuardia's and Randolph's suggestions into subsequent drafts. Eleanor monitored the proceedings from the Roosevelts' retreat at Campobello, Maine. Their cottage had neither telephone service nor electricity, so the first lady had to hike a half-mile down the road to the island telegrapher's home, where she sat on the front steps waiting for another call from Washington or New York.

Heavy from late nights, Rauh slumped with relief once everyone finally came to terms. The resulting document offered less than Randolph demanded. It said nothing about discrimination in the military or the government. Randolph's insistence on abolishing segregation in the military was long forgotten. What remained nevertheless represented a great leap toward economic justice. Rauh's document forbid discrimination in defense industries and job training programs. It established a new board, reporting directly to the president, to enforce it. "Fix it up for me quick," FDR scrawled on his copy.[43]

After a minor polishing from the attorney general's office, the order was ready for the president's signature. Randolph, by now in Houston for the NAACP convention, solicited input from several MOWM executive committee members before wiring the first lady to advise her that a march was "unnecessary at this time." Randolph expected FDR to sign the document at an "appropriate ceremony" that included LaGuardia, White, and himself. He anticipated orders outlawing discrimination in the government and the military in the near future.[44]

Roosevelt, contrary to Randolph's expectations, enacted Executive Order 8802 with neither pomp nor circumstance. As temperatures in the capital climbed into the mid-nineties, the president fled north to join his wife in Campobello. From his refuge in Maine, FDR signed a statement marking the approach of July 4, then a minor amendment to civil service rules, then the defense industry nondiscrimination order, then a proclamation continuing the one-and-a-half-cent-per-pound postage rate on books. He offered no grand flourishes and no florid words—no words at all, in fact. No press conference, no radio announcement, no newsreel cameras.

A few papers ran small notices about the president's order and the agency it created, the Fair Employment Practices Committee (FEPC). Randolph and MOWM played minor roles in these pieces; the *Washington Evening Star* explained that the order caused an unnamed black organization to cancel some kind of "parade." It never printed Randolph's name.

Most papers ignored these developments altogether. After a tumultuous decade in which the sprawling New Deal intersected with an enormous defense buildup, new bureaucracies simply weren't newsworthy anymore. Other stories seemed far more important. Germany, for example, had invaded the Soviet Union while Joe Rauh was sweating over his draft. Both president and press were busy making sense of the overseas war. Informed observers claimed the Soviets would soon fall. Hitler stood on the brink of dominating the continent.[45]

Randolph beamed as he mounted the pulpit at Houston's Good Hope Baptist Church to address the second day of the NAACP convention. War talk permeated the meeting, but not the war overseas, the one dominating American newspapers. "Defend Democracy at Home," was the conference's theme, a provocative slogan intended to highlight the gap between the nation's rhetoric and its deeds.

"Playful" was not part of Randolph's usual repertoire. But today, with a charged atmosphere in the church and Executive Order 8802 in the bag, the Chief was feeling mischievous. "I am laboring under an interesting and strange sensation tonight in that I find my own voice indistinct to my ear," he teased. "It is the result of a long trip I have just completed from Washington to Houston in an American airplane. My ears are still stopped up." Randolph reviewed his call to march, the conferences with ever-tightening circles of powerbrokers and, finally, his tête-à-tête with Roosevelt. He then revealed the contents of 8802. MOWM had achieved its primary objective, he told the delegates, and was postponing its march. He neglected to mention his tactical retreats in the face of Roosevelt's persuasive skills.

Randolph predicted additional victories in the near future. "It is interesting to watch the transitions that have taken place," he said in a rare moment of immodesty. "At one time Negro leaders were seeking the government. ... But the tables turned, and even the President of the United States began seeking a conference with Negro leaders." Roosevelt hadn't changed his tune because he suddenly saw the justness of their cause. Rather, he finally grasped the power of the mobilized black masses. African Americans were learning how to translate their latent economic and political strength into favorable policy decisions. The crisis of wartime facilitated that shift, as did the budding relationship between the black streets and charismatic leaders. MOWM, having seized the initiative, had no intention of fading away. "POWER! POWER! That is the thing we have got to have," Randolph roared. The march was over for now. The movement had just begun.[46]

For all Randolph's bluster, his constituents gave 8802 mixed reviews. The ever-skeptical *Pittsburgh Courier* deemed the FEPC "pretty useless" because it lacked an enforcement mechanism. The paper believed Roosevelt wanted African Americans in defense jobs, but not badly enough to force employers to accept them. The *Philadelphia Tribune*, on the other hand, labeled the executive order "an event of historical importance." The *New York Amsterdam Star-News* compared it to the Emancipation Proclamation, and the *Washington Afro-American* dubbed it "the new Magna Charta." Even with these plaudits, cynicism reigned in black America. African Americans had heard too many pretty words to put much faith in the most recent batch. Most African American papers paid closer attention to Marva Louis's impending divorce from her husband Joe, the heavyweight champion of the world and a god within the black community, than they did to 8802.[47]

Randolph had attained the pinnacle of black leadership. One admiring paper compared FDR to Abraham Lincoln, but placed Randolph's photo above both of theirs. According to the *Amsterdam Star-News*, he was "the man of the hour. ... The nation's No. 1 Negro leader." There was an irony to his new status. Randolph had dedicated his life to building mass movements grounded in the notion that

Cartoon from the *Washington Afro-American*, 28 June 1941. Black leaders celebrated Executive Order 8802 but wondered whether President Roosevelt would uphold his promises. *Courtesy of the* Afro-American *Newspapers Archives and Research Center*

everyone's voice carried the same weight. He spoke in similar terms about MOWM, insisting that it had neither leaders nor followers, but rather represented a true grassroots effort that invested power equally in all its members. That simply wasn't true. MOWM could not have existed without Randolph. He was its face, its mouthpiece, its guide. He had declared the march, given it shape, and called it off. In a very real sense, he *was* MOWM.

Randolph never overcame that irony. His personal following never developed into a truly decentralized mass movement. That was a problem for the future. For now Randolph could celebrate a significant achievement. Devoted to working-class blacks, committed to upholding his principles, and uninterested in personal glory, he had proved that shouting worked better than begging. Executive Order 8802, although an imperfect document, gained African Americans a foothold in defense employment. It pointed the way toward a brighter economic future. MOWM had shoved the president from a timid silence on discrimination to a reluctant if vocal acknowledgment of it. For the first time in American history, a mass, grassroots, nonviolent black movement, albeit one dominated by a charismatic leader, had forced the federal government to take steps toward racial equality.[48]

"I consider the fight for the Negro masses the greatest service I can render to my people, and the fight done is my complete compensation, especially when I see them getting jobs, justice, freedom and equality," Randolph told an interviewer. Confident in public, inside he felt fortunate to have won half a loaf. "We weren't sure of a 100,000 turnout for the March on Washington," he admitted years later. "We weren't sure of 10,000." No one knew whether the March on Washington Movement would ever actually march and, if not, what exactly it was supposed to do. It had won an order promising nondiscrimination in the defense industry and a fair employment board. Whether the FEPC would, or could, do its job remained to be seen.[49]

July 1, 1941 was a scorching day in the nation's capital. As temperatures hovered in the mid-nineties, sweltering Washingtonians fanned themselves on shaded porches or spent a quarter to watch *Billy the Kid* or Abbott and Costello's war-themed comedy *In the Navy* in the comfort of a movie theater. The real war, the one overseas, was heating up, too, as German legions pushed deeper into Soviet territory. President

Roosevelt reaffirmed American neutrality even as he expelled German diplomats and condemned the Nazis' sinking of the American merchant vessel *Robin Moor* as an act of piracy. The war abroad was creating jobs at home—skilled jobs, high-paying defense work offering a salary a man could feed his family on. The ironic Depression-era anthem "We're in the Money" finally rang true: "The long-lost dollar has come back to the fold/With silver you can turn your dreams to gold."

A sullen, sweaty hush hung over the city. Congress was out of session. FDR was in upstate New York dedicating his presidential library. Like every other sports fan, the president was keeping close tabs on Yankee center fielder Joe DiMaggio's remarkable hitting streak. Dago, as many fans called him, had just stroked a hit in his forty-fourth consecutive game, tying the record Wee Willie Keeler set in 1897.

Blistering heat kept all but a handful of sightseers away from the National Mall. The few people milling around the Lincoln Memorial that day witnessed an unusual sight. A group of 1,000 African Americans representing something called the March on Washington Movement had gathered on the building's Watergate steps. Mayor LaGuardia shook hands with well wishers as a tall, distinguished black man with a dark suit and a remarkable voice addressed the rally. Few of the tourists recognized A. Philip Randolph delivering what amounted to a victory speech. With the Washington Monument rising over his shoulder and the Potomac River flowing nearby, Randolph congratulated the crowd for validating his faith in the black masses. Their combined strength would produce additional triumphs in the future, he promised.

Randolph's address represented the final shot in the opening battle of a long war for equality. It merited one sentence in the next day's *Washington Post*.

CHAPTER 4

....

No Place to Put You

Randolph has a lot of explaining to do," *Pittsburgh Courier* columnist Horace Cayton observed. "Our race is great at passing resolutions and planning but when it comes time to act, very few show up," lamented another correspondent. "It will take years before I will have the same faith in these leaders," remarked a third.[1]

This sense of betrayal surprised Randolph, who defended his decision to suspend the march in front of several thousand followers at Harlem's Salem Methodist Church. "Simply stated," he said, "the march was postponed because its main objective—the issuance of an executive order banning discrimination in national defense—was secured." His explanation failed to appease critics, including those within his own organization. The March on Washington Movement's (MOWM) youth division accused their leader of selling out. Randolph, in a fit of pique, retorted that communists had manipulated the "infantile, ridiculous, and tragic" dissidents into making foolish arguments. Black youth was "bogged down in hopeless intellectual and moral confusion and uncertainty," he sniffed.[2]

Randolph had spent a decade badgering the Pullman Company to recognize the Brotherhood of Sleeping Car Porters (BSCP). He was reimagining MOWM as a similarly long-term endeavor, a sharp turnaround from his earlier insistence that it existed solely to organize a one-off march. MOWM would have triumphs and defeats, he said. It would accept partial victories to advance its larger ambitions.

Soon after his Lincoln Memorial victory rally, Randolph departed on an around-the-country recruiting swing. With the steady clatter of wheels in the background, he pondered ways to transform MOWM into a permanent advocate for social and economic justice. He plotted a program to increase MOWM's membership to 1 million. He considered starting a monthly MOWM magazine. Neither project was possible until he overcame his money woes. MOWM had sixty-five dollars in the bank.[3]

With no march on the horizon, Randolph also faced the challenge of distinguishing MOWM from other civil rights groups, especially the NAACP. They both fought discrimination. They both opposed segregation. Their memberships overlapped. Many asked whether MOWM was redundant, dividing attention and resources without contributing anything new to the discussion. Randolph didn't have a good answer.

Critics attacked the all-black MOWM for answering segregation with segregation, just as Marcus Garvey had in the 1920s. Randolph dismissed the "antiwhite" charge. The League of Women Voters was not "antiman," he noted. MOWM existed to teach African Americans to stand up for themselves. Change would come when they used their own strength to clear obstacles, not when they found new ways to gain white support. "Most Negroes are afraid to be in an all-Negro movement," he told a friend. "They want some white people hanging around to whom they may run as though they were their parents when they get into difficulties." In Randolph's mind, black America needed to grow up.[4]

He journeyed through a country that, although technically at peace, felt like a nation at war. Men still too young to vote opened draft notices. Uniformed soldiers dotted buses and trains. Defense plants hummed with activity after years of Depression-enforced silence. Americans grappled with life on an incomprehensible scale—thousands of planes, millions of men, billions of dollars. "Negroes must no longer think in terms of little units or small maneuvers," Randolph argued. Being right wasn't enough to bring change. It would take huge numbers of African Americans—black voters—to enlist the government in their cause. Randolph's vision depended on people power, not omnipotent leaders. In contrast to the top-heavy NAACP, in MOWM "the highest will be as low as the lowest and the lowest will be as high as the highest."[5]

The year following Randolph's postponement of the march brought tremendous challenges for African Americans, MOWM, and the United States. Many of Randolph's supporters believed he had trapped lightning in a bottle only to let it skitter free, perhaps never to be recaptured. Randolph needed to explain what the movement would do if it wasn't marching. Executive Order 8802 committed the Roosevelt administration to guaranteeing equal access to defense jobs. Exactly how it would do that, and how forcefully, remained to be seen. Roosevelt's order said nothing about a military that marginalized black soldiers.

Progress on these fronts was uneven. External pressures would force the military to take halting steps toward equality. A new federal agency, born from 8802, would assail racism within the defense industry. And Randolph's great mass movement would reach its apex of popularity before entering a decline that muddied black America's future prospects.

"What happened to call off the March on Washington?" the president of the NAACP's Duluth, Minnesota branch asked. "It certainly must have been something very, very interesting."[6]

The new Fair Employment Practices Committee (FEPC), the "very, very interesting thing" in question, produced intense political jockeying from the outset. Randolph assumed the Roosevelt administration would give him carte blanche to name its members. Many African Americans thought Randolph himself should be on the committee. Roosevelt never asked him, and Randolph said he would rather oversee MOWM than be part of a bureaucracy. Walter White signaled his interest in a job, but no one in Washington signaled back.[7]

Randolph and White pushed their administration contacts to stock the FEPC with high-profile names. Roosevelt's staff generally accommodated their views, although their nomination of Wendell Willkie, FDR's opponent in 1940, was dead on arrival. Mayor LaGuardia, citing a crushing workload, refused Randolph's pleas to head the committee. *Louisville Courier-Journal* editor Mark Ethridge accepted the position with Randolph and White's blessing. Having a white Southern chairman, even a liberal like Ethridge, might make the FEPC more palatable to Dixie. David Sarnoff, a Jewish American and head of the Radio Corporation of America, signed up, as did Philip Murray of the Congress of Industrial Organizations (CIO), and William Green of the American Federation of Labor (AFL). Randolph, eager to get union leaders on the committee, championed

Murray and Green despite Green's subpar record on race. Over a dozen AFL unions discriminated against African Americans. After intense debate, Randolph also won a seat for BSCP vice-president Milton P. Webster. Earl Dickerson, a black lawyer and Democratic alderman from Chicago, rounded out the six-man committee.

Randolph was pleased with his work. "You have gone right down the line with the Negroes' effort to secure equal participation in national defense employment and the Negroes throughout the country are grateful to you for it," he told FDR. Roosevelt, however, minimized public awareness of the blue-ribbon panel. Press Secretary Stephen Early announced its membership without fanfare, saying only that the FEPC came into existence "after a long howl from the Colored folks." The president waited five weeks before hosting the committee at the White House. Early downplayed the significance of the meeting. "That is the Negro thing?" a reporter asked of the FEPC. "Yes, mostly," Early replied.[8]

Chairman Ethridge embraced a gradualist approach to racial progress. "It is obvious that the Negroes have been led to believe a good deal more than the truth by their own leaders," he told Early, a close friend. "I think the agitators had got themselves into such a position with a threatened march that they wanted to make the abandonment of the march appear to come as the result of a great victory." Ethridge tried to dampen the enthusiasm of the FEPC's black members. Discrimination had been around for a long time, and would take a long time to eliminate, he told them.[9]

The FEPC's undersized quarters in the Social Security Building had no filing cabinets, few desks, and an inadequate staff. The bureau's budget came out of executive branch funds. Congress had not voted to create it, nor did legislators have any control over it, points sure to inspire grumbles in the Capitol. Most white Southerners hated it. Nevertheless, optimism pervaded the agency. Recruiters hired idealistic, hardworking people, without regard to race or gender, from labor unions, civil rights organizations, universities, and law schools. Black and white worked together in an age when segregation divided many government offices. And they worked hard, fielding more than 1,600 complaints between October and December 1941 alone. Citizens could initiate an investigation simply by writing a letter describing an incident of alleged discrimination. Correspondents accused defense contractors of refusing to hire or promote them because of race or ethnicity, complained about pay disparities and unfair firings, and blasted unions and training program administrators for turning them away. The FEPC's skeleton crew could not keep pace with the deluge.

Ethridge's FEPC kept a low profile, working behind the scenes to persuade contractors to obey Executive Order 8802. Only when that failed did it convene public hearings intended to shame companies into compliance.

Its first hearing occurred in October 1941 in Los Angeles. FEPC investigators had accumulated evidence of widespread discrimination among area aviation plants. North American Aviation Corporation had 12,500 employees, just eight of them black, all of them janitors. Company officials claimed African Americans never applied for jobs. A similar situation existed at Douglas Aircraft, where only ten of its 33,000 employees were black. Executives again blamed a lack of applications. Lockheed provided a bright spot of sorts. Although blacks comprised about one one-thousandth of its workforce, it was implementing a plan to educate supervisors and personnel managers about Executive Order 8802. Lockheed's application form no longer asked for candidates' race or ethnicity, and the company focused on hiring exceptional African Americans whose competence would ease resistance to an interracial workforce. Ethridge praised Lockheed's methodical approach as a model for other businesses.

Throughout the hearings Ethridge acted like a confidant rather than an adversary, searching for ways to uphold 8802 without inconveniencing corporations. Still, some exchanges left him scratching his head. "Does your company discriminate against colored people?" one committee member asked an executive.

"No sir," he replied.

"How many men do you employ?"

"Two thousand eight hundred and eighty."

"How many of them are colored?"

"Two."

"When were they hired?"

"Today."

Witnesses complicated matters by claiming their contracts with labor unions prevented them from hiring minorities. Several cited the

International Association of Machinists, an AFL union whose initiation ritual required new members to promise not to "propose for membership in this Association any other than a competent, white candidate."[10]

Committee members proved unable to sort out who bore ultimate responsibility for discrimination. The hearings as a whole proved a bit of a muddle, producing reams of testimony but no clear verdict, abundant coverage in black newspapers and almost none in white ones. And with no enforcement powers, the FEPC could scold malefactors but not punish them.

After a grueling, ten-week national tour, Randolph returned to Harlem on December 5, 1941, two days before Japan bombed Pearl Harbor. He did not know that FBI chief J. Edgar Hoover had recommended "custodial detention" for the race troublemaker. As the United States entered the fight, Randolph noted a profound lack of interest on 125th Street and other bustling venues. "Whitey owns everything," observed the young Harlemite Malcolm Little. "He wants us to go and bleed for him? Let him fight."[11]

Such apathy horrified Randolph. African Americans had a stake in democracy and would fare far worse under Axis rule than in an imperfect republic. "What shall the Negro do?" Randolph asked in an essay written several days after Congress declared war. "There is only one answer. He must fight. He must give freely and fully of his blood, toil, tears and treasure to the cause of victory." Unlike W. E. B. DuBois, who had favored suspending civil rights activity during World War I, Randolph asked African Americans to win their rights at home while defending them overseas. "Negroes cannot ask for anything more, nor can they accept anything less," he wrote.[12]

Randolph's argument coincided with the wartime "Double V" program. This movement first took shape with twenty-six-year-old James G. Thompson's January 1942 letter to the *Pittsburgh Courier*. Thompson reported seeing "V" signs everywhere, solid walls of propaganda for victory over fascism. "If this V sign means that to those now engaged in this great conflict," Thompson wrote, "then let we colored Americans adopt the double VV for a double victory. The first V for victory over our enemies from without, the second V for victory over our enemies from within!"[13]

Thousands of African Americans registered as air raid wardens and civil defense officers. Like their white countrymen, blacks huddled around radios, keeping a safe distance from doors and windows and ready to seek shelter in case of bombing. Frustrations endured despite these commonalities. "The colored races as a whole would benefit if Japan should win the war," one man told the *Baltimore Afro-American.* "This could be the first step in the darker races' coming back into their own." An early 1942 survey revealed that nearly one in five African Americans believed they would be better off under Japanese rule. The same poll showed that 90 percent of whites considered defeating the Axis more important than making democracy work at home. African Americans split evenly between the two options. Two thirds of whites thought African Americans enjoyed equal access to defense jobs. Only one third of blacks agreed.[14]

Pro-Japanese sentiment was broad but shallow, reflecting dissatisfaction with the status quo rather than a genuine thirst for Emperor Hirohito's rule. Widespread black support for the Japanese was short-lived. Black newspapers ignored perhaps the greatest affront to civil rights during the entire war: President Roosevelt's February 1942 order to relocate Japanese Americans living on the West Coast to internment camps in the interior. Not even Randolph, who often discussed the war's potential to liberate dark-skinned victims of imperialism in China, India, and Africa, denounced the move.

Inequality remained a basic fact of life. African American unemployment hovered around 20 percent, far above the white rate. Other minorities, including Mexican Americans, also suffered as defense plants integrated at a glacial pace. "Most of 'em didn't say right out they wouldn't hire me," said Bob Jones, the black protagonist of Chester Himes's 1945 novel *If He Hollers Let Him Go.* "They just looked so goddamned startled that I'd even asked. As if some friendly dog had come in through the door and said, 'I can talk.'" Employers' stubbornness reinforced employees' resistance to change; if the boss favored an all-white workforce, then so did they. In one of many race-based strikes, workers at the Curtiss-Wright plant in Columbus, Ohio, walked off the job in November 1941 when the company hired an African American for its tool and die department.

Inequality remained a basic fact of military life. Over half of the 115,000 African Americans in the Army served in the South, where most locals viewed them with contempt. "We would rather be in jail or dead than to remain here under the conditions to which we are subjected," one draftee stationed in Mississippi wrote his mother. A mere handful of black cadets served in the Army's air corps. The Navy still limited black recruits to the messman branch. The Marines shut them out altogether. "If it were a question of having a Marine Corps of 5,000 whites or 250,000 Negroes, I would rather have the whites," Marine Commandant Major General Thomas Holcomb argued."[15]

"What happens to Negroes after the war will be determined a great deal by what happens to them during the war," Eleanor Roosevelt told an audience at Virginia's all-black Hampton Institute. If this were true, then nothing good was going to happen to them after the war. Double V faced double jeopardy as the military suffered a catastrophic first six months of combat. American troops ceded ground in the Gilbert Islands, Guam, Wake Island, Corregidor, Leyte, and Bataan. At home, African Americans endured slight after slight. The black press snorted when President Roosevelt denounced "discrimination in any of its ugly forms" in his January 1942 State of the Union address. Editorialists challenged FDR to heed his own advice by eliminating racial bigotry within the government.[16]

Tales of injustice proliferated in the black press. One story in the *Chicago Defender* described three black men who visited an Army recruiting center. "We've been ordered not to accept any Negroes," an officer told them.

"Why?" they asked.

"Well, I don't know," he replied. "They ain't got no place to put you."

Another outrage occurred in an Army camp near Marcus Hook, Pennsylvania. Colonel Riley McGarragh, the Georgia-born commander of the 77th Coast Artillery Regiment, posted an order declaring that "any cases of relations between white and colored males and females whether voluntary or not are considered rape, and during time of war the penalty is death." The War Department quickly rescinded the order, but the damage was done. McGarragh's explanation enraged African Americans. "Unless you have lived in the South you can't understand the problem a thing like this raises," he said of black–white romances. "I was afraid some of these Negroes might get ideas."[17]

Military segregation even reached inside GIs' bodies. Bowing to the wishes of white Southerners, the Army and Navy asked the

Red Cross to separate blood plasma into white and black donations. Red Cross chairman Norman Davis of Tennessee scorned criticism from African American newspapers. "It is a highly sensitive question and I don't believe agitation will help it," he said. "The Red Cross's job is not to solve racial questions but to administer to all races." Congressman John Rankin of Mississippi blamed talk of plasma integration on communists, calling it "one of the schemes of these fellow travelers to try to mongrelize this Nation." Even Benjamin Davis, the Army's lone black general, claimed that black soldiers "would be happier" with blood "from their own people." Randolph saw the blood-segregation policy, which held throughout the war, as further evidence of the Roosevelt administration's quiet subversion of equality. "Refusal of the blood of a citizen ... on account of race, color, creed, or nationality is a subtle advocacy of racial superiority, the cult and curse of Hitler and Hitlerism, Japanese and Italian fascism," he explained.[18]

Homefront morale sagged even farther when twenty-six-year-old Cleo Wright of Sikeston, Missouri, became the wartime era's first lynching victim. Wright was no angel; on the night of January 25, 1942, he broke into a white woman's home, stabbed her with a six-inch knife (she survived), and fled into the darkness. Two searchers spotted Wright walking down a road. They opened fire when he brandished his blade. Four bullets ripped into his body, badly wounding him. News of his arrest filtered through town. Hundreds of armed whites gathered outside City Hall to demand the criminal. They forced their way in when authorities rebuffed them. Stuffing Wright into the trunk of a Ford, they half-drove, half-dragged him to a Baptist church in Sikeston's black district. Lynchers dumped a five-gallon can of gasoline over Wright and set him ablaze as the congregation watched in horror. Even with hundreds of witnesses, no one was ever indicted for the murder.

For a time the NAACP adopted "Remember Pearl Harbor ... and Sikeston, Mo." as its slogan. Randolph considered the lynching part of a larger wave of anti-black violence. A recent scuffle over a bus seat near Fort Bragg, North Carolina, ended with military police herding hundreds of black soldiers into the stockade, where guards brutalized them. A riot pitting white civilians against black GIs from Camp Claiborne broke out in Alexandria, Louisiana, at nearly the same time. The brawl, which wounded twenty-eight enlisted men, followed several incidents where locals had mistreated African Americans. Randolph predicted more bloodshed unless FDR tackled racial prejudice head on.[19]

Roosevelt hoped to avoid interracial violence. He wanted to maximize black contributions to the war effort. At the same time, he could not risk agitating the South by aligning with controversial black activists. The military's innate conservatism presented an additional obstacle. The War Department saw African Americans as problems rather than potential assets, concluding that increasing their role in the war would undermine white support for it.

Army officials argued that force effectiveness declined as the number of African American GIs rose. "There is a general consensus of opinion that colored units are inferior to the performances of white troops," one April 1942 memo concluded, "due to the inherent psychology of the colored race and their need for leadership." The Army solved this problem by handing black troops shovels rather than rifles. Its Air Corps invented fancy titles to conceal the menial jobs its few black enlisted men occupied. "Aviation squadrons" performed housekeeping duties. "Air base transportation platoons" did general service tasks. "Air base security battalions" guarded against the unlikely possibility of a parachute attack.[20]

FDR searched for ways to open the military without angering either the brass or the South. He suggested to Navy Secretary Knox that his service might "invent something that colored enlistees could do in addition to the rating of messman." Secretary of War Stimson backed Roosevelt because the Navy's restrictions pushed black recruits toward the Army, which could not take many more "without adverse effect on its combat efficiency." Prospects for change were dim. A recent Navy study concluded that "the enlistment of Negroes (other than as mess attendants) leads to disruptive and undermining conditions." Knox obligingly convened another committee that, not surprisingly, stonewalled the president's mild proposal.[21]

African Americans kept up the pressure. Eager for examples of black valor, editors elevated Dorie Miller, a black cook on the *U.S.S. West Virginia* who manned an antiaircraft gun during the attack on Pearl Harbor, into an example of what African Americans could do if they only got a chance.

Rumors that the Navy would soon modify its policies percolated in the black press. Secretary Knox indeed announced new regulations

"above and beyond the call of duty"

DORIE MILLER
*Received the Navy Cross
at Pearl Harbor, May 27, 1942*

Recognizing black dissatisfaction, the U.S. Navy used Pearl Harbor hero Dorie Miller as a recruiting tool but failed to substantively improve its treatment of African Americans. *Library of Congress, Prints and Photographs Collection, LC-USZC4-2328*

in April 1942. The Navy, Marines, and Coast Guard agreed to accept African Americans for general service and promote them by merit into the lower ranks of the officer corps. Randolph and other disappointed black leaders noted that Knox left segregation intact, although it was unclear how this would work on ships. Further, the Navy could fill labor battalions with black seamen without violating the plan. Knox framed the revision as a wartime emergency move rather than a permanent about-face. Under its terms, black servicemen could not reenlist after the war. The new rules, Knox explained, aimed to "make the maximum use of Negroes in the most effective way to avoid difficulties of a racial character."[22]

The Navy opened its recruiting offices to African Americans in June 1942. Black Marine recruits started reporting to Montford Point, a segregated training facility in North Carolina, in August. Roosevelt believed these gestures addressed African Americans' concerns and might lead to further incremental gains. Secretary Knox thought the service had done all it could to foster equality without disturbing tranquility.

Black newspapers credited the president for chipping away at racism. The NAACP registered only mild objections to the Navy's new plan. "We are glad that the Navy's policy has been revised, but we wonder if the change is not more apparent than real," it observed in a press release. Randolph, in contrast, blasted Knox for perpetuating segregation. The new policy was "a definite insult," he stated in a public letter to the secretary. "It holds colored Americans in contempt. ... It officially proclaims segregation as the policy of the American Government." In Randolph's mind, Knox's message proved that the government cared more about victory than democracy. The government's emphasis on appeasing whites rather than cultivating justice demonstrated that Washington actually considered segregation essential to victory.[23]

Administration officials noted that blacks comprised 9 percent of government employees, roughly proportional to their share of the national population. Reformers observed that 62 percent of those black employees worked as custodians. Defense companies and labor unions still preferred whites, whether male or female, over black men. Many training programs for defense jobs accepted only white applicants. The state and local officials running the programs saw no reason to train African Americans because employers would not hire them anyway.

Signs of improvement dotted the far horizon. With the war going poorly and the white labor pool drying up, discriminatory hiring practices were starting to smack of disloyalty. "Any firm which refuses to complete a bomber because it does not want to employ a Negro or Jew is just as much a saboteur as a man who would throw a monkey wrench into a machine," one FEPC field representative declared. Businessmen agreed; a 1942 pamphlet from the American Management Association argued that "today's urgent need for manpower effectively removes Negro employment in industry from the realm of social reform." Wartime needs were transforming a hot-button social issue into a national-security priority.[24]

Randolph's anger deepened during the war's disastrous first months. He saw democracy slipping away, and with it African Americans' hopes for overcoming economic, social, and cultural inequality. It took mass power to move great institutions, and Randolph wanted to forge the black masses into a sledgehammer that struck blows for freedom. "Certainly," he wrote FDR, "you must know that colored people are reaching such a point of desperation that they are beginning to express a willingness and determination to die right here in America to attain a democracy which they never had." He excoriated Roosevelt for refusing to meet with MOWM and for accepting the Southern "stranglehold" on the capital. Action, or the threat of it, had changed FDR's mind in 1941. Randolph believed he could change it again in 1942.[25]

In April 1942 Randolph invited a few black reporters to MOWM's Harlem office. "This is our hour of greatest opportunity," he told them. "To wait until the war is over, we will be where we were before." FDR might sympathize with African Americans but would not act unless mass pressure compelled him. To that end, MOWM was preparing a series of huge demonstrations of black power. Plans for a rally in New York's Madison Square Garden were well underway, with additional gatherings to follow.[26]

Gas rationing and other wartime travel restrictions made an actual march on Washington unlikely. To stay relevant, the March on Washington Movement needed to find other ways of gaining attention. The Madison Square Garden event would be the organization's high-water mark. It also revealed the group's weaknesses. Randolph's agenda encompassed a vast sprawl of complaints. He wanted to combat segregation, discrimination, lynching, violence against black soldiers, the Red Cross's blood policy, and the shortage of defense jobs, all at the same time. His sense of outrage had outstripped his pragmatism. He oversaw a budding mass movement with no clear direction. Randolph was stretched too thin. Despite his desire for a grassroots movement, MOWM was top-heavy. Randolph plotted overall strategy, planned demonstrations, recruited new chapters, and maintained his national contacts while at the same time directing the Brotherhood of Sleeping Car Porters. It was more than one man could do.

Madison Square Garden was a boxy, unattractive arena located a few blocks south of Central Park and several miles from Harlem.

Randolph took a huge gamble in renting it. He needed to raise thousands of dollars just to cover costs for the rally. The arena could accommodate 20,000 people, twice what Randolph had initially summoned to march on Washington. An empty house would leave MOWM bankrupt and humiliated.

Although exhausted, Randolph worked tirelessly to pull off the rally. He solicited donations from black churches, fraternal organizations, labor groups, and individuals. The NAACP, whose support for Randolph's movement coincided with a huge bump in its own membership numbers, kicked in a considerable sum. The invaluable porters' union not only contributed money, but also carried the fundraising message to whistle-stop towns around the nation. Randolph used the BSCP as a financial safety net. "The Brotherhood might have to make up any deficit in the funds if they don't collect enough money before the meeting," he confided to Milton P. Webster. White liberals circled the rally without committing resources. MOWM's blacks-only policy discouraged them, as did Randolph's nebulous agenda.[27]

"The affair is to be colossal and dramatic," promised the *New York Amsterdam Star-News*. Reverend Adam Clayton Powell, after securing a spot on the program, demanded 100 percent attendance from African Americans living within one hundred miles of the Garden. Black papers printed donor lists to reward the faithful and shame slackers. Flyers plastered every flat surface in Harlem. "Winning Democracy for the Negro Is Winning the War for Democracy," one proclaimed. "Wake Up, Negro America!" screamed another. Randolph asked Harlemites to darken their homes during the rally as a sign of solidarity.[28]

Mainstream newspapers ignored the upcoming event, just as they had the previous year's march. The NAACP and the Urban League also kept silent despite contributing money. Leaders of both groups feared MOWM might become a permanent organization, and therefore a competitor. The *Pittsburgh Courier*, Randolph's longtime nemesis, condemned the meeting. "What ... does the March-on-Washington committee propose to do or protest that is not already being done or protested by every Negro individual and organization?" columnist P. L. Prattis asked. "If Mr. Randolph arouses and organizes the discontented, what does he [propose] to do with them?" Their anger might escalate into violence if Randolph stoked the flames too high. A race riot could tarnish the civil rights movement for years to come. "I hope they are going to be able to help us without hurting us," Prattis fretted. Prattis had a point, but Randolph could not have changed course even if he wanted to. Too much was riding on the rally.[29]

On Tuesday, June 16, 1942, around 18,000 African Americans streamed downtown in their Sunday best. Women wearing festive hats and men in solemn ties jammed buses and subway trains. They walked the last blocks to the Garden through the dying rays of the midsummer sun. A few celebrants slung their jackets over their shoulders in a slight concession to the heat. Most remained rigidly formal. Some cast sidelong glances at the occasional white face in the crowd. Uniformed sleeping car porters swapped stories about troublesome riders and their favorite haunts along the line. Communists distributed pamphlets lampooning Randolph as a socialist stooge.

Sixty blocks uptown, quiet reigned in Harlem. Children ran free, but few adults ventured outside to break the silence. A rare light here and there interrupted the eerie darkness stretching from 110th to 165th Street and from Madison to Amsterdam Avenue. For one night, Harlem's boisterous street culture fell silent out of respect for Randolph's audacity.

More than a few people breathed sighs of relief as they settled into their seats. Contrary to fears, a respectable crowd had turned out. Not enough to fill the cavernous building, and certainly not enough to spill into the streets, as Randolph had predicted, but enough to create a stir. Dignitaries glad-handed each other before taking chairs onstage. Randolph shelved his distaste for theatrics to make the night's grandest entrance. Resplendent in his crisp, dark suit, with a white pocket square as an exclamation mark, he strode to the stage surrounded by a vanguard of porters. The crowd rose to its feet as a band struck up the old union song "Hold the Fort, For We Are Coming": "We meet today in freedom's cause/And raise our voices high/We'll join our hands in union strong/To battle or to die."

After this burst of excitement, the throng settled in for what proved to be a long, long night. "We have here assembled the national leaders of the Negro people," meeting chairman Lawrence Ervin began. He spoke a literal truth. Randolph, in a bid for unity, had invited nearly every important black activist to speak. He begged them to keep their remarks brief. When presented with an immense, excited audience, none of them followed instructions. "This is the first time in all of my speaking career … when I have been limited to but five minutes," labor organizer Frank Crosswaith shouted from the platform. "Frank Crosswaith," he continued, "is utterly unable to disclose the corners of his soul in five minutes."[30]

Randolph spent hours squirming in his seat as the hall teetered between elation and boredom. Crosswaith electrified the meeting when he declared it "the first funeral I ever attended in Madison Square Garden." "Like every other black man, woman and child here tonight," he continued, "I am here to bury in the grave of forgetfulness the type of black man that America too long has known." Adam Clayton Powell snatched the spotlight when he used his speech to announce his candidacy for Congress. Speaker after speaker denounced injustice after injustice. They deplored discrimination, lynching, poll taxes, segregation, and FEPC's gradualism. They called for black representatives on the postwar peace delegation, criticized the Southerners who controlled congressional committees, and ripped European rule over dark-skinned people. All of them—Crosswaith, Mary McLeod Bethune, Walter White, and a dozen more—demanded an end to delays and half measures. "We have grown tired of turning the other cheek," Bethune seethed. "Both our cheeks are now so blistered they are too sensitive for further blows."[31]

The anger emanating from the rostrum fueled the rowdy crowd. FBI informants in the stands jotted down statements they considered seditious. An exchange in "The Watchword Is Forward," a one-act play composed for the occasion, attracted particular attention, along with the loudest applause of the night. Attendees hooted and hollered through the drama, which pitted a white Army officer against a reluctant black draftee, played by actor and civil rights advocate Canada Lee, whose recent portrayal of Bigger Thomas in Orson Welles's staging of *Native Son* had wowed audiences. Lee's character recited a list of grievances against the Army, particularly its abuse of black recruits in Southern camps. He pounced when the arrogant officer questioned his bravery. "I want you to know I ain't afraid," he replied. "I don't mind fighting. I'll fight Hitler, Mussolini, and the Japs all at the same time, but I'm telling you I'll give those crackers down South the same damn medicine!" Thousands leapt to their feet, loosing a roar that rocked the

Garden. "Say that again!" a woman screamed from the balcony as the din faded, unleashing a second wave of cheers.[32]

Randolph sat for five hours before finally approaching the microphone. The crowd, shrugging off its fatigue, rewarded him with a three-minute ovation. Randolph waved for silence not just from modesty, but also because MOWM had only reserved the Garden until midnight. Setting aside his prepared speech, he spent his few minutes introducing Annie Waller, the mother of Virginia sharecropper Odell Waller, who was facing a death sentence for murdering his landlord.[33] He then bid attendees a good night and left the stage.

"I think it was a grand meeting," Randolph deadpanned. Bloated as the rally was, he had pulled off an extraordinary coup. The $1,000 MOWM netted from the Garden event swelled its coffers. More important, Randolph had mounted a spectacle unlike anything since Marcus Garvey's rowdy parades. Black America viewed Randolph as a hero, a new Moses, its leader of leaders. "A new day [is] dawning in the life of the Negro," Frank Crosswaith crowed. Most white papers ignored the sunrise, never mentioning Randolph's triumph.[34]

Randolph convened a second rally on June 24 at the Chicago Coliseum. Randolph's micromanaging of the event reinforced impressions that MOWM was no grassroots organization. Randolph approved publicity stickers, selected the songs (he forbade depressing spirituals), and set the number of ushers. MOWM's national office did not trust the Chicago division to make arrangements on its own. Milton P. Webster feared "a grand, A-1 mess up" unless Randolph took charge. An inept fundraising campaign forced the BSCP to scrape together enough money to rent the hall.[35]

"Storm the Coliseum!" MOWM's publicity posters read. Around 12,000 people did just that, enough to create an overflow crowd but a far cry from the 25,000 Randolph expected. South Side neighborhoods observed a fifteen-minute blackout during the event. Overzealous local MOWM activists had proposed a two-hour blackout. Randolph convinced them to adopt a more reasonable goal.[36]

This time Randolph delivered the speech he had prepared for Madison Square Garden. Randolph's orations rarely soared. Lacking in fluidity, rhythm, and stylistic flourishes, they consisted of thudding blows of logic punctuated with provocative calls to action. American democracy was "a miserable failure" because it applied only to whites.

We Hope, We Hope!

Cartoon from the *Star-News*, 27 June 1942. Randolph's Madison Square Garden rally appeared to mark the start of a new era of black militancy. *Courtesy of the* New York Amsterdam News

"Better that Negroes face extermination than a life of segregation with its degradation and bitter humiliation." He blasted the federal government for embracing Jim Crow, the Army for mistreating black recruits, and the Red Cross for segregating blood. In a single hour he attacked the poll tax, lynching, maldistribution of federal funds, discrimination in training programs and defense plants, and the FEPC's relative impotence, as evidenced by its microscopic budget and lack of enforcement powers. Racial problems were getting worse, he insisted, and African Americans could not suspend their demands until after the war.

The crowd followed Randolph all over the thematic map, yelling and applauding as accusations piled up. "Negroes are going to MARCH and we don't give a damn what happens," he rumbled. Those last seven words, which endorsed mass action regardless of

the consequences for a nation engaged in a global struggle to determine mankind's future, crystallized two years of black outrage.
This was no intemperate ad-lib, but rather a scripted thumb in
Roosevelt's eye. Randolph's face betrayed no surprise when the
ovation literally shook the Coliseum's rafters. He knew he had
thrown down the gauntlet.[37]

"What now?" the *Pittsburgh Courier* asked. "All we have so far are
ear-splitting generalities and blowsy platitudes. We do not have a program." Randolph had created MOWM as a temporary organization
with a single purpose. Although its members stayed home in 1941, its
name suggested they would march at some point. When, and for what,
remained unclear, but the rank and file expected a summons at any
moment. In contrast, Randolph saw marching as a last option, the
equivalent of a union voting to strike. It was a weapon brandished at
critical moments, not a tool to employ against every grievance. "The
objective of this committee is not an actual physical march," he told
reporters.[38]

"There must be an actual march on Washington," one of his militant backers retorted. "If there is not, the majority will conclude that
we are the same docile, begging, cringing, handkerchief-head Uncle
Toms of yesterday." Followers wondered whether Randolph's patience, which contrasted with his urgent rhetoric, masked a paralyzing
uncertainty.[39]

The New York and Chicago mass meetings, along with an August
1942 gathering of 10,000 in St. Louis, generated an enormous amount
of energy. Randolph's shapeless agenda dispersed that energy in a
dozen directions. The focused demands of 1941 evolved into an
ad-hoc assortment of proposals based on whatever gripped Randolph
at the moment. MOWM's creeping transformation into a comprehensive civil-rights organization endangered its financial support from the
NAACP and other groups reluctant to nurture a rival. MOWM's
superior street appeal and working-class constituency threatened the
NAACP's status as the nation's premier civil rights advocate. Roy
Wilkins, Walter White's assistant, implored his boss to deflate
MOWM's ambitions. "They intend to seize upon all the issues which
ordinarily we would handle," he said, "and because they have a lot of
public enthusiasm over the Madison Square garden meeting, they
might be able to do something."[40]

MOWM's rift with the NAACP undercut both organizations' effectiveness and threatened to scuttle the Double V campaign. Randolph's subordinates foreshadowed disputes that shook the 1960s-era civil rights movement when they mocked the NAACP as out-of-touch elitists dependent on white liberal support. Much of the black press agreed. "It is an organization whose membership rolls read too much like the roster of a more or less select club. ... It has nothing of the real vigor of the people," the *Los Angeles Tribune* said. White responded with a media blitz designed to blunt MOWM's appeal by promoting the NAACP's efforts to stop lynching, its legal victories over segregated schooling, and its close ties to influential lawmakers. He considered using his financial clout to somehow wrest control of MOWM from Randolph. This carried its own risks, as a close association with the black masses might undermine the NAACP's respectability.[41]

Randolph tried to soothe inflamed passions. He knew that talk of the grassroots versus the elite was just overheated rhetoric. There was actually significant overlap between MOWM and NAACP membership, as well as between the NAACP and the porters' union. Hoping to coexist, he insisted that his group supplemented rather than supplanted the NAACP. MOWM's mass pressure agenda distinguished it from the NAACP's legalistic approach, he said. And although MOWM's top-heavy structure suggested otherwise, Randolph still believed he was creating an economic justice movement with a broadly dispersed power base. Along these lines, he offered to concentrate his fundraising efforts on the poor and lower middle class, leaving big donors to the NAACP. "No good contributors to the NAACP should be lost by raising another movement," he wrote White. Despite this assurance, the NAACP head lost interest in helping MOWM once he decided that his friend's creation wasn't going away any time soon.[42]

Riding a wave of success, Randolph ignored these red flags. In fall 1942 he assembled a conference in Detroit to draft a constitution, a necessary step toward giving MOWM a permanent structure. Randolph dismissed White's warning that the move would cost him the NAACP's backing. The Chief electrified delegates with a take-no-prisoners keynote address. "Some of us will be put in jail," he said, "but this will give the Negro masses a sense of their importance and value as citizens and as fighters in the Negro liberation movement and the cause for democracy as a whole. It will make white people in high places and the ordinary white man understand that Negroes have rights that they are bound to respect." His intemperate words dismayed the NAACP, whose executive board cut off contributions to MOWM, shattering any illusion of black unity.[43]

Randolph's group seemed to have momentum. MOWM chapters hosted events throughout 1942. Units in St. Louis, New York, Chicago, Detroit, and Cincinnati picketed companies with discriminatory hiring practices. Fundraising dances, cocktail parties, and parades boosted MOWM's public stature.

Its St. Louis chapter, led by BSCP organizer T. D. MacNeal, proved especially effective. St. Louis presented a mixed bag in terms of employment. Some businesses hired black workers with little fuss, whereas others retained all-white workforces in the name of labor peace and productivity. MacNeal sought to tip the balance toward equality. He operated largely on his own authority, periodically updating Randolph but never taking orders from him.

MacNeal began attacking high-profile employers during the buildup to MOWM's mass meetings. On a blazing hot day in May 1942 he led five hundred silent marchers around the enormous U.S. Cartridge Company complex. Only 600 of the company's 21,000 workers were black, all of them porters and general laborers. That very day, U.S. Cartridge announced plans to put African Americans on the production lines. It raised porters' wages two days later, then hired seventy-two black women, the first to work for the company, two days after that. Hundreds of African Americans were training for production line jobs by August, when MOWM held its mass meeting in St. Louis's Municipal Auditorium.

The St. Louis chapter's weekly meetings drew several hundred devotees to a downtown YMCA. Emboldened by success, MacNeal led three hundred demonstrators to the Carter Carburetor Corporation, a downtown plant producing fuses for artillery shells. Despite the year-old Executive Order 8802, none of its 2,700 employees were black. "Fight the Axis, Don't Fight Us," one placard read. MacNeal next turned his attention to public utilities. Union Electric, Laclede Gas, and Bell Telephone faced angry protesters. "LET'S STOP WOULD-BE HITLERS AT HOME," one of the chapter's pamphlets screamed. "LET'S PRACTICE DEMOCRACY AS WE PREACH IT!"[44]

"The organization is endeavoring to rid the Negro of a mental attitude to accept certain un-American practices as some inherent right of one class to discriminate against another," an editorialist noted in the *St. Louis American*, a black newspaper. MacNeal's passionate leadership inspired his equally ardent followers. He led a local fight not just for economic equality, but also for black pride. "No Negro who believes in standing on his feet as a red-blooded citizen can fail to join this Movement," he argued. MacNeal figured his chapter's activities led to 15,000 African Americans getting jobs by the end of the war.[45]

Enthusiasm was hardly universal. Some chapters existed mostly on paper. Money was always short. What was advertised as a huge rally in New York's Union Square attracted only five hundred marchers. Speakers talked from ladders leaned against trucks because MOWM could not afford to build a platform. A MOWM-sponsored prayer protest at New York's City Hall drew barely one hundred people. Disinterested black bystanders ate their lunches on nearby benches, chatting away as if nothing was happening. The event offered soul-stirring speeches, "but unfortunately," one attendee said, "there were not many souls for it to stir." Even rallies in St. Louis attracted fewer people than MacNeal anticipated.[46]

MOWM was losing steam. Part of the blame lay with Randolph, who never hired enough reliable subordinates to spread the workload. His tendency to micromanage was especially unfortunate because he was juggling multiple organizations and causes. More than a year after the postponed march, MOWM had yet to establish a reliable fundraising network or an effective recruitment operation. Publicity campaigns foundered for lack of money or creativity. MOWM's national headquarters was a dysfunctional snakepit rife with personal rivalries that Randolph never quashed.

African Americans admired Randolph's integrity and plainspoken ways. They applauded his role in winning Executive Order 8802 but wondered why MOWM still existed. Although it had thrown some great parties, it had produced no tangible victories since June 1941. Its agenda closely paralleled that of the more established NAACP. Many African Americans rejected its talk of mass protests during wartime as unpatriotic.

By late 1942 the war overseas was turning in the Allies' favor. The Navy, after a disastrous first six months following Pearl Harbor, crippled the Japanese fleet at Midway. In Europe, Soviet legions starved out a Nazi army at Stalingrad and began pushing toward Germany. At home, however, the war for equality suffered a string of defeats. Black leadership had fractured. MOWM was fading. The federal government's halfhearted commitment to civil rights wavered as the administration placed victory overseas above all other concerns. As the nation's military fortunes rose, African Americans' confidence in the war, and in their country, declined.

CHAPTER 5

An Hour of Crisis

Randolph's ability to mobilize thousands of African Americans despite poor organization and a shoestring budget reflected the depths of black disenchantment during the war's first year. An African American truck driver from Philadelphia faced treason charges for calling a black soldier "a crazy nigger ... out fighting for white trash." In Harlem, Malcolm Little, desperate to escape the white man's war, put on a crazy act to evade the draft. His hair dyed a flaming red, he stormed into the induction center wearing a garish zoot suit and yellow knob-toe shoes, then began spouting gibberish at the startled recruiting officer. His behavior earned him a spot on an Army psychiatrist's couch. Little feigned paranoia, jerking compulsively and peering under doors as if Hitler were waiting on the other side. Creeping close to the doctor, he whispered in his ear, "Daddy-o, now you and me, we're from up North here, so don't you tell nobody. ... I want to get sent down South. Organize them nigger soldiers, you dig? Steal us some guns, and kill up crackers!" The doctor classified him as 4-F, unacceptable for military service.[1]

America's overseas military fortunes had improved, but the twelve months after the triumphant Battle of Midway proved troublesome for domestic race relations. The armed forces' incremental lowering of racial barriers and the FEPC's halting advances proved double-edged swords. These small victories inspired race advocates to amplify their efforts. MOWM and other civil rights organizations now believed they could smash injustice once and for all. At the same time, the slow pace of change in an era of heightened expectations fueled anger among African Americans eager to match their country's actions with its rhetoric. Dissatisfaction ran rampant by the summer of 1943, when a series of race riots rocked the nation. As the dust settled, Americans had to wonder whether their internal divisions had caused the Good War to go bad.

In the summer of 1942, just as the March on Washington Movement was peaking, the Office of War Information (OWI), the government's largest producer of war propaganda, set out to determine why African Americans lacked enthusiasm for the war. The well-intentioned project epitomized Washington's inability to comprehend black America. OWI racial advisor Milton Starr's report exonerated the military from blame. Nor did it dwell on the pervasive racism still infecting defense industries one year after Roosevelt signed Executive Order 8802. Starr also minimized frustrations about persistent economic gaps between the races. He instead blamed African Americans' indifference on radicals such as Randolph, whose demands for revolutionary change discouraged ordinary blacks from appreciating how far they had come. "The Negro has *not* been recently deprived of any privileges," Starr observed, yet "a large part of the [black] press and leadership takes the attitude that unless all rights are granted to the Negro now, the support to the war effort of 13,000,000 Negroes will be withheld, resulting in our losing the war."[2]

Starr thought Randolph's poisonous rhetoric polluted the entire wartime landscape. His confrontational speeches discouraged patriotism among African Americans and compelled moderate black leaders to adopt extremist rhetoric to stay relevant. Randolph's talk of marching on Washington raised concerns about race war. Demands for social equality aroused white fears of miscegenation. Satisfying their calls for political equality in the South "would require an army of occupation as in Reconstruction days." Ending discrimination in the military meant putting black officers in charge of white enlisted men, a prospect Starr found "inconceivable." Besides, he continued, "War Department files indicate that records of all Negro soldiers in all wars are bad."

Like most of Roosevelt's subordinates, Starr viewed African Americans in terms of morale rather than justice. "The Negro has a large potential for patriotic response, which if properly developed, would to a large extent allay the unrest caused by his violent leaders," he said, glossing over the face that neither Randolph, Walter White, nor any other mainstream black leader had endorsed violent protest.

Executive Order 8802 and the FEPC brought more African Americans into the defense industry without quieting black discontent. Government agencies such as the OWI issued a steady stream of propaganda images designed to convince blacks that the country valued their contributions to the war effort. *Courtesy Franklin D. Roosevelt Presidential Library*

He proposed a multipronged propaganda assault to get blacks on board with the war. The Army and the Justice Department's Civil Rights Division should send more material to black papers. Newsreels and patriotic short films needed more footage of African Americans. Perhaps OWI could produce a comic strip for black newspapers. Starr also suggested a half-hour weekly radio show about black GIs, featuring celebrities such as Joe Louis, Cab Calloway, and Paul Robeson.

Starr's insistence that popular culture could win over reluctant blacks seems to reveal an almost willful refusal to address the issues driving their dissatisfaction. But many in the Roosevelt administration saw those problems as unsolvable in the immediate term. Economic and social inequalities that had survived for centuries could not be eliminated overnight. An uncompromising fight for civil rights would turn the South, and much of the North, against the administration, and perhaps the war. And besides, the president was already bearing a tremendous burden. Few in the White House believed he could simultaneously manage a war against fascism and a war for racial equality.

Perhaps the soothing balm of popular culture could cool black passions. Movies and radio programs profoundly influenced national understandings of the war. Most Americans could not see the conflict firsthand. They instead saw the war through cultural lenses, prepackaged by newspaper editors, newsreel executives, and motion picture screenwriters. Although none of these culturemakers faced the kind of censorship encountered overseas, they all felt government officials looking over their shoulders, and they all wanted to contribute to victory.

Hollywood was the most important mass culture industry. In August 1942, the same month Randolph addressed 10,000 followers in St. Louis's Municipal Auditorium, Paramount Pictures released a trifle of a film that introduced one of the defining pieces of World War II-era culture. *Holiday Inn*'s whisper-thin story of a song-and-dance man who abandons city life to open a charming countryside hotel served mostly as an excuse for its star, crooner Bing Crosby, to sing a new collection of songs from America's favorite composer, Irving Berlin. Everybody would win. Crosby could sell some albums, Paramount could cash in on his popularity, and Americans could enjoy a hundred minutes of escapist entertainment.

Critics dismissed the film as well-meaning schmaltz. They ignored the single Crosby recorded to promote the picture. But something strange happened as the cold grayness of winter set in. People started packing screenings of *Holiday Inn*. They snatched Crosby's record off the shelves. Crosby hadn't thought much of the song, which he recorded in two quick takes before rushing from the studio to play golf. Yet movie audiences swooned when Crosby, looking dapper in a checked shirt and soft smoking jacket, sat at a piano to play "White Christmas." Costar Marjorie Reynolds, flanked by a trimmed tree and a roaring fire, watches with watery eyes as Crosby sings about a world where treetops glisten, sleigh bells ring, and every Christmas is white.

War songs were supposed to be about war. Oldtimers still hummed "It's a Long Way to Tipperary," "Over There," and other hits from the last big one. Martial music dominated the airwaves throughout 1942. Listeners still steaming from Pearl Harbor snapped up such forgettable tunes as "You're a Sap, Mr. Jap," "The Japs Don't Have a Chinaman's Chance," and "We're Gonna Find a Fellow Who's Very, Very Yellow, and Beat Him Till He's Red, White and Blue." But "White Christmas" was different. It was a war song without guns, anger, or even an enemy. Everyone bought the record—white and black, male and female. Most surprisingly, Berlin announced at the dinner table one night, "The boys overseas are buying it."[3]

Crosby's visit to an American paratrooper unit stationed in post–D-Day France confirmed how intensely soldiers identified with the tune. A roughneck sergeant approached the singer before the show. "You gonna sing 'White Christmas?'" he asked. Yes, Crosby promised—soldiers all over Europe had demanded it. "Well, in that case, I guess I'll duck out," the sergeant replied. You might like my other numbers, a dismayed Crosby assured him. "I like the song all right," said the sergeant, "but I'll listen from behind the portable kitchen. It's no good for the men's morale to see their sergeant crying."[4]

"White Christmas" spoke to both the past and the future. It conjured up powerful, if idealized, images of home, reminding listeners of a time when families sat around the hearth sipping cocoa and assuring them that those days would return. Berlin wrote for a nation at war, for separated lovers, for the millions leaving for jobs in unfamiliar cities. His song defined the goal of the war as simply the end of war. He anticipated the return of normalcy and envisioned a sepia-tinged stability replacing the steel-plated brutality of wartime life.

Berlin was not thinking about black listeners when he wrote "White Christmas." There are no black characters in Holiday Inn, and no reason to strain for racial undertones in the song's title. But his work resonated with them as much as it did with whites. Even if fewer of them had experienced the romanticized holiday it depicted, they too longed for the serenity of peacetime. They too experienced the dislocation the song sought to alleviate. Around 600,000 African Americans migrated from rural areas to cities between 1940 and 1943. They poured into New York, Chicago, Detroit, and Los Angeles. They pursued shipbuilding jobs in New Orleans, Mobile, and Charleston, and aircraft manufacturing positions in Dallas and Atlanta. This demographic upheaval disrupted families. War forced children to grow up without fathers. Delinquency rates climbed as latchkey kids roamed the streets without parental supervision. Overstretched municipalities could not meet the rising demand for recreational facilities. Families doubled and tripled up in overpriced homes and apartments.

"White Christmas" exemplified the kind of cultural power Milton Starr hoped to harness. But the song's fuzzy war aims had little to do with the administration's goals. Nor did it offer a clear vision of American unity or of black involvement in the war. But efforts were already underway to recruit Hollywood for the cultural crusade to make blacks feel like America's war was their war, too.

Major studios had forged close relationships with the Roosevelt administration. They relied on the Commerce Department to update them on overseas markets, the State Department to resolve thorny international disputes, and the Justice Department to ignore what closely resembled an oligopoly designed to prevent new competitors from entering the movie business. In 1939, when Europe went to war, studio executives, most of them Jews with Eastern European roots, began green-lighting pictures that correlated with the White House's foreign policy.

Those prewar bonds tightened after Pearl Harbor. Patriotic film executives wanted to prove their loyalty. Washington encouraged them to produce big-screen messages that matched its own priorities. The OWI's Bureau of Motion Pictures (BMP) acted as a liaison between the coasts. BMP officials, who had no experience making movies, established nonbinding guidelines for Hollywood. Each film should somehow help win the war. Movies should present it as a fight for democracy relevant to every American. "We must emphasize that this is a people's war, that we must hang together or we shall all hang separately. ... We must emphasize that this country is a melting pot, a nation of many races and creeds, who have demonstrated that they can live together and progress," explained the OWI's 1942 *Government Information Manual for the Motion Picture Industry*. "Can we not portray on the screen the fact that ... the Negroes have a real, a legal, and a permanent chance for improvement of their status under democracy and no chance at all under a dictatorship?"[5]

Filmmakers struggled to implement the BMP's utopian vision. Studios had long cast blacks as servants, porters, or comic relief. Screenwriters and directors often reflected prevailing social prejudices.

And profit-driven studios needed to book their films in Southern theaters, which would reject pictures with African American leads. Dependent on audience goodwill, studios hesitated to inject hot-button racial issues into programmatic melodramas, or earnest discussions of black–white relations into a comedy. Whenever possible, they simply avoided racial landmines by using all-white casts.

The BMP swung into action when Metro-Goldwyn-Mayer announced *The Man on America's Conscience*, a biographical film about Reconstruction-era president Andrew Johnson. Although Johnson's reputation has declined since the 1940s, at the time many whites praised his mild treatment of the defeated South, perceiving him as a force for national reconciliation after the Civil War. MGM seemed unaware that African Americans demonized Johnson for opposing black voting rights and for turning a blind eye to state laws restricting former slaves' freedoms. MGM not only intended to praise Johnson, but also to portray Pennsylvania congressman Thaddeus Stevens, a champion of black rights, as a vindictive drunk. One scene had Stevens playing cards with John Wilkes Booth, a fictionalized encounter sure to infuriate African Americans.[6]

BMP officials urged MGM to reconsider. The project grew into a cause célèbre as government bureaucrats, in conjunction with political liberals (Wendell Willkie and Walter White made their feelings known), pleaded for greater sensitivity toward black feelings. Resenting these intrusions, MGM inserted minor script revisions that eased some of Stevens's rough edges. It solved the race problem by essentially writing blacks out of the picture. Only four African Americans appeared in the final film, retitled *Tennessee Johnson* (1942), all of them in trivial roles as servants. These cosmetic changes satisfied BMP monitors reluctant to antagonize the studio. "We want to encourage the studios to make films with real guts, films that can cause complaint from pro-Fascist minorities," one administrator advised Walter White, but in the case of *Tennessee Johnson*, "we have to ... register our complaints and be willing to lose a battle and win a war."[7]

Soon after the *Tennessee Johnson* imbroglio, the OWI took another stab at divining black attitudes toward the war. Its researchers spent five months, from November 1942 to March 1943, compiling a sweeping survey of racial attitudes and of mass culture's portrayals of African Americans, two subjects they saw as inextricably linked.

Their work uncovered yawning chasms separating white and black perceptions of the war and of each other. When asked whether "most colored people are pretty well satisfied with things in this country," 64 percent of whites responded "yes." Fifty-seven percent of whites said African Americans had good opportunities to help win the war, whereas 68 percent of blacks said they did not. The survey revealed broad support among whites for segregation. Three quarters voted for segregating public transportation, nine-tenths for segregating restaurants, and 96 percent for segregating housing. Whites backed segregating the military by a nine-to-one ratio. Just 18 percent of blacks endorsed military segregation.

OWI reviewers argued that the lack of African American radio and film characters prevented whites from understanding blacks' contributions to the war and dissuaded blacks from embracing the cause. Monitors tracking twenty-nine national radio commentators heard only two stories in five months about African Americans' role in the war. Blacks figured in less than 1 percent of newsreel clips. They appeared more often in movies and radio serials, but almost always as servants or comic relief. "Negroes are presented as basically different from other people, as taking no relevant part in the life of the nation, as offering nothing, contributing nothing, expecting nothing," the OWI report concluded.[8]

The OWI tried, albeit without much conviction, to change Hollywood's ways. It did have a few modest breakthroughs. *Sahara* (1943), a Humphrey Bogart film about a tank platoon battling its way across North Africa, included a gallant Sudanese sergeant major, played by Illinois native Rex Ingram. *Bataan* (1943) placed a black man in an ethnically diverse squadron fighting a heroic delaying action against a Japanese horde. The movie never mentioned segregation in the real military.

This Is the Army (1943), a Warner Bros. Technicolor extravaganza that clothed a classic "hey, let's put on a show" story in khaki, unwittingly presented a more honest depiction of segregation. It is an airy confection of a film, a breezy musical about a company of GIs that mounts a song-and-dance review to benefit the Army Emergency Relief Fund. Screenwriters included a cameo for Sergeant Joe Louis, who mumbled a few lines about God being on the Americans' side. *This Is the Army*, however, reinforced rather than challenged racial stereotypes. Other than the famous Louis, blacks never share the screen with whites, except for a single, extreme long shot of the troupe. A score of whites perform a "minstrel number" in blackface, singing Irving Berlin's "Mandy" while wearing boater hats and oversized bow-ties. The black soldiers perform a wild swing tune called "That's What the Well-Dressed Man in Harlem Will Wear," punctuating their exuberance with frenetic kicks and spins while Louis works a speed bag. Enormous, zoot-suited figures in the background reinforce the caricature of childlike African Americans living for good times and flashy clothes. An all-white audience thunders its approval. OWI reviewers offered no objections to the picture. Their tacit endorsement reflected the agency's ambiguous position. Washington wanted to incorporate African Americans into mass culture, but lacked the determination to overcome entrenched attitudes.

At times even the OWI stereotyped African Americans. A confidential 1944 manual for white officers characterized blacks as "gregarious, extrovertive ... easy-going ... loud in speech ... easily hurt by criticism ... appreciative of praise ... hot-tempered ... mentally lazy, not retentive, forgetful ... ruled by instinct and emotion rather than by reason ... keen sense of rhythm ... lacks mechanical sense ... works at slower pace than whites ... physically strong regardless of size ... weak feet ... evasive ... lies easily, frequently, naturally."[9]

Randolph frequented vaudeville houses in his younger days but was too busy now to be much of a music fan. Although no doubt familiar with "White Christmas," the song's syrupy vision of postwar ease clashed with his sense of where the country was headed. His correspondence never mentions *Tennessee Johnson* or *This Is the Army*. In fact, someone reading his papers might conclude that he never saw a single movie during the war. Neither did he engage in the broader discussions about how mass culture depicted African Americans. In avoiding the conversation, he missed an opportunity to influence one of the underlying perpetuators of discrimination.

He focused on familiar targets, concentrating on organizing the grassroots and on the administration's treatment of minorities. By late 1942, when "White Christmas" was dominating the airwaves, both areas were trending south. His March on Washington Movement was entering its decline phase. The military was digging in its heels on the use of black soldiers. With his other goals proving elusive, Randolph began redirecting his attention toward the FEPC, a bureau essential to African Americans' economic future.

The FEPC's youthful enthusiasm survived its fall 1941 Los Angeles hearings. Its investigators tracked down reports of discrimination from around the country. Staffers negotiated scores of settlements and filed dozens of cease and desist orders against defense contractors violating Executive Order 8802. African Americans increasingly viewed it as a means for attaining economic justice. "If it does its job successfully, the American Negro will truly get a New Deal," the *Pittsburgh Courier* enthused.[10]

Serious problems lurked beneath this rosy surface. FEPC's $300,000 budget made it the federal government's smallest agency. Its tiny staff could not process the thousands of grievances pouring in. "The FEPC is meaningless unless its present staff is augmented to carry out the terms and provisions of the executive order," Randolph complained. Even other federal agencies, including the United States Employment Service and the United States Office of Education, ignored its directives with impunity. Enemies in Congress demonized it as a symbol of executive-branch overreach and federal intrusion into local affairs. Perhaps most damaging, although the agency could expose discrimination and recommend modifications, it could not enforce its edicts. Putting a happy face on the FEPC's weakness, Executive Secretary Lawrence Cramer noted that "our nuisance value is tremendous."[11]

Speakers at the summer 1942 MOWM rallies highlighted these weaknesses but could do nothing about them. The FEPC's black members, Earl Dickerson and Milton P. Webster, felt the heat. Their passion for the committee's mission exceeded that of their white peers. They believed the FEPC's white members did not understand, or did not want to understand, the magnitude of America's racial problems. Dickerson and Webster thought Chairman Mark Ethridge's habit of moving quietly so as to avoid agitating opponents or embarrassing the administration undermined the group's potential. For his part, Ethridge believed the FEPC had already achieved its purpose. "We paralyzed any idea of a march on Washington and we have worked honestly for a better measure of justice for the Negro," he told White House Press Secretary Stephen Early. "They have less cause for complaint than they ever had, and they know it."[12]

Ethridge, citing his responsibilities at the *Louisville Courier-Journal,* resigned as chair in early 1942, although he remained on the committee. Roosevelt chose Hampton Institute president Malcolm MacLean to replace him. MacLean accepted the premise that so infuriated Randolph—that wartime was no time for social protest. MacLean believed discrimination resulted from ignorance rather than maliciousness. Employers did not know skilled minority workers were available, and minorities did not know how to apply for defense jobs. His mission, therefore, was not to attack discrimination so much as to mount a slow, steady educational campaign against it. He wanted the FEPC to succeed, but only enough to keep people like Randolph from complaining.[13]

The FEPC's June 1942 hearings in Birmingham, Alabama, marked its first foray into the South. Its location and timing— between MOWM's Madison Square Garden and Chicago Coliseum events—created a tense atmosphere. "A bunch of snoopers, two of whom are Negroes, will assemble in Birmingham … to determine whether the South is doing right by Little Sambo," the *Gadsden (Alabama) Times* announced. Southern papers warned of a socialist-led drive to abolish segregation, encourage intermarriage, and elevate blacks over whites. Sensing danger, Ethridge telephoned Dickerson a few days before the committee journeyed South. "Earl, perhaps you shouldn't go down there," he suggested. "The South is part of the United States," Dickerson responded, and the FEPC had an obligation to uphold the law. FEPC member David Sarnoff also voiced concern. "I can sympathize with your deep feelings," he told Dickerson, "but if you are going down to Alabama to try the persecution of the Negro race, which has been going [on] ever since the country started, I am not in sympathy." A white, six-foot-four-inch-tall U.S. Marshal accompanied Dickerson throughout the trip.[14]

Ethridge's opening remarks, delivered in a segregated courtroom, confirmed the board's modest intentions. Executive Order 8802 "is a war order and not a social document," he said. Ethridge denied accusations that the FEPC aimed to abolish Jim Crow or destroy racial hierarchy. "No power in the world—not even in all the mechanized armies of the earth, Allied or Axis—could force the Southern white people to the abandonment of the principle of social segregation," he explained. He chided "Negro leaders and … Negro newspaper editors" who imagined 8802 as a second Emancipation Proclamation, accusing them of sowing dissent at a time when unity was of paramount importance.[15]

Ethridge sent the White House a copy of his address, telling Press Secretary Stephen Early that his words would "do a great deal to ease the tension" in the South. Roosevelt's advisors agreed that Ethridge had offered "sound and constructive" advice. Even Mrs. Roosevelt approved.[16]

Ethridge's statement eased Southern fears of social revolution. "It was an intelligent, constructive effort to deal with minority problems in war industries," the *Birmingham Herald-Age* noted. The *Richmond Times-Dispatch* applauded Ethridge's "sane and levelheaded counsel to the Negro." Even the *New York Amsterdam-Star News* accepted Ethridge's logic. "We are inclined to view President Roosevelt's Executive Order 8802 in the same light as seen by Mr. Ethridge—a war document, not a social proclamation," one of its editorials opined. *Pittsburgh Courier* columnist George Schuyler, a prominent black conservative, agreed. "Some Negroes have written a social meaning into [8802] which is contrary to its meaning," he noted. Washington would not force the South to grant equality, and the South would not willingly surrender its traditions.[17]

Randolph was having none of it. "Mr. Ethridge should also know ... that it is also true that all of the power in the world ... could not force the Negro to the abandonment of his fight for the destruction of racial discrimination, segregation and Jim Crow," he fumed. The *Chicago Defender* and several other black papers called for Ethridge's resignation. Dickerson and Webster ripped the Kentuckian in the press. At the next FEPC meeting, they pushed the committee to announce a position on segregation. As tempers flared, Ethridge left to catch a train. Sarnoff departed soon after to attend to other business. Lacking a quorum, the meeting broke up without resolving the question.[18]

In a sense, everybody was right. Roosevelt never intended 8802 to bring social equality, nor did he expect the FEPC to force the issue. Randolph was right to assert that African Americans were tired of waiting for their rights. Conservative white Southerners were correct to claim that the FEPC threatened racial traditions. On a subconscious level they grasped what Randolph had long argued—that economic equality, in the form of equal opportunities to get jobs, would eventually produce an America free from segregation, discrimination, and prejudice.

The Birmingham inquiry upset the region's social conventions despite Ethridge's disavowal of social tinkering. Few Southerners had ever encountered systematic, outside scrutiny of their racial politics. Black professionals testified as expert witnesses. Black workers denounced white-only labor unions. Black committee members forced white executives to admit discrimination. Moreover, the hearings changed some companies the FEPC cited. The Coca-Cola Corporation, for example, abandoned its racially tinged hiring practices. The number of blacks working for firms the FEPC investigated at Birmingham more than doubled over the next six months. FEPC staffers deemed the proceedings a success despite the Ethridge flap.

Their enthusiasm was short lived. A few days after Birmingham, the administration cancelled hearings on anti-Latino discrimination in the southwestern United States. The edict shocked field investigators who had spent months pursuing reports of employers paying Mexicans less than whites, or of limiting them to menial positions. Interviews with workers, union reps, and corporate managers revealed a widespread belief that Mexicans were too stupid to handle skilled positions. After denying him a promotion, one foreman told an American-born Latino, "I don't give a damn if you were born in China, you are still a Mexican."[19]

Assistant Secretary of State Sumner Welles urged Roosevelt to stop the proceedings. Welles was finalizing agreements to enable the short-term importation of much-needed Mexican laborers. Evidence of mistreatment might sour Mexico's government on the deal. Fixing discrimination required "time, tact and patience," Welles argued. Hearings might also fracture national unity while fueling the Nazi propaganda machine. And, Welles concluded in a perverse turn of logic, because anti-Mexican discrimination was so common, hearings were unlikely to turn up any revelations.[20]

Roosevelt ruled in the diplomat's favor. He stunned the bureau again when, in August 1942, he revoked its independent status and transferred it to the War Manpower Commission (WMC), an agency created that spring to maximize the efficient use of manpower. WMC chair Paul McNutt, a former governor of Indiana with presidential ambitions, lobbied for the move, which consolidated his control over manpower functions. Roosevelt's motivations are unclear, but he seems to have acted from political considerations. Needing Southern votes in the upcoming congressional elections, he effectively buried the hated FEPC by imposing bureaucratic distance between it and him.

The shift made sense on an administrative level, as it merged departments with similar duties. Moreover, McNutt had a solid record on racial matters. In World War I he volunteered to command an all-black brigade. In the 1920s he opposed the Ku Klux Klan, at the time a major social and political force in Indiana. In recent years he had condemned the poll tax and praised black soldiers. He endorsed the Double V campaign at a July 1942 "Unity for Victory" rally in Harlem.

Randolph called the transfer "a grave warning to the Negro people of the revival and threatening growth of the sinister Ku Klux and lynch-rope spirit." He accused the administration of sacrificing African Americans on the altar of Southern votes. Some agencies within the WMC discriminated against blacks, he noted. The realignment felt like a personal betrayal. Roosevelt had promised to make the FEPC an independent agency, funded from the executive branch's budget, that reported directly to him. A year later, the FEPC was taking orders from McNutt and the WMC. African Americans' hopes for a better economic future now rested with Congress, which appropriated funds for the WMC. "It is just going to be a stooge committee," Milton P. Webster advised Randolph.[21]

FEPC chair Malcolm MacLean asked Roosevelt to mollify protestors with a strong statement on minority rights. Roosevelt resisted. The uprising was "a lot of smoke and very little fire," he said. FDR pleaded ignorance when a reporter inquired about the transfer. "I don't know," he responded, in a bald-faced lie. "I just got a memorandum on that last night, and I have got to look into it." He offered a clarification ten days later, telling reporters that he moved the FEPC to strengthen it. With the WMC's larger staff at its disposal, the FEPC would have broader powers and be more effective than when it was an independent board.[22]

Randolph hit the roof. He shot off a fiery telegram to Walter White, blasting the move as a "complete surrender to [the] Ku Klux spirit of [the] South ... an insult to [the] race." He sent the president a milder note. "Negroes shocked and disturbed to hear Fair Employment Committee submerged in Man Power Commission," he wrote.

"Am confident you have been wrongly advised." When this protest failed to bring results, he made his anger public. Relocating the FEPC "amounts to complete emasculation and destruction of its usefulness," he told the black press.[23]

Randolph's fusillade was part of a barrage of complaints hitting the White House. MOWM and NAACP chapters voiced their disapproval, as did the sleeping car porters and various labor, church, and civic groups. With the FEPC in danger, many African Americans realized for the first time how much its fate affected their future. "This one agency with its skeleton staff, woefully inadequate methods of dealing with a nationwide problem, and its powerlessness to compel even the giving of testimony, did more to build colored morale than any agency in the country," lamented George F. McCray of the Associated Negro Press, ominously referring to the board in the past tense.[24]

At first the backlash had little impact. The FEPC wallowed in bureaucratic limbo for several months despite McNutt's promises to strengthen it. The committee exhausted its budget in October. McNutt assigned WMC staff to take over the FEPC's field work. Investigations ground to a halt. The FEPC could not hold hearings without McNutt's approval. "Any damn thing the Manpower Commission wants to do they can do," Webster complained. "The committee is being stripped down to its last legs," lamented Earl Dickerson.[25]

Pressure from African American groups eventually forced a partial retreat. McNutt finally funded the FEPC, at a far lower level than Randolph wanted, and allowed it to appoint its own field representatives. McNutt retained the right of approval over proposed public hearings. Overwhelmed staff members kept swimming upstream against a torrent of claims they could never hope to properly investigate.

In January 1943 McNutt ordered the FEPC to postpone its imminent hearings on discrimination in the railroad industry. Investigators had spent months accumulating evidence of railroad companies' violations of 8802. The railroads were a major employer of African Americans. Many of them, especially those based in the South, restricted blacks to the most physically demanding jobs and paid them less than white employees. Several large railroad unions barred African Americans. Canceling the hearings was "good strategy," he explained, because it freed him to quietly work out a deal rather than publicly embarrass the railroads. African Americans "have got to recognize me as their friend and not crack me on the head every time my neck is out," he complained.[26]

Randolph called the cancellation "a slap in the face." "It seems to show further that the FEPC was just a sop, an appeasement, in the first place to stop the March On Washington," MOWM's St. Louis chapter claimed. Randolph ordered MOWM chapters to picket government buildings. Malcolm MacLean resigned from the FEPC. William Hastie, Secretary of War Stimson's civilian advisor, also quit. Ever the organizer, Randolph assembled representatives from fraternal, labor, civic, and religious groups into a Committee to Save the FEPC. Hotheaded MOWM members wanted to march. Sensing the chaos within his organization and fearful of inflaming racial tensions at a pivotal moment in the war, Randolph ignored their demands.[27]

He instead opted to become a backroom negotiator. He spearheaded a clear-the-air meeting between himself, Walter White, and about twenty other black leaders, on the one hand, and McNutt and a few other WMC officials on the other. The conference, held in the Social Security Building in February 1943, devolved into an angry airing of grievances, with Randolph leading the charge. He demanded immediate restoration of the FEPC's independent status and a rescheduling of the railroad hearings. Using his most provocative language to date, he charged the administration with selling out to reactionary Southerners. "The government today is the primary factor, the major factor, in the country in propagating discrimination against Negroes," he fumed, because it allowed unequal treatment in the military, in defense industries, and in its civilian bureaus. Washington, Randolph concluded, was the enemy.

He took the floor again as the meeting broke up, calmer now but no less defiant. "I want to say ... with respect to my observation about the Negroes being required to fight the Government, that I don't make any reservations about that statement," he said, "because the Government itself has a very definite policy with respect to segregation in relation to the Negro, and the Negroes and liberals in this country have got to fight to change that policy."[28]

"This is an hour of crisis," a MOWM press release insisted. "Negro Americans are frustrated. Growing discontent is visible among the multitude. Eager eyes and questioning faces are turned toward leadership in search of a way out. ... The patience of Negro America is sorely tried." Randolph sensed the anger wherever he traveled. He knew the odds of violence on the home front increased with every passing day.[29]

The United States in 1943 was an angry, nervous, unsettled place, a twitchy nation certain of trouble coming but unsure of how to avoid it. African Americans, sensing an opportunity to improve their lives and increasingly suspicious of moderates bearing promises of future rewards, demanded democracy now. Militancy was on the rise. A new organization, the Congress of Racial Equality (CORE), began staging sit-ins in hotels and restaurants that refused to serve blacks. A black youth in Lexington, Kentucky stabbed a white driver who ordered him to the back of his bus.

Southern whites grumbled that ignorant Northerners, radical black troublemakers, and idealistic federal bureaucrats (with the meddling Eleanor Roosevelt leading the parade) wanted to force racial equality, which to them meant black rule, on the region. "White people are going to be working for the Negroes after the war," they worried. Some Northern whites were starting to feel the same way. With wartime migration upending their communities' traditional racial, class, cultural, and political dynamics, they could no longer pretend that African Americans did not exist.[30]

Rumors of impending racial violence were everywhere. The whispering in Atlanta, New Orleans, and Washington, DC grew so loud that race riots almost broke out simply because residents were convinced they were coming. Stories of arsenals concealed in black churches, rifles hidden in coffins, and African Americans stockpiling shells passed from ear to ear. Whites cast wary eyes on black soldiers, any of whom might be the leader of the coming revolution. Many believed Axis agents had organized African Americans into secret cabals—the Black Dragon Society, the Yellow Shirts, the Swastika Club. Undercover FBI agents dismissed these tales; J. Edgar Hoover's men thought communists, not fascists, were sowing unrest among black Americans.

President Roosevelt saw the United States' enormous industrial capacity as the key to victory. By 1943, however, racial tensions were throwing wrenches into the gears. In March, white employees at a Packard plant in Detroit walked off their job making aircraft engines when the company hired four black women as machine operators. The administration had no good answers for this or for similar strikes occurring around the country. Philleo Nash, the OWI's liaison with the White House, suggested making "a large number of small concessions in Negro employment, training, upgrading and in the armed forces" while reassuring whites that these tweaks would not endanger "social segregation." A slightly strengthened FEPC might "smother the Negro problem" so long as the controversial agency maintained a low profile.[31]

Pent-up tensions exploded in the summer of 1943. White shipyard workers in Mobile, Alabama, rioted when companies promoted black welders. In June roving gangs of soldiers and sailors in Los Angeles incited a week of violence when they attacked Mexican Americans wearing zoot suits, a sartorial mark of ethnic pride. Smaller zoot suit riots broke out in Baltimore, Philadelphia, Pittsburgh, and elsewhere. Black soldiers clashed with military police at Camp Stewart, Georgia, just hours after the Los Angeles unrest subsided.

Many looked to Detroit, long a racial tinderbox, as the next likely problem spot. The city had swelled as auto manufacturers accumulated defense contracts. Around 200,000 whites, most of them rural Southerners, poured in, along with 50,000 African Americans. A tight housing market forced migrants to sleep in boxcars, tents, churches, and jails. Detroit's ethnic minorities, especially the Poles, discouraged blacks from entering "their" neighborhoods. New black arrivals crammed into the city's overcrowded black districts. One of these ghettoes, Paradise Valley, housed 65,000 African Americans in a one-and-a-half square mile area. Some single-family residences held 150 people. Schools were similarly packed. Whites zealously guarded access to recreation areas. Belle Isle, a riverfront park near Paradise Valley, experienced black–white violence on a regular basis.

Detroit nearly came to blows a year earlier, when hundreds of armed whites blocked a few dozen black families from entering the federally financed Sojourner Truth housing project. State troopers finally moved the families in two months later. Detroiters predicted more trouble but did nothing to prevent it. The KKK expanded its activities in the area. Walkouts at defense plants became everyday occurrences. "I'd rather see Hitler and Hirohito win the war than work beside a nigger on the assembly line," one employee growled. Fistfights broke out in schools. African Americans' relations with the police deteriorated. With municipal budgets strained and young men heading overseas, Detroit's police department, like many in the United States, shrank during the war despite the city's booming population. Only 1 percent of its officers were black. "Sooner or later there is going to be a blow-up," people muttered.[32]

The explosion came on June 20, 1943. Allied forces had just mopped up the last Axis resistance in North Africa and were two weeks from invading Sicily. War was on its way to Detroit, too. Over 100,000 people descended on Belle Isle to escape the scorching Sunday heat. Police broke up fistfights throughout the day. Sundown, rather than cooling passions, brought additional violence. Scuffling between individuals escalated into mass brawls. At this moment of almost unbearable racial tension, a black man grabbed the microphone at the Forest Club, an African American hotspot in the heart of Paradise Valley, to announce that whites were assaulting blacks at Belle Isle. The nightclub emptied as blacks started looting white-owned businesses. Rumors that whites had killed three blacks sent more rioters into the streets. Flare-ups continued through Monday. Blacks continued their rampage while blue-collar whites assembled downtown to go "nigger huntin.'" Police and soldiers finally stopped the violence late that night. Nine whites and twenty-five African Americans lay dead. A post-riot investigator thought Detroit resembled "bombed-out London." "We'll win next time, by God!" he heard a white man say.[33]

Local leaders pointed fingers while seeking ways to parlay ethnic and racial tensions into votes. White Detroiters blamed the riots on communists, Eleanor Roosevelt, uppity blacks, and any other convenient target. "Sure we want the Negro to make a good living," one middle-class white man said, "but damn it let him spend his money on his side of town."[34]

Washington struggled to comprehend what had happened. Eleanor Roosevelt urged her husband to denounce racial injustice. Attorney General Francis Biddle proposed a law barring black Southerners from migrating to "communities which cannot absorb them, either on account of their physical limitations or cultural background." Secretary of War Stimson cast the riot as part of a "deliberate effort ... on the part of certain radical leaders of the colored race to use the war for obtaining ... race equality and interracial marriages." Congressman John Rankin of Mississippi pinned the disturbance on the "crazy policies of the President's Committee on Fair Employment Practice in attempting to mix the races in all kinds of employment." FDR, after hearing these opinions, elected to do nothing.[35]

The dust was still settling in Detroit when Harlem burst into flames. Mayor LaGuardia had felt trouble brewing. In the aftermath of Detroit he used his weekly radio address to celebrate New York City's diversity and plead for a calm discussion of racial inequality. He met with black leaders, asked white clergymen to condemn racism, and promised new housing projects in overcrowded Harlem after the war. Although offered sincerely, none of these gestures addressed blacks' immediate problems. With the war consuming all available manpower and resources, LaGuardia had no way to alleviate African Americans' woes.

Just before dusk on August 1, Private Robert Bandy, a black MP with the New Jersey-based 730th regiment, escorted his mother through the crowds clogging the sidewalk outside the Braddock Hotel, a popular hangout spot for entertainers performing around the corner at the Apollo Theater. Minutes later, a police officer struck thirty-three-year-old Margie Polite, a black woman he accused of disturbing the peace. When Bandy rushed to her assistance, the officer shot him in the shoulder. The fracas attracted passersby who started whispering about a white cop who had murdered a GI. Young men started sprinting through the streets shouting, "White man kill black soldier! Get the white man! Get the white man!"[36]

Harlemites returning from work or Sunday errands found the district in an uproar. One of them, a dishwasher named Sidney Poitier, exited the subway at the 125th Street station. "There was chaos everywhere," the future Oscar-winning actor remembered. Cops and looters streamed past as he walked up Lenox Avenue. Pops of gunfire rang out from somewhere nearby. Reflections off shards of broken glass transformed busy streets into twinkling landscapes. It would have been beautiful if it weren't so horrifying. Poitier, one of Harlem's many West Indian imports, succumbed to the anarchic spirit around him. He dove into a department store and looked for something to grab.

A fresh round of gunfire, this one close by, sent him scurrying into a storeroom. He hid behind a flour sack, waited for the police to pass, then ran for his rented room on 127th, dodging bullets all the way. One bullet tore through his calf, leaving a permanent scar.[37]

A few blocks away, small-time hustler Malcolm Little surveyed the chaos from the corner of 125th Street and St. Nicholas Avenue. Rioting blacks carrying armloads of furniture, clothes, and booze hustled past. Mayor LaGuardia and Walter White whizzed by in a red fire car, using its loudspeaker to implore people to go home. Little instead joined a jovial band of looters who were laughing at the sign a terrified Chinese businessman had stuck on his store's door. "Me Colored Too," it read.[38]

On Monday the sun rose over a scene resembling the devastation in Warsaw, London, Stalingrad, and other war-torn cities. Pedestrians confronted blocks of broken windows and stripped store shelves. Iron gates meant to protect businesses lay twisted on the ground. Thousands of police officers and air raid wardens patrolled the street as martial law, in fact if not officially, descended on Harlem. Six people lay dead and hundreds injured.

"Looting is just a natural instinct," a white policeman commented. "They don't know better. They're just like savages. Don't belong in a civilized country in my estimation ... belong back in a tree ... only thing missing is a tail." Editorialists blamed the riots on black inferiority, the black press, and fire-breathing black leaders. Panic gripped the nation. The mayor of Barnesville, Georgia promised to arrest any African American not in the military or working as a cook or a nurse. South Carolina's House of Representatives passed a resolution demanding that "the damned agitators of the North leave the South alone." Residents of Lawrenceburg, Tennessee erected a marker at the city limits reading: "NIGGER, READ AND RUN. DON'T LET THE SUN GO DOWN ON YOU HERE. IF YOU CAN'T READ, RUN ANYWAY."[39]

Mayor LaGuardia and President Roosevelt recognized the deeper social, economic, and cultural problems underlying the riots. With the war consuming their attention, they did little to answer those concerns. So black frustration mounted as hopes for Double V waned. Even Eleanor Roosevelt got crossways with the black masses when she wrote a clumsy *Negro Digest* article entitled "If I Were a Negro." Some found her title insulting. Others saved their vitriol for what followed. "If I were a Negro," the first lady wrote, "I would take every chance that came my way to prove my quality and ability and if recognition was slow, I would continue to prove myself, knowing that in the end, good performance would be acknowledged." The *Amsterdam News* observed that African Americans had already proven their quality and that her husband was more responsible for slow recognition than anyone else. "They don't understand what's happening in the United States," the paper claimed.[40]

America's war was moving in two directions. Battlefield affairs were shifting into the Allies' favor. American and British forces steamrolled across North Africa in late 1942, squeezing the Axis occupiers off the continent. In the Pacific, the Japanese kept backpedaling after losing the Battle of Midway. American forces retook Guadalcanal and the Solomon Islands and prepared to start island hopping toward Japan.

Hopes for victory on the home front waned at the very moment when Americans could taste victory overseas. MOWM was struggling to define itself. American culture either caricatured or ignored blacks. The FEPC appeared on its last legs. The military refused to open additional opportunities for blacks. Riots shattered the nation. President Roosevelt was too distracted by the war and political considerations to follow his better angels. Conservatives swept the November 1942 congressional elections, enhancing the South's power in Washington and lengthening the odds against action on lynching or the poll tax.

It seemed everyone was angry at everyone else. Whites, blacks, Mexican Americans, the North, the South, the West—no one and nowhere was tranquil. Randolph, for one, stuck with the argument he voiced at the fractious meeting with McNutt's WMC. Asserting that the government had become the enemy, he looked to cultivate "a moral and spiritual force which the southern cracker will not be able to ignore or brush aside." Randolph's view of the future mirrored that of the generals and admirals; all of them were preparing for a long, grinding fight against an implacable foe. And all of them were confident of victory.[41]

CHAPTER 6

....

Bad and Getting Worse

Most white Americans thought the war was going well in summer 1943. Even though peace lay in some distant, almost unimaginable future, they found hope in Allied offensives that had the Axis retreating in Africa, Asia, and, beginning with the July 1943 invasion of Sicily, the fringes of Europe.

Black Americans agreed that the military situation was improving but denied that the war itself was going well. They were fighting for Double V, and victory at home seemed an increasingly remote possibility. It was unclear whether the recent riots vented pent-up frustrations or were the leading edge of a tidal wave of domestic violence. Segregation and discrimination in the military remained substantively intact. The FEPC was hanging by a thread, starved for money and paralyzed after War Manpower Commission chair Paul McNutt canceled its investigation into the railroad industry. A. Philip Randolph's March on Washington Movement, a bright beacon of possibility two years earlier, was limping along, its idealism fading and its influence on the wane.

The next two years brought a mixed bag of triumphs and defeats. Allied forces liberated Europe and backed Japan into a corner. At home, the war for equality raged on. MOWM's tailspin continued after summer 1943. Randolph tried, with limited success, to reassemble its pieces into new movements dedicated to saving the FEPC and ending military discrimination. FEPC survived into 1945, if barely. A combination of political pressures and military necessities drove the armed forces to modify their policies in ways that would have been unthinkable before Pearl Harbor. It was clear by early 1945 that a new world was coming. Its exact outlines and contours remained unclear.

One small incident from the Harlem riot amused NAACP chief counsel Thurgood Marshall. In a letter to a friend, the future Supreme Court justice shared the news that some thug had shattered one of MOWM's windows. Marshall assured his correspondent that rioters left the office itself untouched. Then he twisted the dagger. "Maybe it was not looted for the reason that there is nothing in there to be looted," he laughed.[1]

"We are not authorities on organizing marches to Washington," the *Pittsburgh Courier* editorialized, "but it is difficult to see why it should require all this time to get down to the business of marching." Once full of promise, Randolph's movement entered 1943 in dire straits. MOWM had only a few thriving chapters. As of September, the national office had $125 in the bank and a sheaf of unpaid bills. Randolph wrote personal checks to cover expenses. MOWM's dwindling staff often went weeks without pay. They unleashed their frustrations on each other, escalating minor disagreements into an all-out office war. Randolph's juggling of a half-dozen causes, all of them top priority, infuriated subordinates and confused African Americans who were waiting for the March on Washington Movement to march. Randolph knew the organization's name no longer reflected its amorphous agenda but could not change it without creating more confusion. It "has its limiting character," he admitted.[2]

MOWM's troubles made it a slow-moving target for critics. Dwight MacDonald, a liberal white journalist, contributed perhaps the most scathing indictment. MacDonald charged Randolph with turning a grassroots movement into a cult of personality. MOWM was too top-down and too poorly organized to translate the heat of rhetoric into the light of action. If anything, Randolph was too magnetic. His forceful character awed subordinates into acting only when he told them to. His overcrowded schedule prevented him from devoting enough time to MOWM. With their leader absent, paralyzed national office staffers conducted long, pointless conferences that settled nothing. No one could articulate a cohesive plan of action. MacDonald thought MOWM's blacks-only policy "a bad mistake" that "split the two races at a time when racial antagonism on both sides is growing dangerously." MacDonald found no joy in his takedown.

"We want to see the MOWM develop into the kind of powerful movement it can potentially become," he said, "but its weaknesses are at present very disturbing to its friends."[3]

Randolph pleaded for more time to whip MOWM into shape. "I have had some experience in organizing workers," he told MacDonald. "I know this business of organizing anybody or anything isn't done over night and it is full of headaches." It took time to get a movement running smoothly. MOWM's "inner strength and objective clarity of vision" would soon become clear to all, he promised. Randolph remained adamant about keeping MOWM all black even though it invited detractors.[4]

Randolph stayed the course, making little effort to right the listing ship. He hoped MOWM's upcoming "We Are Americans Too" conference, scheduled for July 1943 in Chicago, might reinvigorate the faltering group. MOWM had announced the event with typical bombast in late 1942. African Americans "are engaged in a great world revolution testing whether this nation or any nation so conceived and so dedicated to double standards of citizenship and justice can long endure," a press release blared. Randolph envisioned letter-writing campaigns, marches on city halls, and a week of rallies that would shake the Windy City. A more select gathering would debate whether MOWM should march on Washington, outline new offensives against racial inequality, and, in a nod toward Randolph's increasing interest in linking African Americans' fight with a global struggle against oppression, consider ways to end colonialism in Africa and the West Indies.[5]

Most provocative, Randolph asked followers to celebrate "We Are Americans Too" week with a nonviolent resistance campaign against segregation. Randolph had long admired Mohandas Gandhi's crusade for an independent India. He also watched with fascination as the new Congress of Racial Equality (CORE) began staging sit-ins at public institutions that denied service to black patrons. Inspired by these movements, Randolph advised African Americans and sympathetic whites to "refuse to obey any law ... which violates the fundamental human and citizenship rights of the Negro people." Blacks should invade segregated restaurants and movie theaters. Parents should withhold their children from segregated schools. Black office workers should stay home. Black passengers on Southern railroads should infiltrate the dining car rather than carry food aboard. "If we go to a café and are refused breakfast, we will return for lunch," he told the *Kansas City Call*. "If we are refused again, we will return for dinner."[6]

"They are talking foolishness," the liberal newspaper *PM* wrote of Randolph's call. "No matter how great the grievance … civil disobedience in wartime cannot be the answer." The *Pittsburgh Courier* accused Randolph of "the most dangerous demagoguery on record." Even the plan's supporters harbored doubts. Randolph rejected fears of disrupting the war effort or of starting a race war. He saw an opportunity to answer critics who mocked him as all talk and no action. He denied being a revolutionary. His "non-violent goodwill direct action" program aimed only to realize promises made in the Declaration of Independence and the Constitution. Spreading democracy would preserve civil government, not destabilize it.[7]

The "We Are Americans Too" conference represented a crucial test of MOWM's viability. Randolph demanded support from black civic, social, and fraternal groups. MOWM stretched its limited resources to promote the event. Members sold hats and buttons to raise money. Ads plastered black newspapers.

Randolph was desperate to recapture last summer's enthusiasm. He mounted a vigorous counteroffensive against the skeptics. "MOWM proposes that the Negro people no longer rely solely upon the Republican, Democratic, Socialist or Communist parties but that they should build a powerful non-partisan political block without the benefit of the flesh-pots of either of the parties," he said. He would not renounce the use of mass pressure. He would not alter MOWM's blacks-only membership requirement, with its message of "self-reliance to the Negro people." And he would not, would never stop, fighting for economic justice.[8]

Defiant though he was, Randolph needed allies. He asked NAACP executive secretary Walter White to participate in the Chicago conference. White demurred, telling his friend that the NAACP's board would decide whether to endorse the event. White passed the request to his directors, along with his opinion that "it would not further our common objective to divert any considerable part of the energies of the Association to the establishment of the proposed new, permanent organization (the March-On-Washington Movement)." Taking this cue, the board formed a committee that talked the issue to death.

White skipped the Chicago gathering. Randolph also invited Adam Clayton Powell to speak. The good reverend declined.[9]

Shrugging off these rejections, Randolph plowed forward. MOWM's predictions of an audience in the thousands proved wildly optimistic. Undercover FBI agents counted around seventy delegates at the July 1 opening session, held just ten days after the Detroit riots. Half the attendees belonged to the Brotherhood of Sleeping Car Porters. Public forums attracted several hundred people, a far cry from the throngs who had packed Madison Square Garden, the Chicago Coliseum, and the St. Louis Municipal Auditorium last year. Pass-the-hat sessions raised about $750, far below what Randolph needed to cover costs.

Walter White had dispatched an assistant, Roy Wilkins, to act as his eyes and ears in Chicago. Wilkins could not believe what he was seeing. No one seemed to be in charge. Con artists sold piles of stolen MOWM literature on the street. Dispirited delegates endured sessions that started late, dragged on long past schedule, and drifted far off topic. Their red, white, and blue crepe-paper hats wilted in the summer heat, their fading glory a sad reflection of MOWM's own sagging fortunes. MOWM was no longer a "serious competitor," he wrote in a private memo to White.[10]

The few delegates at the "We Are Americans Too" conference made two consequential decisions. To no one's surprise, they voted to make MOWM a permanent organization. Their move cost them their last chance of winning support from the NAACP and other civil rights groups willing to back a one-time event, such as the proposed 1941 march, but not to fund a competitor.

Delegates also reaffirmed MOWM's black-only requirement as a means of "inject[ing] militancy into large numbers of Negroes who of necessity must be leaders in their own fight for freedom." White newspapers, which had long ignored MOWM, suddenly started paying attention. Reporters focused on MOWM's restricted membership while ignoring its demands. In the wake of Detroit, it was easy to see MOWM as a peddler of racial animosity. "These are times that require responsible citizenship of all Americans," the *Chicago Sun* complained.[11]

Black journalists who had supported an all-black movement before Pearl Harbor now joined in the denunciations. Longtime Randolph supporter the *Chicago Defender* branded him a "Negro isolationist" who espoused "the racial theory of history ... so terribly exploited by

Hitler." Writing in the *Kansas City Call*, another pro-Randolph sheet, Frank Marshall Davis blasted MOWM's determination to "establish a jim crow clan to fight jim crow." MOWM wasn't a mass movement, he continued, it was "a mess of a movement." He advised its members to switch allegiances to the more reasonable NAACP.[12]

MOWM's slide continued. Its national office had $92 on hand at the end of 1944. Local meetings drew handfuls of diehards. Chapters folded. MOWM's most public outlet, its bookstore on the corner of 124th and 7th in Harlem, never became the profit machine its founders anticipated. It survived by selling an odd mix of such race-conscious literature as *Uncle Tom's Cabin*, Booker T. Washington's *Up from Slavery*, and Richard Wright's *Native Son*, alongside seamier titles, including *The History of Prostitution*, *The Encyclopedia of Sexual Knowledge*, and *Sex in Prison*. In 1944 it netted $197.23. Randolph's subordinates begged him to devote more time to MOWM. The Chief still talked a good fight. He advised an overflow crowd in Denver to "expect instructions and the call to march on Washington" soon. Yet he failed to distinguish MOWM from other civil rights groups looking to desegregate the military, end discrimination, and gain political equality. He was losing interest in an organization clearly past its prime.[13]

"I could not give all of the time necessary to building a mass organization, and it is not easy to convince people that it is worth their while to become a part of a mass movement," Randolph later told an interviewer. He still thought an all-black organization could help develop young leaders and channel the fervor for equality. Catholics, Jews, union members, and businessmen joined exclusionary bodies designed to promote their interests, and so should African Americans. But the March on Washington, a title that galvanized the most dynamic mass movement in black history, had become an empty threat, a painful reminder of the greatest civil rights demonstration that never happened. Chapters in St. Louis and a few other cities spent the last years of the war picketing public utilities, insurance companies, and other businesses with discriminatory hiring practices. Elsewhere, MOWM faded into obscurity.[14]

Pathetic as it last years were, MOWM laid the foundations for the next generation of civil rights activity. It aroused African Americans to understand that mass protest, and even the threat of mass protest, could affect national policy. It raised the possibility of combating inequality with nonviolent resistance. It urged blacks to take pride in their own potential, to rely on their own strength to achieve economic justice. Finally, it gave Randolph the clout he needed to force policy-makers to hear his persistent message of democracy, freedom, and equality.

Randolph was in many ways the author of MOWM's demise. His ham-handed leadership and inability to focus on one cause led to mismanagement, poor organization, mission creep, and an unpredictable agenda that overlapped with other activist groups. His oversized sense of outrage and stubborn inflexibility made him not just a powerful opponent, but also a prickly partner in collaborative ventures. His radicalism scared off potential supporters reluctant to appear unpatriotic during wartime.

With MOWM dying, Randolph transferred his energies to other battles, choosing new terrain for his war for equality. Like General Eisenhower, he operated on multiple fronts, shifting his attention from one army to another as he deployed his forces. The porters' union still occupied him, of course, but he directed the bulk of his firepower to two causes crucial for Double V. He maintained a relentless assault against discrimination in the military. At the same time, he battled to save the FEPC from bureaucratic extinction. Randolph took the FEPC's fate personally. He took credit for its creation and could not stomach its demise. His brainchild was in trouble, crippled from its move to Paul McNutt's WMC and the cancellation of its railroad hearings. Like a father racing into a burning building, he was determined to save it whatever the cost.

The FEPC lay dormant through early 1943. Randolph bombarded the White House with demands to resuscitate the agency. In February, around the same time he lost his temper in McNutt's presence, and as he was organizing the "We Are Americans Too" meeting, Randolph convened a "Save the FEPC Conference" in Washington, DC. At it, he defended the FEPC's record and urged the president to order McNutt to reschedule the railroad hearings. The FEPC must regain its bureaucratic independence, Randolph said. It should stage more public hearings and gain the power to enforce its rulings. The fate of Double V depended on the FEPC. "Unless there is an awakening of the progressive forces, with the unity of labor, the organization of the Negro, and the cooperation of white liberals there can be no real hope to safeguard and protect social, labor and racial gains in the future," Randolph declared.[15]

Randolph's reference to white liberals revealed his inconsistent thinking on race. He attended the conference as a representative of MOWM, an all-black organization. Saving the FEPC, however, was also important for white ethnic and religious minorities. Randolph envisioned MOWM as part of a broader pro-FEPC coalition. Critics could be forgiven for failing to understand why MOWM worked with whites when Randolph deemed it necessary but refused to collaborate with them on other issues.

Randolph also tried to mend fences with the NAACP. Despite Walter White's misgivings about MOWM, Randolph invited him and other prominent civil rights, labor, and church figures to join a picket line that circled the WMC office that March. "This will not be a picket line of the masses," Randolph warned, lest anyone think he was trying to repeat his big splash of 1941, "but of the leaders for the purposes of focusing national attention on this question of the future of FEPC."[16]

President Roosevelt refused to show his hand. He handed the FEPC issue to subordinates who debated the agency's future at a leisurely pace. It is "the symbol and center of agitation of the Negro question," one staffer maintained. Keeping it "provides a more fertile field for the professional troublemakers among the Negroes." Others argued for reviving it. "It may only be a symbol but the Negroes now want the Committee," influential South Carolina Senator and New Dealer James Byrnes told Roosevelt.[17]

"There is no more explosive, no more emotional question on the American home front," noted Jonathan Daniels, part of FDR's nearly all-white circle of advisors on racial issues. "I wish I thought it could be patched up," Daniels continued. "I wish it could be handled by subordinates. I am sure it no longer can be. This needs and deserves the thought and the courage of the President himself." Still Roosevelt delayed, choosing to listen to his own internal political clock. He signaled his interest in saving the committee but made no public statement. Finally, in May 1943, amid rising racial tensions and an unrelenting campaign from Randolph and his allies, Roosevelt issued Executive Order 9346, establishing a new FEPC with powers similar to the previous one. The order removed the FEPC from McNutt's control and returned it to the executive branch, but denied it the authority to enforce its edicts. Publicity and moral suasion remained its sole bargaining tools. Nor did the order end discrimination within the government. Federal agencies involved in defense training only had to "take all measures appropriate" to ensure equal opportunity.[18]

The resurrected FEPC's new chair, Monsignor Francis Haas, was a Catholic priest who had held several positions under FDR. African Americans responded to his appointment with suspicion. Haas was a relatively obscure figure with more experience resolving labor disputes than with civil rights. He felt like a conciliator, not a crusader. But Haas proved more passionate than many blacks suspected. He saw equality as a biblical mandate, citing, for example, the Apostle Paul's insistence that "there is neither Jew nor Greek; there is neither slave nor freeman; there is neither male nor female. For you are all one in Jesus Christ."[19]

Haas revived the stalled railroad hearings, which he gaveled open in September. A few hundred African Americans, most of them wearing jackets and ties, filled the Department of Labor's auditorium. Railroad attorneys and the few corporate executives who showed up sat stone-faced as black railroad workers and FEPC lawyers spent four days laying out evidence of discrimination. The railroads offered no defense and declined to cross-examine witnesses. They insisted that they were focused on winning the war rather than on solving social problems. Besides, they asserted, the FEPC had no legal right to investigate their labor practices.

Haas resigned after the hearings to become the Bishop of the Diocese of Grand Rapids. New chair Malcolm Ross lacked his predecessor's zeal. Personnel shifts and Ross's foot-dragging delayed the FEPC's decision for two months. Finally, it ordered twenty railroads and seven unions to end their discriminatory practices. Most refused. Their defiance threw the FEPC's legitimacy into question. If it could not enforce its edicts, and could not shame malefactors into submission, it had no reason for existing. "This is a major crisis in the industrial life of the Negro," Randolph exclaimed. MOWM, on life support after the disastrous "We Are Americans Too" conference, ginned up another publicity blitz, accusing railroad companies of aiding the Nazis by exacerbating social divisions. Eyes across black America turned toward the White House, waiting for FDR to defend the agency he had twice created. "It's up to Mr. Big now," *Pittsburgh Courier* columnist Horace Cayton wrote.[20]

"Mr. Big" kept silent. With acrimony building on all sides, Roosevelt bottled up the explosive topic through one of his favorite methods: forming a committee. As he had hoped, the study group studied and studied without reaching any conclusions. Black anger faded as months dragged on without resolution. Exhaustion set in. "No news" could only make headlines for so long.[21]

Randolph scrambled to rebuild support for the FEPC. Rather than employ the discredited MOWM, in September 1943 he convened another Conference to Save the FEPC. From that gathering sprang a new pressure group, the National Council for a Permanent FEPC. The move marked a new phase in Randolph's war. To this point he had focused on strengthening the FEPC. Now he sought not only to enhance the agency's power, but also to pressure Washington into keeping it alive after the war.

Randolph and the Reverend Allan Knight Chalmers acted as cochairs. Randolph stacked the council with trusted allies. He stumped across the country, setting up local chapters. Some MOWM branches simply changed their names to match the new organization. As with MOWM, Randolph's porters were key to promoting and financing the nascent council. Senators Robert F. Wagner of New York and Arthur Capper of Kansas signed on as honorary chairs. In a publicity move, Randolph asked Eleanor Roosevelt to join. The first lady declined, fearing her membership "would open the way to criticism and brand you as a political organization."[22]

The FEPC's woes continued. FDR pigeonholed requests for a meeting with the committee. Barring an infusion of new resources, its tiny staff could never keep up with the torrent of discrimination reports. Committee members were barely on speaking terms. From the beginning, most of the board's whites had favored quiet, incremental change, whereas its black members demanded a more aggressive posture. As tensions mounted, meetings became touchy affairs. Milton P. Webster interrupted one discussion to describe his trip up from Atlanta on a segregated train. "*You* white people are all right," he said, wagging his finger at his colleagues. "*You* recognize this is a shocking condition. *You* want to do something about it. But after all *you* don't know what discrimination is. *You* have never been discriminated against."[23]

FEPC's congressional foes circled the wounded agency. Its insu-
lated status had long angered opponents. Congress had never voted to
create the board, nor could it directly control FEPC's budget so long
as it resided within the executive branch. In early 1944, a clever political maneuver from Georgia senator Richard Russell nearly sunk the
FEPC. Exploiting conservative frustration with Roosevelt's ad-hoc
expansion of the government, Russell tacked on an amendment to an
appropriations bill that would abolish any agency that had existed for
more than a year without congressional authorization and funding.

The Russell amendment put the FEPC's fate in Congress' hands.
Southern Democrats mounted withering attacks on it. Congressman
John Rankin called the FEPC "the beginning of a communistic dictatorship." If it was allowed to survive, he claimed, Washington could tell
people who to hire, who to eat with, and who to marry. Mississippi's
Theodore Bilbo warned Senate colleagues that the FEPC would
compel them to hire African American aides. "All the B.O. powders on
Earth will not dissipate the odoriferous aroma they will find permeat-
ing their offices," he said. Fellow Mississippian James Eastland leapt to
his feet, screaming "White girls [w]ould be forced to take dictation
from a group of burr-headed niggers and nigger supervisors!" The race
baiters found allies among congressional conservatives eager to shrink
the government and undermine the liberal president.[24]

Randolph's forces defended the federal government's smallest
agency. The National Council for a Permanent FEPC issued a steady
stream of press releases. Randolph never proposed the kind of mass
protest he envisioned in 1941 or a civil disobedience campaign, à la
1943. Neither of those had come off as planned, and the council
couldn't afford them anyway. Despite generous support from the
sleeping car porters, it had less than $1,000 in hand.[25]

Randolph rallied just enough support to save the FEPC. It
squeaked through Congress with a $500,000 budget and a massive
target on its back. This near miss brought unprecedented attention to
an agency that generally kept out of sight. In so doing, it broadened
support for civil rights, which was already gaining momentum as more
Americans struggled to square the fight against Nazism with their
own country's inequalities. Randolph's council attracted white liberals
and labor unions. Members of religious minorities also came on board.
Most employers no longer required job candidates to declare their race

on application forms, but often stamped "Jew" or "Hebrew" on those forms. Catholics, Jehovah's Witnesses, and other non-Protestants feared similar winnowing. Also significant, both in the short and the long term, was the growing involvement of black churches. Randolph's father, Reverend James, would have applauded his son's ability to convince black ministers who preached a social justice theology but steered clear of politics to speak on the FEPC's behalf. Black ministers would play a crucial part in the generation-long civil rights drama that lay ahead.[26]

Roosevelt, his political instincts as sharp as ever, sensed the changing wind. Facing rising enthusiasm for the FEPC and a tough reelection bid in November 1944, he suddenly had to worry about losing his liberal base. His Republican opponent, New York governor Tom Dewey, backed a permanent FEPC, and the Republican party platform endorsed civil rights. Roosevelt was also taking heat for jettisoning Vice President Henry Wallace, a staunch civil rights advocate, in favor of Missouri senator Harry Truman. FDR made the switch to mollify conservative Democrats. According to false but persistent rumors, Truman was a former member of the Ku Klux Klan.

Now, with the election just weeks away, FDR pacified liberals by hosting his first meeting with African American leaders since June 1941. He shunned Randolph, instead inviting moderates Walter White, Mary McLeod Bethune, and Channing Tobias to the White House. The president radiated charm, reassuring them of his desire to eliminate segregation and discrimination in the military. He expressed his desire for a permanent FEPC. "Didn't I invent it?" he quipped. "Of course I'm for it."[27]

African Americans challenged the president to repeat in public what he said behind closed doors. Feeling the pressure, Roosevelt endorsed a permanent FEPC in an election-eve address to Congress. In it he linked the FEPC with a broader postwar vision of an America where "all persons, regardless of race, color, creed or place of birth, can live in peace, honor and human dignity," enjoying the protections guaranteed under the Constitution and the Bill of Rights. FDR's speech helped him lock down the vast majority of black votes. African Americans provided Roosevelt's margin of victory in several Northern states.[28]

For the moment, the FEPC had survived the conservative reaction that had chipped away at New Deal programs since the late 1930s.

More whites were beginning to see how civil rights and economic justice benefited them. Activists could point to other positive signs. The Supreme Court's 1944 *Smith v. Allwright* decision nullified Texas's "white primary" system, which barred blacks from voting in primaries. The decision raised hopes for abolishing other limits on democracy, especially within the military. Double V might yet come to pass.

Lieutenant Charles Hall, a twenty-two-year-old native of Brazil, Indiana, kept a firm grip on the controls of his P-40 Warhawk. The western tip of Sicily unfurled thousands of feet beneath him. Up ahead and just below his plane, the lumbering B-25 bombers he was escorting disgorged their deadly cargo on the Castelventrano air base. Hall's brown eyes, shielded behind flight goggles, scanned the sky for Germans.

Hall's outfit, the 99th Pursuit Squadron, had arrived in North Africa about six weeks earlier, on May 31, 1943. It was the first black air unit to see action overseas. His first seven missions had passed without incident. Today looked like more of the same. The P-40's engine hummed, maintaining the almost leisurely pace required to shadow the plodding bombers. Suddenly, as fires engulfed the target below, Hall spied what every pilot both feared and anticipated: a pack of Focke-Wulf 190s, the pride of Hitler's *Luftwaffe*.

The American snapped into combat mode. Focke-Wulfs were far speedier and nimbler than his P-40. He gunned the engine, interposing himself between the bombers and the oncoming fighters. Although piloting the inferior plane, Hall outmaneuvered his adversary, gaining an inside position that left the enemy vulnerable while putting him outside the Nazi's field of fire. The American squeezed his trigger, sending a burst of bullets speeding toward the Focke-Wulf. He watched the German plane bank to the left before plummeting groundward. Hall mirrored its fall, pulling up just before his victim smashed into the earth. His compatriots chased off the remaining German pilots as he regained altitude. The victorious squadron restored their formation, minus two planes lost in the dogfight, and headed back to base.

Lieutenant Colonel Benjamin O. Davis, Jr., the son of the Army's only black general, greeted the survivors when they landed. Davis then presented a special guest, Dwight Eisenhower, commanding general of the European theater, who offered his congratulations. Lieutenant

Charles Hall had just become the first African American to down an Axis plane. His feat earned him the right to crack open the bottle of Coca-Cola the pilots had kept on ice in anticipation of their first kill.[29]

Although few whites learned of Hall's feat, the black press made him a hero. His action marked a rare bright spot for African Americans hungry for uniformed idols. Allied forces were gaining the upper hand in the war, but progress toward racial equality in the armed forces had stalled. As of mid-1943, African Americans could not serve as bombardiers, gunners, or navigators, positions the brass considered too technical, and requiring too much teamwork, for them to handle. African Americans lionized the Tuskegee Airmen, so named because some of their training occurred at the famous, all-black institute in Alabama, while criticizing Tuskegee itself for participating in a segregated program.

Other services, especially the Navy, kept blacks even farther on the margins. One year after Navy Secretary Knox promised to promote African Americans by merit, the fleet still had no black officers. Even if there were black officers they would have had no post. Regulations forbid African Americans from commanding whites, and the Navy had no all-black crews. Blacks could not serve in naval aviation. Black women could not join the WAVES, the Navy's auxiliary branch. The Navy's much-publicized decision to abolish the messman rank proved cosmetic, as the service simply recategorized "messmen" as "stewards."

African Americans looked more favorably on the Army, which had 2,000 black officers and more than 60,000 black GIs overseas, most of them in service roles. Still, a thousand indignities created friction. Evidence of inequality was everywhere. Many white officers regarded assignments to a black unit as a mark of shame. Black soldiers at Fort Logan, Colorado, stood at attention outside the mess hall until their white comrades finished eating. Arrivals at Davis-Montham Field in Tucson found black tarpaper covering barracks and other facilities intended for African Americans. A white, Southern officer greeted black Pennsylvanians to Camp Claiborne, Louisiana by shouting, "We want you to know we're not takin' any foolishness down here, because we don't shoot 'em down here, we hang 'em." Camp Claiborne "is a living hell," one serviceman wrote in 1944.[30]

Prejudice extended overseas. British civilians displayed a friendly sense of curiosity when black GIs started hitting their shores in 1942 as part of the long buildup to D-Day. Unused to black faces and unfamiliar with American racial mores, many Britons found the visiting army's policies ludicrous. Some openly criticized discriminatory regulations. Offended white soldiers demanded a crackdown lest their black compatriots get too many ideas. Officers denied African Americans passes into town, hoping to minimize their contact with whites. Military policemen locked up black GIs caught speaking with locals. For the most part, British officials tolerated their ally's prejudices. Great Britain needed the Americans and had no desire to start an international incident over their handling of blacks. "Colored troops themselves probably expected to be treated in this country as in the United States, and a markedly different treatment might well cause political difficulties at the end of the war," British Secretary of War James Grigg rationalized.[31]

A series of racial disturbances tore through Southern bases in summer 1943, the same time that Detroit burst into riots. The worst of these occurred at Camp Stewart, an antiartillery training center in eastern Georgia infamous for abusing African Americans. White officers there told recruits to disregard orders from black officers. Camp officials provided blacks with substandard food and sanitation facilities. Its nurses turned away black patients. The nearby town of Hinesville offered few recreational opportunities, a hostile police force, and an abundance of signs denoting segregated facilities. We are "in deadly peril," warned one black veteran of the European theater. Violence finally erupted after a white civilian allegedly attacked a black soldier's wife. MPs arrested the private when he tried to leave the camp carrying a rifle and thoughts of revenge. Rumors of additional insults against black women flew around the barracks. Black troops clashed with white MPs. An exchange of gunfire left one MP dead and four more wounded.[32]

Camps in the North could be equally inhospitable. Officers at Camp Shenango, Pennsylvania, denied African Americans access to the post exchange, the servicemen's club, and the base's five movie theaters, while welcoming German prisoners into those forbidden places. Black enlisted men lived in cramped barracks near a forest, as far from the main gate as possible. "If you went through camp as a visitor, you'd never know black soldiers were there, unless they happened to be working on some menial detail," one former trainee remembered.[33]

In July 1943, a month after the Camp Stewart shootout, and between the Detroit and Harlem riots, a gang of white soldiers from Camp Shenango kicked out a black private's eye when he asked a PX worker for a beer. The victim's friends were plotting retaliation when a fleet of six trucks pulled up. Uniformed whites jumped from the vehicles, surrounded the area, and opened fire. A half-dozen blacks crumpled to the ground, their blood staining the road. Medics swept through the scene. "He'll make it," one said as he examined a wounded man, "Niggers don't die when you shoot 'em in the head."

The wounded groaned in pain as medics tossed them into ambulances. "Why we be doin' this to our own soldiers?" a bleeding man asked his driver. "Who ever told you niggers were our soldiers?" the driver replied. "Where I come from we shoot niggers like we shoot rabbits."[34]

Dempsey Travis, a black infantryman stationed at Camp Shenango during the firefight, captured the prevailing mood as well as anyone. "I think of two armies, one black, one white," he said.[35]

"The abolition of segregation in the armed forces has become the central and dominating issue in the life of the Negro people of America today," Randolph observed in a MOWM press release. Throughout 1943, and until the war's final days, he exhorted FDR to follow in President Lincoln's footsteps by advocating "freedom and democracy" during a time of crisis.[36]

MOWM, wobbly though it was, threw itself into the fight. It commissioned Dwight MacDonald to write a condemnation of military segregation. "The War's Greatest Scandal: The Story of Jim Crow in Uniform," sold for five cents, recounted the most spectacular acts of anti-black violence, associated American racism with Hitler's master race theories, and decried the disproportional use of African American soldiers as service troops. "Jimcrow in uniform ... violates the most basic principles of the democracy our leaders say we are fighting for," MacDonald wrote. "It spreads the most vicious of Hitler's doctrines among the very soldiers and sailors who are dying in battle with Hitler's armies." MacDonald closed his pamphlet with an apocalyptic warning that the coming of peace might unleash a wave of race riots that dwarfed the chaos following World War I.[37]

Randolph also involved MOWM in the case of Winfred Lynn, a landscape gardener from Long Island facing trial for refusing to enlist.

Lynn, on receiving his draft summons, proclaimed his willingness "to serve in any unit of the armed forces of my country which is not segregated by race," but would not join "a unit undemocratically selected as a Negro group." Randolph, with typical enthusiasm, helped form the National Committee for Winfred Lynn to raise money for his defense. The committee's early meetings occurred at MOWM's Harlem headquarters. Largely because of these efforts, Lynn became a well-known figure in black papers, although the white press paid him little attention.[38]

President Roosevelt felt the growing black anger. He too was frustrated with the slow pace of change in the military. Whenever possible, he nudged the services to liberalize their racial policies. Segregation bred inefficiency, as it required the military to build duplicate facilities for black and white soldiers. It muddied the clean moral lines he hoped to draw between the Allies and the Axis. It also contributed to domestic unrest, manifested in letter-writing campaigns, protest rallies, and, finally, riots.

Roosevelt's concerns for justice conflicted with his need to mollify the South. He asked rather than ordered the military to reform—and he asked as quietly as possible, so as not to upset racial conservatives. Still, the deteriorating situation troubled him. He assigned an aide, Jonathan Daniels, a liberal North Carolinian, to gather material on African American grievances. Daniels urged FDR to speak out on racial issues and to hold the military to its vague promises. He also pushed Roosevelt to acknowledge that black discontent weakened civilian morale, wasted available labor, and undermined defense production. Winning the war demanded winning over African Americans.

This renewed outreach extended into the cultural sphere, as the OWI, the government's wartime propaganda wing, stepped up efforts to sell the war to African Americans. "The Negro problem is bad and getting worse," an early 1944 OWI report asserted. "Discrimination and prejudice are engendering a widespread resentment and a condition favorable to racial disorders." Images of "mutual friendship and understanding and respect" could ease tensions. OWI bureaucrats placed more stories about black combat soldiers in black newspapers and urged radio networks to work favorable portrayals of African Americans into their productions.[39]

The Negro Soldier (1944), directed by Stuart Heisler as part of Frank Capra's "Why We Fight" series of propaganda films, epitomized the OWI's rededication to diversity. The movie's opening section combined documentary footage with Hollywood reenactments to showcase black contributions to military history. Viewers watched black heroes helping to win American independence and participating in the War of 1812. The Civil War presented a challenge to the national unity message. Accordingly, the filmmakers limited their treatment of the conflict to a brief reading from the Gettysburg Address ("that government of the people, by the people, and for the people, shall not perish from the earth"). After dodging this bullet, *The Negro Soldier* showed black pioneers crossing the frontier, black laborers building the railroads, and black doughboys following General Pershing to victory in World War I.

The movie next sought to humanize individual blacks. It shifts to a present-day church service. An African American woman rises from her pew to read a letter from her son, Robert, whom the Army has just promoted to lieutenant. Scenes of Robert's time in boot camp—familiar to every soldier watching the picture—flash by as she reads.

Heisler and his screenwriter, black leftist Carlton Moss, circumvented War Department censors who discouraged onscreen conversations about segregation by condemning segregation through visual imagery. White and black inductees stand together at a reception center. They sit in the same room, with the black recruits in a separate section, to hear a chaplain speak. But the whites disappear the moment Robert receives his uniform. Columns of black troops march past with nary a white face in sight. The camera lingers on black pilots, black gunners, black infantrymen, and black tankers. It then gives a glimpse into the possible future. A black West Point cadet snaps to attention next to a white cadet. Blacks and whites sit together in officer training school. Unlike *This Is the Army*, there are no shuck-and-jive routines, no blackface performances, and no tributes to the Old South.

"It is refreshingly free of any condescension or Uncle Tomism," the *Pittsburgh Courier* raved. Although *The Negro Soldier* performed poorly at the domestic box office, it revolutionized attitudes within the military. Officials required every GI to watch it as part of their training. For the first time, black soldiers became real people, full of relatable experiences and emotions. An Army survey revealed that two thirds of white GIs had a "highly favorable" response to the film.[40]

War Department brass still viewed black soldiers as burdens. "Negroes can't expect to elevate themselves through the Army," Georgia-born major general Frank Hunter told his staff. "The Negro hasn't been able to obtain equality in two hundred years and probably won't, except in some distant future." Many generals agreed that integration, or even equal treatment, would increase racial conflict. They were fed up with African American protesters intent on wringing every possible concession from the crisis. They resented having to factor civilian complaints into their decisions. "The Army is not concerned primarily with problems of race, social and economic justice, or civilian educational opportunity," a 1944 training manual stated. "It is concerned with the development of soldiers out of the available manpower."[41]

But the tide was clearly turning. Randolph kept calling on blacks to agitate for desegregation. Walter White used his well-publicized tour of the Mideast, North Africa, and Europe to alert mainstream newspapers to segregation at overseas bases. Elements within the military began to argue that segregation might incite additional race riots. "The Negro seems determined to take advantage of the war situation to better his own position," one internal memo noted. It observed, in disapproving tones, that troublemakers such as Randolph had whipped the black press into a frenzy. Tensions might explode in St. Louis (a city with a strong MOWM chapter, the report noted) and other communities.[42]

Black activism, the need for manpower, and a desire for efficiency compelled the high command to reconsider its racial policies. American forces were sprawled across the globe, battling the Axis from New Guinea to Italy. Invading Nazi-occupied France would require additional millions of troops, plus an untold number of ships, planes, jeeps, tanks, bombs, and rifles. By early 1944 even Secretary of War Stimson, who had long denigrated African American GIs, conceded that "we have got to use the colored race to help us in this fight."[43]

This realization produced incremental changes over the war's final eighteen months. General Dwight Eisenhower, planning the D-Day invasion, electrified the black community with a directive stating that "equal opportunities for service and recreation are the right of every American soldier regardless of branch, race, color or creed." A few weeks later the Army distributed an order desegregating military posts and transportation for soldiers, whether on or off post.[44]

The Navy also began lifting barriers. A handful of African Americans entered its officer training program in early 1944, less than a month before the christening of the *U.S.S. Mason*, a destroyer escort with a white commander and an all-black crew. Progress accelerated when Secretary Frank Knox died in April. James Forrestal, his replacement, was no crusader, but widespread institutional discrimination offended his sense of fair play. Further, he saw integration as the best way to end the riots and mutinies rocking the service. Forrestal delighted the black community when he named Lester Granger, his former class-mate at Dartmouth and executive secretary of the National Urban League, as his civilian aide. The Navy started accepting black women into the WAVES, the women's reserve unit, in late 1944, and began enlisting black nurses a few months later.

African Americans who had felt detached from the war suddenly began seeing black faces in combat roles. In Italy, the 92nd Infantry Division used flamethrowers to expel German troops from fortified mountain positions. The 24th Infantry Regiment helped push the Japanese off Guadalcanal, Saipan, and Tinian, and the 37th division helped expel them from the Philippine capital of Manila. Black drivers guided supply convoys along the treacherous road linking India with China, and black antiaircraft gunners supported the D-Day landings.

Launched in December 1944, the Battle of the Bulge, Hitler's last-ditch effort to halt the Allied juggernaut, proved a turning point in the war for equality. The German offensive decimated American reserve forces. Needing infantrymen, General Eisenhower initiated a crash program to retrain black service units for the front lines. So many soldiers volunteered that thousands had to be turned away. In just six weeks, African American volunteers who had spent the war wielding shovels and cookpots mastered rifles and grenades. They hustled to the front, where officers assigned black platoons to white companies. This arrangement represented a compromise; Eisenhower briefly considered total integration before adopting an approach that preserved segregation, but at the smallest possible unit level. These quasi-integrated companies endured grueling fights at Remagen and Mainz as they smashed into Germany. The shared battle experience proved trans-formative. Surveys conducted before this hasty experiment showed that one third of white soldiers approved of having African American soldiers in their company. Follow-up polls taken after the Battle of the

Bulge revealed that over three quarters of white GIs were more open to the idea than before.[45]

Front-line duty proved a life-changing experience. Charles Gates of the 761st Tank Battalion found his introduction to General George S. Patton's 3rd Army to be an exhilarating, revelatory moment. "You're the first Negro tankers ever to be used in the American army in combat," the fiery general told the unit. "I want you to establish a record for yourselves and a record for your race. I want you to make a liar of me. When you get in combat—and you will be in combat—when you see those kraut S.O.B.'s, don't spare the ammunition!" The tankers erupted into cheers, thrilled to hear a white man order them to shoot other white men. Patton's words stuck with them as they manhandled the Nazis across France, Belgium, and Holland over the next several months, earning 293 Purple Hearts, sixty Bronze Stars, and eleven Silver Stars along the way. These combat veterans could never again accept second-class citizenship.[46]

An interracial squad of American GIs display a captured Nazi flag, March 1945.
U.S. Army, Courtesy of Harry S. Truman Presidential Library

Military necessities and domestic pressures had cracked the door to equality. Randolph wanted to shove it open the rest of the way. He challenged President Roosevelt to abolish military segregation. FDR refused to take this dramatic step. His silence infuriated African Americans grown accustomed to change. Black newspapers scrutinized every word coming from the administration for insights into the president's thinking. Secretary of War Henry Stimson got into hot water for suggesting that black GIs' relative lack of education made them better suited for service roles than combat duty. Black reporters summarized his statement as "Negro troops are too dumb to fight." Cries for Stimson's resignation permeated the press.[47]

Military segregation was on the defensive. Progress, however, depended on local conditions. The War Department was in no position to force civilians, camp staffs, and field officers to implement integration and nondiscrimination orders. A single recalcitrant officer or racist deputy could make life miserable for African Americans regardless of what Washington said. Soon after the Battle of the Bulge, 1,000 black Navy Seabees stationed at Port Hueneme, California, staged a hunger strike to protest a bias toward promoting white sailors. Their commanders arrested the alleged ringleaders, who had just returned from two years in the Pacific, flogged them, and gave them dishonorable discharges.

Southerners reared on a steady diet of white supremacy condemned liberals who demonized their way of life. They saw a New York patrician, his busybody wife, and an inner circle of elite intellectuals hell-bent on imposing alien values on them. To their mind, putting blacks on the same footing as whites implied the elevation of one and the diminution of the other. Integrationist policies threatened to topple their orderly world into a moral cesspool of interracial marriage and social equality.

Southern traditions collided with African American impatience. The July 1944 arrest of Lieutenant Jack Robinson was a single star in a galaxy of incidents. MPs arrested Lieutenant Robinson for refusing to sit in the colored section of a bus bound for Camp Hood, Texas. Robinson's assertiveness perplexed his white interrogators, who could not fathom why he objected to being called "a nigger lieutenant." He faced a court martial for insubordination. His lawyer characterized the case as "a situation in which a few individuals sought to vent their

bigotry on a Negro they considered 'uppity' because he had the audacity to seek to exercise rights that belonged to him as an American and
as a soldier."

Robinson won a "not guilty" verdict. Like thousands of other
black soldiers, however, he felt the sting of prejudice for many years
after the Hiroshima and Nagasaki bombs ended the war. Robinson's
case was unremarkable, reminiscent of countless occasions when black
GIs fell afoul of local mores. This relatively minor incident would have
been forgotten had its protagonist not gone on to desegregate Major
League Baseball three years later.[48]

Most Americans could see the end of the war by early 1945.
General Douglas MacArthur's men had recaptured the Philippines.
America's fleet had annihilated the Japanese navy. Food shortages
demoralized Japanese civilians. In Europe, British and American
forces had liberated Rome and Paris and, with black soldiers among
the vanguard, had pushed into Germany. America's wartime partner,
the Soviet Union, rolled through Nazi-occupied Eastern Europe,
racing to be the first into Berlin.

With victory abroad in reach, Randolph focused on achieving
victory at home. If anything, these military successes compelled him to
fight harder, as an anticipated wave of postwar conservatism might
well reverse the progress of recent years. In late December 1944, while
on a recruiting trip, he sat down at his desk in a segregated hotel in
Durham, North Carolina, to pen a New Year's message. "It is clear that
the [Allies] have no intention of granting freedom and democracy to the
darker peoples of the world," he wrote. African Americans must an-
ticipate a long battle for justice. Their paramount concern was gaining
a permanent FEPC, the best hope for an equitable postwar America.
His other demands sounded familiar to anyone who had listened to
him in recent years: no more military segregation and discrimination,
an Africa free from colonial domination, an end to the poll tax, a
federal antilynching bill, and protection for black voters. He never
mentioned the March on Washington Movement.

Randolph predicted hard times ahead. "If history has provided
any lessons for mankind," he wrote, "they are that wars create new
hates and fears." Peace would open a new and dangerous chapter in the
story of America's troubled race relations. An epic struggle between

good and evil, democracy and fascism, lay ahead. Although MOWM's decline had tarnished Randolph's image, he refused to fade into the background. His people stood on the precipice of a perilous era. They needed leaders who could help them navigate the valley of despair. Randolph intended to lead them to the promised land.[49]

CHAPTER 7

Let Us Win Another Victory

R andolph was in Harlem when the news came. It oozed from apartments and offices like a creeping fog, drifting from radios and through open windows. Minutes later it came crashing down on the streets as leather-lunged newsboys roared out the headlines.

It was April 12, 1945. Franklin Roosevelt was dead.

Across black America people gathered, seeking confirmation that the unthinkable was true. They poured from their homes into the streets, often forgetting to turn off their radios or take food off the stove. They hugged and sobbed as if a family member had died. In a sense, that was exactly what had happened. Roosevelt's photo adorned many of their mantels and side tables, his image displayed alongside those of parents and other loved ones. Many mourners could not remember a time before FDR was president.

Anyone who saw Roosevelt's picture in the paper over the past year, or watched him in a newsreel, could recognize his physical decline. The president avoided discussing or even thinking about his health, but he felt ground down to a nub in his final days. As he had for decades, he retreated to Warm Springs, Georgia to recharge. "The president was the worst looking man I ever saw who was still alive," the station agent thought when an aide wheeled Roosevelt from the train. FDR's detail struggled to transfer him to his car; his once-powerful arm and chest muscles were no longer strong enough to assist their efforts.[1]

A few days in the Little White House worked wonders. The president's mood perked up and his color returned. FDR jested with reporters about his conversations with Soviet premiere Josef Stalin at the recent Yalta Conference while Fala, his hyperactive terrier, nosed around their ankles. He bantered with a crowd that gathered outside the corner drugstore where he stopped for a soda. His spirits soared when Lucy Rutherford, his former mistress and now something-more-than-platonic soulmate, arrived in town with her friend, painter Elizabeth Shoumatoff.

Roosevelt spent April 10 reading paperwork. Shoumatoff circled the president with a sketch pad while FDR teased Rutherford. The following day went much the same, although the president's strength waned once evening came. His hands shook so badly he needed help pouring cocktails. His guests cringed as he strained to shift from his wheelchair to a regular chair, a move he had performed so often as to become second nature. Under doctor's orders, he retired early.

April 12 promised to be a lovely day, clear and mild. FDR sat in his living room, the center of attention as always. He plowed through a sheaf of memos, casting alternating jokes at his secretary and his guests. Shoumatoff set up her easel and started outlining her portrait. Her watercolors treated Roosevelt with kid gloves, showing a man who had thinned during twelve grueling years as president but concealing his ashen pallor. She roughed in his red tie and gray, double-breasted suit, most of it hidden under the blue cape taking shape on the canvas. Her brush captured a most extraordinary look in FDR's eyes. Sober, confident, penetrating, warm, and mysterious, they emerged from the canvas as windows to a soul both inviting and impenetrable.

A butler set the table for lunch. "We've got just fifteen minutes more," Roosevelt told the painter. Suddenly he lost control of his body. His right hand jerked to his forehead. His brow slumped forward as Rutherford rushed toward him. He looked up in confusion. His features tensed. He seemed to be searching for a way to clamp his Cheshire-cat smile back on his face. "I have a terrific pain in the back of my head," he gasped. Then he collapsed. FDR's doctor rushed in a few minutes later. He diagnosed a cerebral hemorrhage. Rutherford and Shoumatoff jammed their clothes into suitcases. They had to be far away before word of the president's condition leaked out.

Two hours later, he was gone.[2]

It took many years for the details of Roosevelt's final days to become public knowledge. At the time all African Americans knew was that they had lost a friend. A frustrating, ambivalent, inscrutable friend, to be sure, but someone who nevertheless had changed their lives. Tributes poured in from everywhere. "[It] is a loss ... almost too great to bear," Walter White lamented. Adam Clayton Powell called FDR "the great emancipator of our century."[3]

Powell was one of many mourners who recognized that Roosevelt had done more for them than any president since Abraham Lincoln. Their tributes recalled federal jobs created during the Depression and blacks holding positions of unprecedented political power. They praised Executive Order 8802 and the FEPC for improving economic opportunities. They lionized FDR for overseeing African Americans' entrance into the Marines, the Air Corps, the WACs, and the WAVES; for appointing the first black general; for opening access to the Navy's higher ranks; for starting to integrate the military.

None of this would have happened without people like Randolph, whose harping forced civil rights into the national consciousness. And African Americans promised an unceasing campaign against segregation, discrimination, the poll tax, lynching, and other grievances Roosevelt stowed on the eternal back burner even as they celebrated the late president's life. "We refuse to retreat, we refuse to even mark time," Powell warned. "We must go forward."[4]

Losing FDR also meant losing Eleanor Roosevelt, revered by African Americans as not just the greatest first lady, but perhaps the greatest white woman in American history. She was a conduit for black complaints who prodded her husband to do the right thing. Her message of tolerance made her a villain to some and a hero to others. Walter White, on hearing of her husband's death, composed a touching letter that conveyed his affection for Eleanor. "We are too stunned by the passing of the world's greatest citizen ... to do more than to tell you our hearts go out to you in deepest sympathy," he wrote.[5]

Randolph participated in the national grieving but maintained a curious public silence. He offered no homage to the fallen leader. His thoughts on Roosevelt remained unsettled for many years. Randolph would be forever associated with Roosevelt, yet he was unable to truly comprehend the enigma he had sparred with on two crucial occasions and lobbied on many others. "FDR was a very great man," a brilliant political strategist who carried African Americans closer to equality, Randolph remarked long after the war. At the same time, Roosevelt's equivocations and gamesmanship confirmed Randolph's belief that social change came through mass pressure, not moral appeals to elected leaders. Being right wasn't enough. "Roosevelt was neither pro nor con on the Negro problem," he said. "I doubt that he knew very much about Negroes and their problems." Randolph resolved that blacks must change future presidents' political calculations by becoming louder, stronger, and better organized.[6]

Uncertainty permeated black America. Roosevelt was gone. So too was Hitler, after he committed suicide in his Berlin bunker a few weeks later. Victory over Japan was only a matter of time. Wartime had seen great leaps toward racial equality. Heightened expectations and demographic shifts had also brought great racial tensions. War-weary whites longed for a return to normalcy. Few would muster much enthusiasm for an ongoing campaign for racial equality. Peace could also end the FEPC, a wartime creation empowered only to monitor defense contractors, not industry as a whole. And no one could claim Double V so long as segregation defined the military.

Randolph had a long to-do list. His first order of business was divining the character and intentions of the White House's new occupant.

Eleanor Roosevelt was in Washington when she learned of Franklin's death. She put on a black dress, cabled her four sons, and summoned Vice President Harry Truman to the White House. Truman, who had held the job for less than three months, had not yet heard the news. When he arrived, the new widow placed her arm on his shoulder as if to comfort him. "Harry," she said, "the president is dead." Stunned, Truman collected himself before asking whether he could do anything for her.

"Is there anything we can do for you?" Eleanor replied, "for you are the one in trouble now."[7]

Harry Truman was a mystery to African Americans, as were they to him. He had spent his life staking out a middle ground on race, indulging in the prejudices surrounding him without becoming a full-blown racist. "Nigger" and "coon" were part of the everyday lexicon in the western Missouri towns of Truman's youth. The future president peppered his speech with enough "niggers," "dagoes," and "chinks" to shock modern ears. Because he encountered few African Americans as a boy, he grew up believing America had no race problem so long as blacks stayed in their place. He tried to join the Ku Klux Klan in the 1920s only to reverse course when he decided membership in the organization would harm his political aspirations.

Truman's attitudes on race evolved as his political career soared. During his 1940 Senate run he affirmed his belief in "the brotherhood of man; not merely the brotherhood of white men, but the brotherhood of all men." Although he favored legal rather than social equality between the races, this was daring stuff for rural Missouri. His self-image as a scrappy underdog compelled him to oppose discrimination in the defense establishment. To his mind, he was successful because the United States provided him a fair chance to prove his merits. Denying the same chance to others struck him as un-American.[8]

Senator Truman compiled a decent record on race. He voted to abolish the poll tax and favored making lynching a federal crime. Whenever possible, however, he avoided the subject. Asked in 1942 about the condition of black Missourians, he replied, "it is a most difficult problem to discuss ... and I would prefer not to discuss it with you until I have had a chance to give it a great deal of thought, which I have been doing for the last ten years."[9]

Black leaders attacked Truman from the moment Roosevelt added him to the ticket. Because Henry Wallace, FDR's third-term vice president, endorsed black equality, replacing him with an obscure border-state senator stank of appeasing racists. Truman conducted several reassuring interviews with African American newspapers. "I have always been for equality of opportunity in work, working conditions and political rights," he told a black reporter visiting his Kansas City office. "I think the Negro in the armed forces ought to have the same treatment and opportunities as every other member of the armed forces." He stopped short of endorsing an integrated military. Truman's goodwill tour eased suspicions, yet discomfort with the Southerner who many African Americans stubbornly believed was once a Klansman persisted.[10]

Randolph pressed the new president to act on discrimination, the FEPC, and other lingering issues. Truman kept his responses vague as he sought his footing in a slippery landscape. He had barely known President Roosevelt, who shut his vice president out of sensitive military discussions. Truman had only the vaguest notions of FDR's secret agreements with Soviet premiere Josef Stalin and British prime minister Winston Churchill regarding the fate of postwar Europe. Soviet armies were digging into Eastern Europe. Great Britain's vast empire was disintegrating. Nazi Germany was collapsing. Truman found the war with Japan equally overwhelming. He had not known about the atomic bomb program until after he took the presidential oath of office. With the weight of the military-industrial complex transferred to his narrow shoulders, and the world's future hanging in the balance, the Missourian needed to get up to speed fast. Civil rights assumed a low priority.

Randolph, worried that peace might kill momentum for civil rights, had already launched a drive to preserve wartime gains. A few months before Roosevelt's death, Randolph, head reeling and joints aching from a bad cold, exhorted the American Federation of Labor's annual convention to endorse a permanent FEPC. Angry retorts from the floor prompted him to blast discriminatory AFL unions as closet fascists. "If anyone thinks the Negroes are going to wait a hundred years to get their rights he is mistaken," Randolph shouted. "You are your own grave diggers and you are sowing the seeds of destruction by approving an insidious form of the theory of a master race." Randolph's motion prevailed in a contentious vote.[11]

Senator Theodore Bilbo of Mississippi offered his reply a few weeks later. If Congress passed a permanent FEPC, he told a session of the Senate Agriculture Committee, "you had better not disband your army when the war is over—you'll need it."[12]

Passions remained high after FDR died. Germany's surrender in May 1945, three weeks into Truman's term, prompted conservatives to accelerate the federal government's conversion to peacetime. An emergency wartime bureau like the FEPC offered a tantalizing target for congressional ax-wielders. Truman, after a lengthy period of indecision, asked Congress not just to fund the agency for the upcoming year, but to make it permanent. Southern senators retaliated by filibustering a military appropriations bill that included funds for FEPC.

The FEPC spent two weeks as a dead agency, its funds exhausted and its renewal suspended in legislative limbo. In July Congress passed a $250,000 appropriation intended to carry it through the next twelve months. It was a token sum, far less than it needed to perform its duties. Agency heads shuttered field offices and slashed staffs.

The FEPC's survival nevertheless renewed hopes for further federal intervention on behalf of minority rights. Its support base widened with each attempt to kill it. African Americans who once avoided political battles now saw it as essential to their future. More religious and labor groups signed "save FEPC" petitions every year. By the war's final days, Randolph's brainchild, an obscure outfit once dismissed as "the Negro thing," had become the touchstone for an interracial civil rights movement.

The awful fire clouds that engulfed Hiroshima and Nagasaki in August 1945 shook up the FEPC debate. The end of the war meant the end of the FEPC, whose mandate only covered the current conflict. "This is it!" a *Chicago Defender* editorial blared. "Grim, frightening, uncertain, zero hour in the life-and-death battle of Negro America to hold its wartime economic gains is here." Companies anticipating reconversion to peacetime production were already laying off black employees. More would follow unless President Truman saved the FEPC. After mulling the issue, Truman extended the bureau through the reconversion period. It was a brief reprieve, and not a particularly meaningful one. The FEPC was down to its last dollars. A few dozen employees kept the lights on in Chicago, Detroit, and St. Louis, the agency's last branches. Broke and understaffed, the FEPC had no hope of completing existing investigations, much less opening new ones. It was alive, but on life support.[13]

The emerging battle over the FEPC was part of a larger struggle to determine the racial dynamics of postwar America. Optimism and anger coincided as civil rights supporters sought to extend their gains, racial conservatives sought to roll back those gains, and apathetic onlookers sought the swiftest path to tranquility after four years of wartime insanity.

In September 1945, Bobbye Williams of Alexander, Arkansas sat down to write a letter to the *Chicago Defender*. In a few simple lines she encapsulated African Americans' hopes, dreams, and desires. "V-J day has finally come," she wrote. "Now let us (I mean Americans regardless of race, creed or color) win another victory—V-N Day, which means Victory for the Negroes in America. Let us pray that those boys come home and live in peace and harmony with their fellow man. Let us pray that they will not be Jim-Crowed in any way."[14]

That same month, a few miles south of the *Defender*'s offices, white students at Gary, Indiana's Froebel High School went on strike to demand a segregated school. Hundreds of parents attended a mass meeting to support their children's protests. The stand-off intensified over the next few weeks as more parents pulled their kids from classes. Similar disruptions hit other Chicago-area districts. Police dispersed groups of angry whites wielding ice picks and clubs. Sympathy movements spread to other cities. "We want this to be a white school," a seventeen-year-old New Yorker told reporters. "We don't want none of that two-tone business in our school."[15]

Frank Sinatra, a gawky crooner idealized by hordes of teenaged girls, thought he could end the crisis. He preached open-mindedness to an interracial assembly at New York's Benjamin Franklin High School. "Sure, you have beefs," he said as shrieking bobbysoxers surged against a line of policemen, "but you settle that with a bust in the eye and then you shake hands. And that's the way it should be." Sinatra then boarded a plane for Chicago, where he delivered a rambling address to a rowdy crowd at Froebel High. "Do me a personal favor," he asked. "I came down here to ask you to go back to school. Please do it."

"Evidently Sinatra's appearance did not do any good," Froebel's principal remarked as the chaos continued. "It confused the issue. I'm confused."[16]

The end of the war left a lot of people confused. An unprecedented demographic upheaval had transformed the nation. More than 16 million Americans had served in uniform. One in five civilians had relocated across county or state lines. Over 3 million people had departed the rural South for Los Angeles, Detroit, Chicago, New York, Mobile, Norfolk, Birmingham, Houston, and other cities. Urban areas faced housing crunches, overcrowded schools, insufficient recreational facilities, jam-packed public transportation, and inadequate infrastructures. City dwellers grew frustrated as a sea of new arrivals, some of them black, some with foreign-sounding last names, and some with hillbilly twangs, clogged their towns.

Millions of African Americans had worked in defense plants, most of them making more money than they ever had before. At war's end, the Army included more than 800,000 black GIs. Some 165,000

African Americans served in the Navy, and 17,000 in the Marines. More than a quarter-million black soldiers were overseas, risking their lives in stations stretching from Wales to Czechoslovakia, from Holland to Egypt, from New Guinea to Iwo Jima. These veterans had suffered too much to accept second-class status. They had fought, and some of their comrades had died, to save democracy overseas. Now they returned to fight for democracy in a country grown exhausted from social, political, cultural, and economic change.

"I'm afraid Negroes will have had a taste of equality in the Army and in war jobs, and will demand their rights as citizens," an elderly woman told an interviewer. "The white people will try to stop them, and there will be trouble." Minority-group veterans had a harder time getting placed in schools and job-training programs than their white compatriots. Personnel managers resumed their prewar habit of specifying "white gentile only" in hiring notices. Reports of burning crosses across the South sparked fears of a Ku Klux Klan revival.[17]

Militant whites used violence to put black veterans in their place. South Carolina policemen pulled a uniformed soldier named Isaac Woodward from a bus and jabbed him with nightsticks, leaving him blind and suffering from partial amnesia. A mob near Monroe, Georgia, snatched two black veterans and their wives from a car, lined them up, and pumped sixty bullets into their bodies. Bigots portrayed such incidents as necessary to preventing race riots. "Red-blooded Anglo Saxon" men should use "any means" to enforce white supremacy, Senator Theodore Bilbo declared. "If you don't know what that means," he smirked, "you are just not up on your persuasive measures." Arsonists in Chicago struck forty-six black-occupied homes between May 1944 and July 1946.[18]

White Americans thought the war was over, but Randolph saw Hiroshima and Nagasaki as part of an ongoing battle for Double V. "No, it is not the end," Randolph had told a Brotherhood of Sleeping Car Porters conference in the war's final months. "While democracy would die if the Axis powers win, it does not follow that democracy will live because the [Allies] win." Randolph had long worried about the fate of African Americans in the postwar era. Now, with blacks getting pink slips and facing demobilization from a segregated military, he redoubled his commitment to rallying them to force the United States to uphold its founding principles.[19]

Randolph concentrated his postwar operations on two interrelated fronts. The National Council for a Permanent FEPC sought to resurrect the agency he saw as critical to achieving economic justice. He also continued his crusade to integrate the military. In the short term, his labors brought mixed success. In the long term, they energized a broad, sustainable civil rights movement that transformed America's racial, social, cultural, and economic landscape over the next several decades.

With the war over, he spent weeks on the road, getting a firsthand look at how reconversion affected African Americans. He hoped to funnel anger over layoffs into support for a permanent FEPC. His frustration mounted as the wartime coalition of FEPC backers disintegrated. Jewish and Catholic groups increasingly prioritized social and cultural inequality ahead of job discrimination. Close affiliation with a "black" cause might do more harm than good, they reasoned. An early 1946 poll showed just four in ten Americans favoring a permanent FEPC. Truman's support withered in the face of implacable Republican and Southern Democratic opposition. Randolph pushed for a meeting with Truman, who pleaded a full schedule and suggested he speak to an assistant instead.

For years, Randolph had demonized the South as racist and ignorant. Now he made a halfhearted appeal to working-class white Southerners. Reviving a socialist, class-based argument he had largely shelved during the war, he urged poor whites to embrace a permanent FEPC. Economic equality for African Americans meant higher living standards for all, he argued, because employers could no longer exploit antagonisms between white and black workers to depress wages.

Randolph doubted his chances of forging an interracial, working-class coalition. He instead stressed a gloomier line, promoting the FEPC as the only way to avoid race riots far worse than those in 1919. "I serve notice on the Congress," he declared in an October 1945 press release, "and this is no more a threat than is a hurricane warning, that if the Congress does not enact FEPC at once, the responsibility for violence which may break out in many cities of our country within a few months rests squarely on the shoulders of Congress." Hoping to recapture the magic of 1942, he announced mass meetings in New York City, Chicago, and other cities. Although Randolph was the prime mover, the interracial National Council for a Permanent FEPC, which had essentially lain dormant since Randolph and white theologian (and future Martin Luther King, Jr., confidant) Allan Knight Chalmers started it in 1943, sponsored the rallies.[20]

Randolph's provocative comment, which many took as a threat despite his claim to be preventing rather than inciting violence, thrust him onto the front pages of black newspapers. Major urban dailies and mainstream wire services ignored his scolding. They also shunned his follow-up press conference in Washington, DC. A row of black scribes jotted notes as Randolph accused Congress of abdicating its responsibility to black Americans and challenged President Truman to carry his support for FEPC beyond mere words. Randolph scribbled an equation on a chalkboard:

$$Un + H - X = R$$

Unemployment, plus hunger, minus hope, equals riots, he explained. Combining a socialist understanding of class grievances with a high-school science lecture, he insisted that "the social chemistry in many cities indicates inevitable violence unless Congress adds an important ingredient to the mixture. This vital ingredient is hope for the minorities."[21]

It took another twenty years for Randolph's dire prediction to come true. Resentment over the lack of opportunities in the ghetto, combined with official indifference to slum conditions, caused the Watts section of Los Angeles to explode in August 1965. Dozens of similarly motivated race riots erupted in subsequent summers.

For the moment, however, Randolph's gloom-and-doom prophecy failed to move policymakers. Even Truman's weak endorsement of a permanent FEPC incensed Southern Democrats, who vowed to defy their party's leader by killing the agency at the earliest possible opportunity. They got their chance in January 1946, when Senator Dennis Chavez of New Mexico brought a permanent FEPC bill to the floor. Senator Walter George of Georgia fired the first shot, declaring, "If this is all Harry Truman has to offer at a time like this, then God help the Democratic party."[22]

With that, the filibuster was on. George's peers droned on for more than two weeks. They promised to keep talking until the Senate dropped the bill. Overt racism permeated the halls of Congress as

Southern senators spun horror stories about uppity blacks menacing white women and assaulting virtuous white men. Most of them came from states whose Byzantine voting laws limited the electorate to a tiny, nearly all-white minority. According to Senator James Eastland (elected in 1942 with just over 51,000 votes, representing 2 percent of Mississippi's population), the FEPC was "an attempt to export the governmental philosophy of Harlem over the United States." Eastland, in a colloquy with another Democrat, Senator John Overton of Louisiana, said African Americans made "a great mistake" when they voted for Democrats. Overton agreed, declaring that white Southerners, "the backbone of the Democratic party," did not want blacks as political allies.[23]

Northern, small-government conservatives also opposed the permanent FEPC bill, but the Senate might have reached the two-thirds majority needed to end a filibuster had moderates and liberals from both parties worked together. Political realities kept this from happening. Republicans who favored the FEPC held their tongues while the South raged. The Democrats were tearing themselves apart, and Republicans saw no reason to pull the opposition party's collective chestnuts from the fire by ending the show.

African American leaders fought to regain momentum. The FEPC represented their last hope for economic justice, the only way to ensure access to the jobs of the future. Randolph's followers packed the Senate galleries. They begged the Chief to announce a march on Washington. Reverend (and, as of 1944, Congressman) Adam Clayton Powell sent hundreds of parishioners into the Capitol as a kind of mobile battalion of door knockers bent on persuading congressmen to support the FEPC.

None of it mattered. On February 9, 1946, a symbolic vote to end debate gained a 48–36 majority, well short of the two-thirds majority needed to stop the filibuster. Alben Barkley of Kentucky, who later served as Truman's vice president, was the only Southern Senator to back cloture. Admitting defeat, Chavez withdrew his bill.

Barring a legislative miracle, the FEPC was dead. Gleeful constituents of South Carolina senator Olin Johnston sent him a funeral bouquet of salmon-colored gladioli with a blue ribbon across the front reading "Rest in Peace."[24]

Randolph, his tie locked in place and his dark suit pressed to perfection, mounted the podium inside New York's Madison Square Garden. His chin cocked slightly above horizontal, he surveyed the gathering of 15,000 people, leaned into the microphone, and declared, "Let me definitely state here, that FEPC is not dead."

The February 28, 1946 mass meeting represented the National Council for a Permanent FEPC's last, best chance of saving the agency. It followed a disappointing rally in the Chicago Coliseum, where just 2,500 people turned out to hear Randolph and an array of local political and religious leaders promise to continue the fight for equal opportunity. Promotional literature for the event had called for 50,000 attendees.

Randolph hoped to rekindle the fervor of 1942. The 1946 Madison Square Garden assembly did echo the earlier event, but not in positive ways. As in 1942, Randolph struggled to raise money, and his organization's top-down nature produced an ineffective publicity campaign. The event itself was poorly run, starting a half-hour late and running deep into the night. Radio stations switched off their coverage long before it ended.

Nevertheless, the turnout proved Randolph could still draw an audience. He attracted several big-name speakers, including Mayor Fiorello LaGuardia; the NAACP's Roy Wilkins, who left angry because radio stations did not carry his speech; and the biggest prize of all, Eleanor Roosevelt. President Truman declined his invitation but, in another coup for Randolph, sent Secretary of Labor Lewis Schwellenbach with a message of support.

Randolph shrugged off a stubborn case of the flu to deliver an upbeat, defiant speech. He promised "relentless warfare" against senators who opposed cloture and attacked President Truman for failing to whip his party into line. Randolph framed the FEPC as a means for preserving America's moral leadership in a world fast descending into a cold war battle between democracy and communism. With the Soviets entrenching in Eastern Europe and expanding their influence elsewhere, the United States needed to set an example by ending exploitation at home. Randolph presented the right to work as essential for human dignity. Trampling the humanity of racial, ethnic, and religious minorities bred desperation, and desperate people were dangerous people. "They may become emotional atomic bombs of destruction and hate," he warned.

A. Philip Randolph, Eleanor Roosevelt, and Fiorello LaGuardia attend a 1946 Save the FEPC rally at Madison Square Garden. *Courtesy Franklin D. Roosevelt Presidential Library. © Bettmann/CORBIS*

Randolph dropped his own bombshell when he announced that the National Council—meaning Randolph—had given "serious consideration to a march on Washington." Unlike the all-black affair of 1941, he now wanted an interracial event. Although he still believed a black-only movement would empower downtrodden African Americans, years of frustration had taught him that a more inclusive crusade could unite disparate groups behind reform. The spectacle of blacks linking arms with whites on Pennsylvania Avenue would offer a suitable kickoff for such a drive.[25]

His big splash fizzled. Mainstream newspapers devoted little space to the Madison Square Garden rally or Randolph's threat. Black newspapers, who had heard all this before, paid only cursory notice. The National Council itself was a mess. It depended on the BSCP for money. Randolph, as he had with MOWM, failed to delegate enough authority to create a decentralized, grassroots interest group. Nor did he hire the executive talent required to impose order on a quarrelsome central office whose workers spent as much time sniping at each other as they did working toward the council's goal.

The FEPC never got the miracle it needed. It passed out of existence on July 1, 1946. Despite persistent staffing and financing shortages, and wavering support from the White House, it had processed more than 12,000 discrimination cases during its five-year existence. African Americans filed 80 percent of the claims, but the agency also defended equal rights for Mexican Americans, Catholics, Jews, Jehovah's Witnesses, Seventh-Day Adventists, and other minorities. It resolved nearly 5,000 cases through quiet negotiations between employers and regional operatives. It initiated legal proceedings in about 3,500 other cases. It is impossible to say how many minority Americans got jobs because of the FEPC. As just one measure of success, twice as many African Americans and Mexican Americans held skilled or semiskilled jobs at the end of the war as at the beginning.

From a more long-term perspective, the FEPC represented a watershed moment for American civil rights. Imperfect though it was, it was the first federal agency devoted entirely to ending job discrimination, and the first to deal with minority organizations so intensely. As the federal government's primary voice on civil rights, it raised awareness of inequality and incited changes in the government and in civilian life. The hasty decision to apply Executive Order 8802 to all minorities paved the way for making civil rights and economic justice relevant to all minorities, not just African Americans.[26]

Randolph took the news hard. "It now seems clear that the so-called fight for democracy in World War II was a subterfuge to millions of citizens of minority status," he remarked.[27]

He never relented in his quest to revive the bureau. Every new session of Congress brought new schemes to overcome the Southern filibuster of permanent FEPC bills. Operating through his National Council, Randolph kept raising money from labor and minority organizations, giving speeches, drafting model bills and executive orders, and lobbying the White House. "It is the biggest job Negroes have ever undertaken since the Civil War," he told one supporter in 1947.[28]

The biggest, perhaps, but not the only job. Randolph and millions of like-minded Americans also championed civil rights bills and demanded an integrated military. President Truman was not ready to push the Army on integration. A combination of ideology and practicality, however, drove him to attack inequality at home. Innate racism aside, Truman viewed himself as a champion of the common man, a president in the mold of Abraham Lincoln, Thomas Jefferson, and Andrew Jackson. Injustice genuinely pained him, and he resolved to alleviate it however he could. Moreover, he understood the importance of winning black support for his 1948 reelection bid. Many African Americans still saw him as a hostile Southerner. The thumping Republicans gave his party in the 1946 congressional elections reinforced the need to shore up his liberal credentials.

The emerging cold war with the Soviets also affected his calculations. Communism and democracy were engaged in a global test of wills, each determined to win allies not just in Europe, but also in Asia, Africa, and Latin America. The hypocritical U.S. posture of preaching freedom while discriminating against minorities provided ample material for Soviet propagandists. As Truman awkwardly explained, "The top dog in a world which is over half colored ought to clean its own hands."[29]

At the same time, Truman's overheated depiction of the cold war as a death match between two incompatible ways of life encouraged a blind, unthinking faith in American supremacy. Cold warriors tarred anyone questioning established political, cultural, social, or racial beliefs as subversives, possible "red" agents hoping to undermine national unity and therefore enhance the Soviet Union's global status.

Truman created the President's Committee on Civil Rights in December 1946. He ordered its fifteen members to determine how best to protect Americans' civil rights, whether through better enforcement of existing laws or passing new ones. "You have a vitally important job," he told committee members when they visited the White House in January 1947. "I want our Bill of Rights implemented in fact." "We will do our utmost, Mr. President," replied Charles Wilson, head of General Electric and chair of the committee. "It's a big job," Truman said. "Go to it!"[30]

The committee spent several months conducting interviews, examining the conditions that cultivated inequality, and designing possible legislative remedies. Its October 1947 report offered "a brutally, and therefore a most healthfully, frank exposure of ills in our society," the *New York Times* declared. *To Secure These Rights* mocked the notion of "separate but equal," a phrase the Supreme Court used to legitimate segregation in its 1896 *Plessy v. Ferguson* decision, as "one of the outstanding myths of American history." It condemned the poll tax, religious discrimination, racist police departments, Southern states' feeble prosecutions of lynchers, and a host of other ills. Segregation within the military was especially pernicious, because soldiers risked their lives defending American values. The report even impressed Randolph. Although skeptical of pious words, he thought the committee might revive interest in fair employment legislation and other elements of his wartime agenda.[31]

Unlike President Roosevelt, who excelled at ignoring blue-ribbon panels, Truman took the committee's recommendations to heart. Not coincidentally, advancing the civil rights agenda furthered his own political needs. His staff began drafting bills based on the committee's findings. As part of this process, Truman resolved to attack military segregation. After a spirited internal debate, he opted to sign an executive order integrating the armed forces rather than try to ram a bill through a Southern filibuster. He kept his decision quiet for the moment, waiting for the right time to release a statement.

The postwar military had made incremental progress toward integration. In 1947, Secretary of the Navy James Forrestal issued an order lifting all restrictions on assignments for African Americans and barring segregation throughout the fleet. The Navy also banned segregation in its housing, mess halls, and recreational facilities. Around the same time, Air Force secretary Stuart Symington ordered his service to dismantle racial barriers to advancement and job placement.

The Marines disregarded the Navy's liberalization, opening only 1,500 spots to African Americans, about 2 percent of its total strength. The Army was another conspicuous holdout. Top brass refused to recognize that segregation undermined efficiency by blocking qualified GIs from jobs and training programs. Officials still viewed integration as a morale issue. Unit cohesion would suffer if whites had to serve alongside blacks, they said. Internal reports indicating that wartime *segregation* had lowered efficiency and bred discontent failed to change their minds. When questioned about desegregating the National Guard, Chief of Staff Omar Bradley responded, "From the military point of view, I still think that any integration of Negroes ... will create problems which may have serious consequences."[32]

A fall 1947 bill requiring all men between the ages of eighteen and twenty-five to register for military service lent immediacy to integration demands. In its original form, the Universal Military Training bill included a nondiscrimination requirement and forbid segregation in the armed forces. Opponents from the Army succeeded in stripping those clauses before the measure reached Congress. There seemed little chance of amending the bill in the face of Southern threats to filibuster an integration clause.

Randolph fumed over this latest injustice. The training bill would introduce a new generation of Americans, including Northerners, to the evils of segregation. Because it imposed a peacetime draft, black men were forced to accept inequality. He summoned a dozen confidants to discuss the crisis in his Harlem office. His guests blustered about Southerners, reactionaries, and American fascists—words Randolph used interchangeably to describe his political enemies—while a cool fall evening blanketed the bustling streets. The fired-up group formed a Committee Against Jim Crow in Military Service and Training. Randolph shared power with Grant Reynolds, a former Army chaplain who got hounded out of the service after repeatedly protesting conditions for black soldiers. Bayard Rustin, a radical pacifist whose wartime sit-ins of segregated restaurants and hotels rattled white America, eventually assumed control over day-to-day operations.

The new committee provided a déjà vu moment for Randolph. In early 1945, with MOWM dying and Nazi Germany collapsing, Randolph had joined other labor leaders and civil rights groups to form the National Committee to Abolish Segregation in the Armed Forces. The group failed to gain much traction or support from other civil rights organizations (the NAACP contributed $5 to its opening fundraiser), and it disappeared with barely a peep.

This time Randolph saw the political, social, and military stars aligning in his favor. Labeling the situation "a crisis as grave as the 1941 job crisis," he forged an interracial alliance dedicated to halting a proposal that normalized segregation while undermining America's moral supremacy. To his dismay, he found that few African Americans were aware of the military training bill. He stoked public familiarity with a barrage of well-publicized letters demanding a sit-down with the president. Truman's secretaries offered an audience with subordinates but shielded their boss from the controversial activist.[33]

Truman nevertheless felt the pressure. He used his January 1948 State of the Union address to reaffirm his liberal agenda. Never a strong public speaker, his calls for a national health insurance program, federal aid for schools, and a higher minimum wage drew little applause from Republicans and Southern Democrats. His promise to send Congress a special message on civil rights also fell flat.

"Phil Randolph ... is an important Negro," Truman advisor David Niles told a secretary seeking advice on how to handle yet another meeting request. The president should probably see him after he completed his civil rights message. That way, Niles concluded, "these people will not be able to say that the message is a result of their visit."[34]

Congress viewed the president's civil rights message, delivered a few weeks after the State of the Union address, with cynicism and horror. Written while Randolph was metaphorically pounding on the White House's door, it offered the most rousing appeal for equality ever to emanate from the White House. "We know the way," Truman declared, "we need only the will." As "a minimum program," Truman demanded a permanent civil rights commission, a new FEPC, an end to the poll tax, a federal antilynching law, and federal protection for voting rights. "We cannot be satisfied until all our people have equal opportunities for jobs, for homes, for education, for health, and for political expression, and until all our people have equal protection under the law," Truman stated. These revolutionary proposals would finally implement the democratic language embodied within the Declaration of Independence and the Constitution. With the cold war settling in, moreover, the world faced "the choice of freedom or enslavement." Congress had the power to put America on the side of freedom.[35]

Truman, who in private still called African Americans "niggers," had placed civil rights squarely at the center of the national debate. "Outrageous," screamed Senator Eastland of Mississippi. "Here's telling President Truman that the Democratic party in Mississippi is through with him, now, hereafter, and forever," seconded the *Jackson (Mississippi) Daily News*. Truman was losing his grip on the South, but he was positioning himself to harvest votes from Northern liberals and African Americans. "Even the great Roosevelt ... did not dare go that far," enthused the *Pittsburgh Courier*.[36]

Randolph finally got his White House invitation in February 1948, one week after Truman issued his civil rights message. Six weeks later he walked through the building's doors for the fourth time. Grant Reynolds, Walter White, Mary McLeod Bethune, and a delegation from the Committee Against Jim Crow in Military Service accompanied him.

Randolph glanced around the Oval Office as he sat down. The room was familiar, yet different. As when Roosevelt occupied the room, it reflected the mind of the man sitting behind the desk. The barely organized chaos from FDR's administration was gone, replaced with orderly, straightforward furnishings suggestive of a man who played it straight and disdained unstructured verbal jousting. "The Buck Stops Here," read a sign on the president's desk. On one wall, looming over the assembly like a ghostly reminder of Randolph's previous visit, hung a portrait of Franklin Roosevelt.

Randolph and Truman began sparring, probing for insights into the other's character. Randolph found the president friendly but firm, a better listener than the gregarious Roosevelt and a stronger presence than "Silent" Calvin Coolidge.

With time at a premium, Randolph came to the point quickly. "Black Americans today are in no mood to shoulder a gun again in defense of this country so long as they are not full-fledged citizens … and recognized as such in the armed forces," he told the president.

Truman glared at his adversary.

"They are well aware of the fact that they have fought and died in every war in this nation," Randolph continued. "Now they want to fight as free men in a free army in a free country."

Truman squirmed in his chair. His expression soured. "I wish you hadn't made that statement," he shot back, "it grieves me."

Truman wanted credit for his bold actions. Randolph wanted to discuss what more the president could do. NAACP attorney Charles Houston jumped in, imploring Truman to appreciate the courage it took to be so honest in such intimidating surroundings.

Everyone calmed down, and Truman told Randolph to continue. His voice easing back into a measured cadence, he asked the president to issue an executive order banning segregation and discrimination in the military. He did not know that Truman, like Roosevelt in 1941, had already decided to issue an order. Randolph interpreted Truman's brief thanks and curt dismissal as evidence that his words had shaken the president into reconsidering his position.[37]

A few weeks later, Randolph testified before the Senate Armed Services Committee about the Universal Military Training bill. His appearance provided a rare moment of mainstream exposure. He seized the opportunity to raise the stakes in the military segregation dispute. As always, Randolph appeared unfazed by the bustle around him. He sat impassively at the witness table, a solidly built man with thinning, gracefully graying hair. A white pocket handkerchief added punch to his dark suit and sober tie. Reporters scribbled notes while Grant Reynolds, sitting to Randolph's right in a gray, striped suit, fussed with the papers in front of him.

Randolph opened with a well-worn recitation of black woes. Then he shifted into uncharted territory. Should Congress not desegregate the military, he advised the panel, America would see "a mass civil disobedience movement" similar to what the British were dealing with in India. "Negro youth have a moral obligation not to lend

A. Philip Randolph (right) and Grant Reynolds prepare to testify before the Senate Armed Services Committee, March 1948. *Library of Congress, Prints and Photographs Collection, LC-USZ62-128074*

themselves as world-wide carriers of an evil and hellish doctrine," he continued. The senators leaned forward as he reached his provocative conclusion. "I personally pledge myself to openly counsel, aid, and abet youth, both white and colored, to quarantine any Jim Crow conscription system," he read. "I shall call upon all colored veterans to join this civil disobedience movement and to recruit their younger brothers in an organized refusal to register. ... We'll be buried in our graves before we will be slaves."

A puzzled silence fell over the room. None of the senators knew that Randolph had made a similar threat back in 1918, landing himself in a Cleveland courtroom. Senator Wayne Morse of Oregon, a liberal Democrat, groped for a clarification from a witness who appeared to be advocating treason. He asked whether Randolph would counsel young men to resist the draft if a foreign enemy attacked the United States. "I would advocate that Negroes take no part in the Army," Randolph replied, because "it is in the interest of the soul of our country and I unhesitatingly and very adamantly hold that that is the only way by which we are going to be able to make America wake up and realize that we do not have democracy here so long as one black man is denied all of the rights enjoyed by all the white men of this country."

Randolph understood the risks of massive, nonviolent resistance. He anticipated retaliatory violence from racists. Detractors would attack protesters as traitors, cowards, and communists. None of that mattered. "I want you to know that we would be willing to absorb the violence, to absorb the terrorism, to face the music and to take whatever comes," he told Morse. "We, as a matter of fact, consider that we are more loyal to our country than the people who perpetuate segregation and discrimination upon Negroes."[38]

"He is perpetuating treason," Congressman John Rankin roared. J. Edgar Hoover stepped up FBI surveillance of Randolph to determine whether to build a case for prosecution. African Americans had mixed feelings about Randolph's latest offensive. Some supported nonviolent resistance. Others applauded Randolph's sincerity while questioning his rationality. Randolph hit the streets to persuade skeptics. Antidraft posters dotted walls in Harlem and other black neighborhoods. Activists shouted news of Randolph's new crusade from busy corners. Polls showed a large majority of black youths supporting the campaign.[39]

Too old to be drafted, Randolph instead placed himself on the front lines of a moral war. He warned his acolytes to expect physical violence and imprisonment. "We will fill up the jails with young men who refuse to serve," he told one of the dozens of rallies he addressed that summer, "and I am prepared to fight the Jim Crow army even if I am convicted of treason and have to rot in jail."[40]

Randolph's supporters hounded Truman. The Chief led a group of picketers demonstrating in front of the White House. When Democrats met in Philadelphia to nominate the president for a second term, Randolph marched outside with a sign reading "PRISON IS BETTER THAN ARMY JIM CROW SERVICE." His backers distributed 100,000 "Don't Join a Jim Crow Army" buttons to urban blacks. Hundreds of people signed pledges to refuse induction should they be drafted. As with the aborted March on Washington, Randolph had no idea whether they would actually uphold their promise at the crucial moment of decision.

Despite these protests, Congress passed the Universal Military Training bill after rejecting amendments safeguarding the rights of black soldiers.

Randolph was exhausted and discouraged. A showdown appeared imminent, and he did not know whether his troops would follow him into battle. President Truman rebuffed requests for a second meeting. Randolph was stretched even thinner than usual. He was running multiple civil rights and labor organizations, managing personal disputes within those organizations, mobilizing a grassroots nonviolence movement, editing the monthly *Black Worker* magazine, agitating for a permanent FEPC, lobbying Truman, and pestering congressmen. Added to this was the strain of caring for his wife Lucille, whose arthritis had recently confined her to a wheelchair. Nearing sixty years of age, he no longer possessed the boundless energy of youth. He needed a victory.

As had often happened during the war, Randolph's radicalism dragged other African American groups into the fight. The surge of publicity behind Randolph compelled other organizations, even those that found him too extreme, to reiterate their opposition to segregation and discrimination. They unwittingly became part of a swelling equality movement that appeared to have Randolph at its head.

The tide hit Truman at precisely the right political moment. Southern Democrats bolted the party when the Philadelphia convention approved a strong civil rights plank. With Dixiecrat candidate Strom Thurmond, a segregationist senator from South Carolina, positioned to snap up Southern states, the president scrambled to lock up votes from Northern liberals and African Americans. Former vice president Henry Wallace's entrance into the race under the new Progressive Party's banner intensified the contest for liberal voters, as did the Republicans' support for civil rights in their party platform.

Randolph was meeting with the BSCP chapter in Denver when he heard that Truman had signed Executive Order 9980, which established fair employment practices throughout the federal government, and Executive Order 9981, which required "equality of treatment and opportunity for all persons in the armed forces without regard to race, color, religion or national origin." It created a new board, the President's Committee on Equality of Treatment and Opportunity in the Armed Services, often dubbed the Fahy Committee in honor of Chairman Charles Fahy, to enforce compliance.[41]

Randolph was wary. Order 9981 appeared to satisfy his demands but never actually used the words "segregation," "desegregation," or "integration." Nor did it establish a timetable for guaranteeing equal treatment. In fact, it did the opposite, as its insistence that implementation occur "as rapidly as possible," seemed an invitation to delay. Randolph's suspicions mounted when Army Chief of Staff Omar Bradley grumbled about the president using the military for social experiments. The Army would stay segregated so long as the rest of the nation did, he said. The general quickly retracted his comments, but the damage was done.

Randolph told supporters to continue their nonviolent agitation. Blasting the order as "deliberately calculated to obscure," he pressured Truman to clarify his meaning. It took several follow-up meetings with Truman's advisors to convince him of the president's sincerity. "Inasmuch as nonsegregation in the armed services is now the announced policy of the Commander-in-Chief," Randolph wrote in an August 1948 *Black Worker* editorial, "we can now place in storage the League for Non-Violent Civil Disobedience Against Military Segregation," the action wing of the Committee against Jim Crow in Military Service.[42]

Randolph soon discovered how difficult it was to stop a revolution. A gang of firebrands under Bayard Rustin's leadership defied

President Harry S. Truman, who spurred the movement to integrate the military, greets an Air Force sergeant in 1950. *Courtesy Harry S. Truman Presidential Library*

Randolph's cease fire. Rustin launched a Pearl Harbor-style sneak attack, denouncing Randolph as a reactionary Uncle Tom at a surprise press conference held just hours before Randolph dissolved the league. Rustin thought the veteran agitator had gone soft, too eager to disband organizations at the first blush of success. He regretted this blindside but felt it necessary. "I was so ashamed that I avoided him for several years," Rustin later remembered.[43]

Seething at this rebellion, Randolph sabotaged his own organization. In a curious public statement, he denigrated the league as a failed attempt to build a mass movement. His personal contribution of $800 represented the bulk of the group's fundraising, he said. Randolph then claimed that "we obtained the Executive Order because our program was morally unassailable." This face-saving gesture overstated the group's actual influence. It also showed the influence of doctrinaire pacifists, including Rustin, on Randolph's thinking. In 1941 he viewed reform purely in terms of focusing mass pressure on political leaders. Now, in 1948, he merged this socialist vision of class-based action with a more pacifistic reform agenda based on defining what was morally right and wrong.[44]

As the Young Turks anticipated, Randolph proved too trusting. The military's determination to preserve the status quo outstripped Truman's desire to desegregate the military. Army brass gave the president's order a chilly reception. Most assumed (wrongly, as it turned out) Truman, whose approval ratings had tumbled to 35 percent since his civil rights message, would lose his reelection bid. Secretary of Defense Louis Johnson directed the various services to compose integration plans. The Army stalled, speaking of desegregation as a fifty- or even hundred-year program. "Amalgamation would place the Negro in a competitive field he is not prepared to face," a group of generals complained. A June 1948 Gallup Poll revealed that two thirds of Americans favored continuing military segregation.[45]

The Korean War finally broke the stalemate. A rush of black volunteers after North Korea's June 1950 invasion of South Korea produced overstrength African American units performing rearguard duties, leaving undermanned white units to face the communist aggressors. Desperate field commanders struck informal deals to import black service soldiers into their weakened units. "I was very, very low on men—less than half strength—and raised hell to get more troops," recalled Lieutenant Colonel Cesidio "Butch" Barberis. "The division called and ... said he had almost two hundred blacks from labor units ... who would transfer to the infantry. I agreed. ... [Major General] Keiser asked me if I realized what a can of worms I was opening up, to which I said, 'So what? They are good fighting men. I need men.'"[46]

As the Pentagon scrambled to figure out what was happening, dispatches from Korea reported that integration improved the quality of black soldiers without harming white morale. By May 1951, 61 percent of infantry companies in Korea were desegregated, and integration was already penetrating other Far East, and even stateside posts. Segregation, long defended as essential to a strong military, crumbled due to the need for a strong military. By 1953, when the war ended, the military was almost entirely integrated, with virtually none of the interracial violence detractors had predicted. "There is no color line in a foxhole," Brigadier General John Michaelis explained.[47]

An integrated platoon of the 2nd Infantry Division confronts North Korean troops near the Chongchon River, November 1950. *National Archives and Records Administration, NARA File# 111-SC-353469*

Executive Order 9981 and actual integration marked significant victories for Double V. Together they fulfilled one of the main demands Randolph had brought to the White House back in 1940. For Randolph, however, the war for equality continued without interruption. He retained his faith in mass, civil disobedience but worried that dogmatic pacifists such as Rustin wanted to exploit the technique without first building a social movement trained to employ it. African Americans and their white allies needed more education on the issues and a stronger grasp of nonviolence's potential uses and misuses before a true civil rights movement could emerge. Grassroots leaders needed to excite the masses, then connect them to a national coordinating network of organizers and speakers—exactly the mission he had pursued for a decade, and one that implied his own shortcomings in that area.

Randolph's activism had brought African Americans to freedom's doorstep. He had proven their ability to overmatch even the savviest politicians and shown them how to organize on a previously unimagined scale. He had merged Marcus Garvey's street-pleasing theatrics with

Walter White's backroom dealings. He had introduced civil disobedience to the black mainstream. And, beginning with his audacious challenge to Franklin Roosevelt, he had concocted a fiery mix of issues that drove black protest for the next generation.

For Randolph, economic opportunity was inseparable from social and political opportunity. Good jobs enhanced equality in other areas. To prove themselves the equals of whites, African Americans first had to seize control of their own destiny. They needed to storm the halls of power, imbued with the conviction that America belonged to them as much as any other group. Although the road ahead was long and treacherous, Randolph knew that one day minorities would reach their destination: an America committed to upholding the principle that all men are created equal.

CONCLUSION

....

May 16, 1979 found longtime civil rights activist Bayard Rustin in Washington, DC, testifying before the House Subcommittee on Africa about the continent's current problems and future hopes. He had reconciled with Randolph years earlier, when the aging leader tapped him to organize the epic 1963 March on Washington. Rustin now headed the A. Philip Randolph Institute, a think tank opened in 1965 to promulgate Randolph's labor and civil rights agendas.

Partway through his testimony someone handed him a note. Rustin opened it, scanned the page, and crumpled into a sobbing heap. His body shook as tears streamed down his face.

A. Philip Randolph was dead.

A maid found him on the floor of his apartment, felled by a heart attack at the age of ninety. His sparsely furnished surroundings reflected a life devoted to serving others. Pages from an autobiography that he never had time to finish filled a desk. Books spilled from a library whose walls boasted an uncountable number of plaques, diplomas, and other honors, including the Presidential Medal of Freedom Lyndon Johnson had bestowed on him in 1964. Randolph's biggest luxury was two black-and-white televisions, used mostly for watching baseball games. He left no survivors and an estate worth about $500. According to his wishes, his body was cremated.

Once considered a dangerous radical, Randolph had gained widespread acceptance by the time he died. Leaders of labor, religious, and educational groups lamented his passing. Randolph's "dignity and integrity, his eloquence, his devotion to nonviolence and his unshake-able commitment to justice all helped shape the ideals and spirit of the civil rights movement," President Jimmy Carter said.[1]

The president's words papered over much of Randolph's record. Carter never mentioned Randolph's socialism and sidestepped his radical pronouncements from the 1930s and 1940s. He ignored Randolph's warnings of race war, his threats to disrupt (or at least inconvenience) the government, and his impassioned defense of an all-black organization. Considering the enormous changes in America's racial landscape over the last generation, Randolph no longer seemed like the radical he was. His involvement in the 1963 March on Washington, a canonical event by 1979, completed Randolph's reinvention. After a lifetime on the outside, he had become mainstream. His ideals remained relatively consistent over the years. The world had finally caught up to him.

Life took Randolph from segregated Florida to the White House, from sweaty union halls to Madison Square Garden. He had by any measure an extraordinary ninety years. Yet his last few decades brought tragedy, frustration, and neglect. His role in convincing Truman to sign Executive Order 9981 represented one of his final triumphs. It did not, however, cause him to abandon his lifelong struggle on behalf of workers and minorities.

Although pushing seventy, Randolph remained active through the 1950s. He traveled 50,000 miles a year, accepted more speaking engage-ments than he should have, and remained a tireless advocate for the sleep-ing car porters. He devoted much of his flagging energy to fighting discrimination in the labor movement, particularly within the AFL-CIO, an umbrella organization encompassing dozens of unions. Randolph spent decades denouncing unfair practices at annual AFL-CIO conven-tions. Delegates either heckled him or left the hall for a cigarette or a drink whenever he spoke. Undaunted, Randolph challenged anyone lis-tening to reconcile cold war America's mission of spreading democracy to Africa, Asia, and elsewhere with its inability to create a true democracy at home. It was Double V all over again, albeit on new terrain.

If the barbs stung, he never let his critics know it. At least in public, he maintained an optimistic determination that change was coming soon. "We are going to break down all the legal barriers to the Negro's equality in this generation, perhaps within the next decade," he told an interviewer in 1958.[2]

His mind sharp but his body deteriorating, Randolph was clearly not the person to lead younger generations to equality. His achievement in helping to pull off the 1963 March on Washington represented more of a last hurrah than a rebirth. He felt out of sync with the young firebrands assuming control of the civil rights movement. They saw the one-time, headline-grabbing events Randolph favored as inadequate remedies for a broken socioeconomic system. Rallies could not repair lives shattered in impoverished ghettoes. Speeches could not bring jobs, education, and hope to inner cities. Randolph had argued much the same with his old friend Walter White. Now he was on the other side of the argument.

Revolutionaries declared Randolph a sellout for endorsing President Lyndon Johnson's Great Society programs, which provided well-intended if hopelessly inadequate federal aid to urban areas. This was an ironic turn, considering the derision Randolph once heaped on moderate blacks. Not even the 1964 Civil Rights Act, which, besides abolishing segregation, created the Equal Employment Opportunity Commission, a close parallel to the World War II–era FEPC, could convince the new radicals that Randolph was on the right track.

A wave of race riots during the mid-1960s confirmed his conviction that the movement was getting out of hand. He understood why poverty produced hotheaded agitators who brandished self-defense rather than nonviolence as a means for winning revolutionary change. He had predicted the rise of violent protests two decades earlier with his $Un + H - X = R$ formula. He disassociated himself from radical civil rights groups, abandoning the angry black underclass he had embraced twenty years earlier. "The time has come when the street marches and demonstrations have about run their course," he said. Sounding much like Walter White, now dead for over a decade, he claimed that "the strategy now in order is to shift from the streets to the conference room." Randolph further infuriated radicals in October 1966 when he signed a full-page *New York Times* advertisement, titled "Crisis and Commitment," that condemned violence, restated his desire for full integration, and appealed to sympathetic whites for support.[3]

Black radicals mocked Randolph's calls for "level heads." They thought of him—when they thought of him at all—as "Uncle Tom No. 2" (NAACP executive director Roy Wilkins occupied the top

spot), an establishment tool whose moderate message was so discon-
nected from reality as to barely deserve comment. Posters plastered
around Harlem denounced Randolph, along with Bayard Rustin and
others, for "Crimes Committed Against the Black People," including
"aiding the enemy" and "being 'traitors' to the black cause." Rarely did
this new generation consider how much Randolph's message had influenced their arguments. Like them, he had linked race with class,
arguing that economic equality went hand-in-hand with true democracy. Like them, he had experimented with all-black organizations.
Like them, he had forced white Americans to confront the importance
of race in everyday life.[4]

Randolph stayed the course. "I *love* the young black militants," he
told an interviewer. "I don't agree with all their methodology, and yet
I can understand why they are in this mood of revolt, of resort to violence, for I was a young black militant myself, the angry young man of
my day." He urged the new angry young men to read history, economics, and sociology. They should study earlier revolutions to see that
violence never produced lasting, positive change.

At the same time, he pushed Washington to address the sources
of their rage by ensuring equal access to cutting-edge jobs in what was
fast becoming a postindustrial society. With the signing of the Civil
Rights and Voting Rights Acts, he explained, "the civil rights revolution ... [has] moved into a new phase which involves social justice and
economic rights—the right to a job, good housing, effective education
and so forth." Achieving these objectives would require a tremendous
amount of people power. Blacks and whites needed to unite to influence public policy. They needed to educate themselves. They needed to
work collectively, through unions, to overcome resistance from corporations and other entrenched interests.[5]

Randolph was also losing influence among organized labor, a crucial force for improving working-class fortunes. Changes in America's
transportation network left the BSCP, the union he had headed for
forty years, a shadow of its former self. He resigned the presidency in
1968, having never made more than $13,000 a year in the post.
Another union, the Brotherhood of Railway and Airline Clerks,
absorbed the Sleeping Car Porters a few months later.

His health declining, Randolph spent most of his days alone or
with his few surviving close friends. Every once in a while he visited

the A. Philip Randolph Institute. He devoted much of his remaining energy to lobbying for the Institute's proposed Freedom Budget, which called for increased federal spending on health care, education, infrastructure, and job training programs as a way to lift the impoverished while undercutting such radical groups as the Black Panthers, who denounced the government as racist and uncaring. Neither Congress nor President Johnson showed much interest in the plan. The escalating cost of the Vietnam War strangled hopes for the ambitious social engineering package.

Randolph gave his final public address at a Waldorf-Astoria gala Bayard Rustin put together to celebrate his eightieth birthday. Hundreds of admirers packed the room. Their presence demonstrated how much America had changed over the last eight decades. New York governor Nelson Rockefeller, scion of one of the world's wealthiest families, and New York City mayor John Lindsay were there to honor the black, socialist labor leader. Coretta Scott King, a widow after her husband's 1968 assassination, represented the mainstream civil rights movement—a paradoxical phrase throughout much of Randolph's career. AFL-CIO president George Meany, a longtime antagonist but now a friend, sat at Randolph's right, smoking cigars. Richard Nixon sent greetings from the White House. Black congresswoman Shirley Chisholm had lauded the honoree on the House floor a day earlier. "Future historians will, I am sure … insure that A. Philip Randolph is remembered as one of the great men of his time, and pay him his just tribute for the role he has played in trying to make this Nation become, someday, truly the land of the free."[6]

After more than three hours of plaudits, Randolph finally rose to speak. His face had sagged and his hair retreated since his younger days. His tuxedo covered a frame grown fragile over the years. His aged legs shaking a bit, he surveyed the expectant crowd and began his talk. The voice was still there, the one that made people feel something important was being said. Thinner and weaker than in its prime, but undoubtedly the same one used for a lifetime spent advancing freedom, justice, and equality. The same one Harry Truman had heard. The same one Franklin Roosevelt had heard. The same one innumerable racists, fence-sitters, skeptics, bullies, admirers, followers, porters, managers, union bosses, congressmen, and generals had heard.

Coretta Scott King congratulates Randolph on his eightieth birthday as (left to right) Bayard Rustin, George Meany, and Nelson Rockefeller look on.
Sam Reiss Photographs Collection, Tamiment Library, New York University. Photograph by Sam Reiss

"Our gathering here tonight is an honoring, and for that I am deeply grateful and humbled," Randolph said. "But in a more profound sense it is a rededication to a cause to which I have contributed my energies, and to principles to which I have dedicated my life." He recalled his exertions for workers and African Americans and described the struggle to organize sleeping car porters. "In my life I have tried to abide by the principles of democracy, non-violence, and integration," he continued. "We cannot reject these principles without also denying ourselves the possibility of freedom."

After this implied warning to militants who preached self-defense and black nationalism, he found words that echoed his speeches from thirty years earlier. "Salvation for the Negro masses must come from within," he told the crowd. "Freedom is never granted; it is won. Justice is never given; it is exacted. But in our struggle we must draw for strength upon something that far transcends the boundaries of race. We must draw upon the capacity of human beings to act with humanity towards one another. We must draw upon the human potential for kindness and decency. And we must have faith that this society, divided by race and by class, and subject to profound social pressures, can one day become a nation of equals, and banish white racism and black racism and anti-Semitism to the limbo of oblivion from which they shall never emerge."[7]

NOTES

....

List of Abbreviations

APR: The Papers of A. Philip Randolph, microfilm edition

BSCP: Records of the Brotherhood of Sleeping Car Porters, Chicago Historical Society, Chicago, Illinois

FBI: FBI File on A. Philip Randolph, microfilm edition

FDRL Early: The Papers of Stephen T. Early, Franklin D. Roosevelt Presidential Library, Hyde Park, New York

FDRL ER: The Papers of Eleanor Roosevelt, Franklin D. Roosevelt Presidential Library, Hyde Park, New York

FDRL OF: Official File, Franklin D. Roosevelt Presidential Library, Hyde Park, New York

FDRL PSF: President's Secretary's File, Franklin D. Roosevelt Presidential Library, Hyde Park, New York

NAACP: Papers of the NAACP Part 13: The NAACP and Labor 1940–1955, Series B: Cooperation with Organized Labor, 1940–1955, microfilm edition

Nash: Papers of Harry S. Truman, Staff Member and Office Files: Philleo Nash Files, Harry S. Truman Presidential Library, Independence, Missouri

Preface

1. Quoted in Lucy G. Barber, *Marching on Washington: The Forging of an American Political Tradition* (Berkeley: University of California Press, 2002), 150.

2. A. Philip Randolph, "Jobs and Freedom," 12 August 1963, APR reel 29.

3. Randolph quoted in Taylor Branch, *Parting the Waters: America in the King Years, 1954–63* (New York: Simon & Schuster, 1988), 840.

4. Branch, *Parting the Waters*, 879; Randolph quoted in Andrew E. Kersten, *A. Philip Randolph: A Life in the Vanguard* (Lanham, MD: Rowman & Littlefield, 2007), 104.

5. A. Philip Randolph, "Address at the March on Washington," 28 August 1963, APR reel 33.

6. www.americanrhetoric.com/speeches/mlkihaveadream.htm. Accessed 20 August 2012.

7. Rustin's introduction to Daniel S. Davis, *Mr. Black Labor: The Story of A. Philip Randolph, Father of the Civil Rights Movement* (New York: E. P. Dutton, 1972), ix.

8. Rustin quoted in Jervis Anderson, *A. Philip Randolph: A Biographical Portrait* (New York: Harcourt Brace Jovanovich, 1973), 332.

9. *New York Times*, 18 May 1979.

10. *New York Times*, 18 May 1979.

11. Jacquelyn Dowd Hall, "The Long Civil Rights Movement and the Political Uses of the Past," *Journal of American History* 91 (March 2005): 1235.

Chapter 1: The Hour and the Man

1. Ralph Ellison, *Invisible Man* (1947; reprint, Vintage, 1972), 3.

2. Jervis Anderson, *A. Philip Randolph: A Biographical Portrait* (New York: Harcourt Brace Jovanovich, 1972), 21.

3. Richard Wright, *Native Son* (New York: Harper & Brothers, 1940), 17, 297, 333.

4. Wright, *Native Son*, 300, 18.

5. William P. Calhoun, *The Caucasian and the Negro in the United States* (Columbia, SC: R. L. Bryan, 1902), 141–42, 8, 21, 20.

6. Claude McKay, *Home to Harlem* (New York: Harper & Brothers, 1928), 14; Langston Hughes, *The Big Sea* (New York: Alfred A. Knopf, 1940), 81.

7. John B. Kennedy, "So This Is Harlem!" *Collier's* 92 (28 October 1933): 50.

8. Nat Brandt, *Harlem at War: The Black Experience in WWII* (Syracuse, NY: Syracuse University Press, 1996), 32, 42; Gilbert Osofsky, *Harlem: The Making of a Ghetto* (New York: Harper, 1966), 135.

9. Quoted in Brandt, *Harlem at War*, 37.

10. Quoted in Robert S. McElvaine, *The Great Depression: America, 1929–1941* (New York: Times Books, 1993), 187.

11. Quoted in Raymond Wolters, *Negroes and the Great Depression: The Problem of Economic Recovery* (Westport, CT: Greenwood, 1970), 145.

12. Conference quoted in Cheryl Lynn Greenberg, *To Ask for an Equal Chance: African Americans in the Great Depression* (Lanham, MD: Rowman & Littlefield, 2009), 53; Smith quoted in McElvaine, *The Great Depression*, 192–93.

13. Quoted in McElvaine, *The Great Depression*, 192.

14. Frank Freidel, *Franklin D. Roosevelt: A Rendezvous with Destiny* (Boston: Little, Brown, 1990), 244–5.

15. Howard W. Odum, *Race and Rumors of Race: Challenge to American Crisis* (Chapel Hill: University of North Carolina Press, 1943), 81.

16. *Richmond Times-Dispatch*, 23 November 1938.

17. *Washington Post*, 28 June 1941.

18. Stephen Early to Malvina Scheider, 5 August 1935, FDRL PSF b. 173, f. White, Walter.

19. Thomas Dyja, *Walter White: The Dilemma of Black Identity in America* (Chicago: Ivan R. Dee, 2008), 130–34.

20. Quoted in Roi Ottley, *New World a-Coming: Inside Black America* (Boston: Houghton Mifflin, 1943), 151.

21. Quoted in Ottley, *New World a-Coming*, 153.

22. Ottley, *New World a-Coming*, 220.

23. Quoted in Wil Haygood, *King of the Cats: The Life and Times of Adam Clayton Powell, Jr.* (Boston: Houghton Mifflin, 1993), 78.

24. Ottley, *New World a-Coming*, 115.

25. Quoted in Haygood, *King of the Cats*, 78.

26. "A. Philip Randolph," *American Labor* (August 1968): 47.

27. A. Philip Randolph, "Vita," [nd], APR reel 33.

28. A. Philip Randolph, "Vita," [nd], APR reel 33.

29. A. Philip Randolph, "Vita," [nd], APR reel 33.

30. Cynthia Taylor, *A. Philip Randolph: The Religious Journey of an African American Labor Leader* (New York: New York University Press, 2006), 31, 38.

31. W. E. B. DuBois, *The Souls of Black Folk*; reprinted in *Three Negro Classics* (New York: Avon, 1965), 209, 215.

32. Jervis Anderson, *A. Philip Randolph*, 60.

33. Jervis Anderson, *A. Philip Randolph*, 66.

34. *Messenger* 1 (November 1917): 1.

35. *Messenger* 1 (November 1917): 1.

36. Quoted in Anderson, *A. Philip Randolph*, 98, 83.

37. Quoted in Anderson, *A. Philip Randolph*, 107.
38. James B. Enos, "Threatening Letter and Human Hand," 16 September 1922, FBI; Anderson, *A. Philip Randolph*, 131–32.
39. George S. Schuyler, *Black and Conservative: The Autobiography of George S. Schuyler* (New Rochelle, NY: Arlington House, 1966), 144.
40. Anderson, *A. Philip Randolph*, 150.
41. Quoted in Anderson, *A. Philip Randolph*, 162.
42. Anderson, *A. Philip Randolph*, 177.
43. Daniel S. Davis, *Mr. Black Labor: The Story of A. Philip Randolph, Father of the Civil Rights Movement* (New York: E. P. Dutton, 1972), 66–68.
44. Quoted in Anderson, *A. Philip Randolph*, 215.
45. Quoted in Davis, *Mr. Black Labor*, 75.
46. Ottley, *New World a-Coming*, 248; Sissle quoted in Anderson, *A. Philip Randolph*, 190.
47. Quoted in Wolters, *Negroes and the Great Depression*, 356.
48. A. Philip Randolph, "The Crisis of the Negro and the Constitution," in *Official Proceedings, Second National Negro Congress, 1937*, reprinted in Francis L. Broderick and August Meier, eds., *Negro Protest Thought in the Twentieth Century* (Indianapolis, IN: Bobbs-Merrill, 1966), 183.

Chapter 2: We Want True Democracy

1. Franklin D. Roosevelt fireside chat, 3 September 1939, http://www.presidency.ucsb.edu/ws/index.php?pid=15801. Accessed 15 August 2012.
2. Franklin D. Roosevelt fireside chat on National Defense, 26 May 1940, in Samuel I. Rosenman, ed., *Public Papers and Addresses of Franklin D. Roosevelt* (New York: Russell & Russell, 1941), 9: 239; Franklin D. Roosevelt speech to Congress, 17 May 1940, Rosenman, ed., *Public Papers and Addresses of Franklin D. Roosevelt*, 9: 199, 200.
3. *New Leader*, 11 May 1940.
4. *Pittsburgh Courier*, 18 May 1940.
5. Karin L. Stanford, *If We Must Die: African American Voices on War and Peace* (Lanham, MD: Rowman & Littlefield, 2008), 2–4.
6. Michele Mitchell, *Righteous Propagation: African Americans and the Politics of Racial Destiny after Reconstruction* (Chapel Hill: University of North Carolina Press, 2004), 62.
7. Mitchell, *Righteous Propagation*, 69.
8. W. E. B. DuBois, "Close Ranks," *Crisis* 16 (July 1918): 62.

9. Richard M. Dalfiume, *Desegregation of the U.S. Armed Forces: Fighting on Two Fronts, 1939–1953* (Columbia: University of Missouri Press, 1969), 15; Sherie Mershon and Steven Schlossman, *Foxholes & Color Lines: Desegregating the U.S. Armed Forces* (Baltimore: The Johns Hopkins University Press, 1998), 6; Nat Brandt, *Harlem at War: The Black Experience in WWII* (Syracuse, NY: Syracuse University Press, 1996), 62.

10. W. E. B. DuBois, "The Black Soldier," *Crisis* 16 (June 1918): 60.

11. *Pittsburgh Courier*, 4 May 1940.

12. *Baltimore Afro-American*, 14 September 1940.

13. Quoted in Brandt, *Harlem at War*, 69.

14. Quoted in Bryan D. Booker, *African Americans in the United States Army in World War II* (Jefferson, NC: McFarland, 2008), 41.

15. Mershon and Schlossman, *Foxholes & Color Lines*, 65; *Pittsburgh Courier*, 5 October 1940.

16. John W. Jeffries, *Wartime America: The World War II Home Front* (Chicago: Ivan R. Dee, 1996), 107–8.

17. Address by Walter White, 23 June 1940, FDRL ER b. 731, f. White, Walter.

18. My reconstruction of this day is based on period photos of the White House; the president's daily schedule, available at the Franklin D. Roosevelt presidential library; William Doyle, *Inside the Oval Office: The White House Tapes from FDR to Clinton* (New York: Kodansha, 1999), ix–x, 6–22; and *Complete Presidential Press Conferences of Franklin D. Roosevelt* (New York: DaCapo, 1972).

19. Memorandum, 27 September 1940, FDRL ER b. 731, f. White, Walter.

20. *Pittsburgh Courier*, 28 September 1940; Eleanor Roosevelt quoted in Doris Kearns Goodwin, *No Ordinary Time: Franklin and Eleanor Roosevelt: The Home Front in World War II* (New York: Simon & Schuster, 1994), 167–68.

21. *New York Post*, 17 September 1940.

22. Brotherhood of Sleeping Car Porters Press Release, 13 October 1940, APR reel 5.

23. Alan Morrison, "Dean of Negro Leaders," *Ebony* 14 (November 1958): 104.

24. A. Philip Randolph, "The Battle for Britain," editorial published by the New York City chapter of the Committee to Defend America by Aiding the Allies [August 1940], in BSCP b. 5, f. Aug–Sept 14, 1940; *PM*, 19 September 1940.

25. A recording of this conference appears at www.whitehousetapes.net/clip/franklin-roosevelt-philip-randolph-walter-white-african-americans-and-us-military. Accessed 21 October 2011. Also see "Conference at the White House," 27 September 1940, FDRL ER b. 731, f. White, Walter; NAACP Press Release, 5 October 1940, FDRL OF 93 b. 3, f. Oct–Dec 1940.

26. Stimson quoted in Goodwin, *No Ordinary Time*, 169.

27. NAACP Press Release, 5 October 1940, FDRL OF 93 b. 3, f. Oct–Dec 1940.

28. Mr. Early's Press Conference, 9 October 1940, FDRL ER b. 731, f. White, Walter.

29. *Chicago Defender*, 19 October 1940; Walter White to David Niles, 10 October 1940, NAACP reel 25.

30. Walter White to Fiorello LaGuardia, 16 October 1940, NAACP reel 25.

31. Walter White to Stephen Early, 21 October 1940, FDRL OF 93 b. 3, f. Oct–Dec 1940; Franklin Roosevelt to Walter White, 25 October 1940, FDRL OF 93 b. 3, f. Oct–Dec 1940.

32. Statement from Franklin Roosevelt, 21 October 1940, FDRL OF 93 b. 3, f. Oct–Dec 1940.

33. Stimson quoted in Dalfiume, *Desegregation of the U.S. Armed Forces*, 42; Stimson quoted in Brandt, *Harlem at War*, 71.

34. A Negro Officer to Sloan, 28 December 1943, in Phillip McGuire, ed., *Taps for a Jim Crow Army: Letters from Black Soldiers in World War II* (Santa Barbara, CA: ABC-Clio, 1983), 47; Jefferson Jordan statement, in Mary Penick Motley, ed., *The Invisible Soldier: The Experience of the Black Soldier, World War II* (Detroit: Wayne State University Press, 1975), 280; Mr. and Mrs. Alexander Kish to Franklin Roosevelt, 25 October 1940, FDRL OF 93 b. 3, f. Oct–Dec 1940; A. P. Allen to Franklin Roosevelt, 25 October 1940, FDRL OF 93 b. 3, f. Oct–Dec 1940.

35. *Baltimore Afro-American*, 2 November 1940.

36. *Philadelphia Tribune*, 12 December 1940.

37. My reconstruction of these events is based primarily on Jervis Anderson, *A. Philip Randolph: A Biographical Portrait* (New York: Harcourt Brace Jovanovich, 1972), 247–48; Tom Brooks, "A. Philip Randolph: A Man for All Seasons" *Tuesday Magazine* 2 (November 1966): 6.

38. Anderson, *A. Philip Randolph*, 248.

39. Lucy G. Barber, *Marching on Washington: The Forging of an American Political Tradition* (Berkeley: University of California Press, 2002), 24, 43.

40. See *Pittsburgh Courier*, 25 January 1941 for this and the following paragraphs.
41. Roi Ottley, *New World a-Coming: Inside Black America* (Boston: Houghton Mifflin, 1943), 291.

Chapter 3: One Hundred Thousand, Mister President
 1. A. Philip Randolph, "Should Negroes March on Washington?" [nd, 1941], APR reel 30.
 2. Nat Brandt, *Harlem at War: The Black Experience in WWII* (Syracuse, NY: Syracuse University Press, 1996), 58.
 3. Malcolm X, *The Autobiography of Malcolm X* (New York: Grove, 1964), 72.
 4. Randolph, "Should Negroes March on Washington?".
 5. *Washington Afro-American*, 1 March 1941; *Chicago Defender*, 18 January 1941.
 6. Walter White to Lowell Mellett, 11 March 1941, NAACP reel 24; *Philadelphia Tribune*, 2 January 1941; *New York Amsterdam News*, 18 January 1941.
 7. *Chicago Defender*, 1 February 1941.
 8. *Washington Afro-American*, 22 February 1941.
 9. *Chicago Defender*, 8 March, 1 February 1941.
 10. A. Philip Randolph, "Let the Negro Masses Speak!" *Black Worker* 7 (March 1941): 4–6, 26.
 11. *Washington Afro-American*, 15 March 1941.
 12. A. Philip Randolph to Walter White, 18 March 1941, NAACP reel 23; Walter White to C. A. Franklin, 21 March 1941, NAACP reel 22.
 13. Roy Wilkins and Tom Matthews, *Standing Fast: The Autobiography of Roy Wilkins* (New York: Viking, 1982), 180; NAACP HQ to all branches, 12 May 1941, NAACP reel 22; Minutes of Subcommittee Hearing, 10 April 1941, NAACP reel 22.
 14. Walter White to A. Philip Randolph, 9 May 1941, NAACP reel 23.
 15. *Pittsburgh Courier*, 5 April 1941.
 16. *Baltimore Afro-American*, 26 April 1941; *Chicago Defender*, 19 April 1941; *Pittsburgh Courier*, 17 May 1941.
 17. *Baltimore Afro-American*, 12 April 1941.
 18. A. Philip Randolph, "Call to Negro America" [May 1941], APR reel 34.
 19. Memorandum, [1941], APR reel 22.
 20. *Pittsburgh Courier*, 14 June 1941.
 21. A. Philip Randolph to William Knudsen, 3 June 1941, FDRL OF 391; William Collins to Stephen Early, 5 June 1941, FDRL OF 391.

22. Robert Patterson to Edwin Watson, 3 June 1941, FDRL OF 391.

23. Franklin Roosevelt to Marvin McIntyre, 7 June 1941, FDRL OF 93 b. 4, f. June–July 1941.

24. Eleanor Roosevelt to A. Philip Randolph, 10 June 1941, FDRL ER b. 748, f. Randolph, A. Philip.

25. Joseph P. Lash, *Eleanor and Franklin: The Story of Their Relationship, Based on Eleanor Roosevelt's Private Papers* (New York: W. W. Norton, 1971), 534.

26. My reconstruction of this conversation is based on "A. Philip Randolph," *American Labor* (August 1968): 53; Tom Brooke, "A. Philip Randolph: A Man for All Seasons," *Tuesday Magazine* 2 (November 1966): 7; *New York Amsterdam Star-News*, 21 June 1941.

27. *New York Amsterdam Star-News*, 28 June 1941.

28. *Washington Afro-American*, 7 June 1941.

29. White House Press Release, 14 June 1941, FDRL OF 93 b. 4, f. June–July 1941.

30. Mr. Early's Press Conference, 14 June 1941, FDRL Early b. 40, f. Jan–June 1941.

31. Minutes of Meeting, Local MOWC, 14 June 1941, NAACP reel 22.

32. Albert Parker, "The Negro March on Washington," *Fourth International* 2 (June 1941): 156.

33. *Baltimore Afro-American*, 21 June 1941.

34. Mr. Early's Press Conference, 18 June 1941, FDRL Early b. 40, f. Jan–June 1941.

35. *Washington Post*, 17, 18 June 1941.

36. A. Philip Randolph to Eleanor Roosevelt, 16 June 1941, FDRL OF 391; Robert Patterson to Edwin Watson, 3 June 1941, FDRL OF 391; Lash, *Eleanor and Franklin*, 533–34.

37. My reconstruction of this conversation is based on A. Philip Randolph, "Employment in Defense Industries," 25 June 1941, APR reel 28; *Pittsburgh Courier*, 28 June 1941; Allan Morrison, "Dean of Negro Leaders," *Ebony* 14 (November 1958): 106; Lerone Bennett, Jr., "The Day They Didn't March," *Ebony* 32 (February 1977): 135–36; Jervis Anderson, *A. Philip Randolph: A Biographical Portrait* (New York: Harcourt Brace Jovanovich, 1973), 256–58; Walter White, *A Man Called White* (New York: Arno Press, 1969), 190–92; and Franklin Roosevelt's Daily Schedule, Franklin D. Roosevelt Presidential Library.

38. Stimson quoted in Brandt, *Harlem at War*, 79; A. Philip Randolph, "Employment in Defense Industries," 25 June 1941, APR reel 28.

39. *Washington Post*, 19 June 1941; *New York Amsterdam Star-News*, 21 June 1941.
40. Bennett, "The Day They Didn't March": 136.
41. Studs Terkel, *The Good War: An Oral History of World War Two* (New York: Pantheon, 1984), 337–38.
42. Robert Patterson and James Forrestal to Franklin Roosevelt, 24 June 1941, FDRL OF 93 b. 4, f. June–July 1941.
43. "Memorandum for the files," 24 June 1941, FDRL OF 4245g b. 3, f. FEPC 1941.
44. A. Philip Randolph to Eleanor Roosevelt, 24 June 1941, FDRL ER b. 748, f. Randolph, A. Philip.
45. *Washington Evening Star*, 26 June 1941.
46. A. Philip Randolph, "Employment in Defense Industries."
47. *Pittsburgh Courier*, 19 July 1941; *Philadelphia Tribune*, 10 July 1941; *New York Amsterdam Star-News*, 5 July 1941; *Washington Afro-American*, 28 June 1941.
48. *New York Amsterdam Star-News*, 12 July 1941.
49. *New York Amsterdam Star-News*, 5 July 1941; Morrison, "Dean of Negro Leaders": 108.

Chapter 4: No Place to Put You

1. *Pittsburgh Courier*, 5, 26 July, 2 August 1941.
2. *Baltimore Afro-American*, 16 August 1941; A. Philip Randolph to Hope Williams, 18 July 1941, APR reel 20.
3. *Baltimore Afro-American*, 16 August 1941.
4. A. Philip Randolph to Bennie Smith, 15 October 1942, APR reel 20.
5. *Pittsburgh Courier*, 13 September 1941; National Negro March-on-Washington Committee, "Report to the Nation," 28 September 1941, BSCP; *New York Amsterdam Star-News*, 13 September 1941.
6. R. J. Simmons to Walter White, 29 June 1941, NAACP reel 22.
7. Harvard Sitkoff, *A New Deal for Blacks: The Emergence of Civil Rights as a National Issue, Vol. 1: The Depression Decade* (New York: Oxford, 1978), 322.
8. A. Philip Randolph to Franklin Roosevelt, 22 July 1941, FDRL OF 4245g OPM b.3, f. FEPC 1941; Mr. Early's Press Conference, 19 July 1941, FDRL Early b. 41, f. July–Dec 1941; Mr. Early's Press Conference, 27 August 1941, FDRL Early b. 41, f. July–Dec 1941.
9. Mark Ethridge to Stephen Early, 20 August 1941, FDRL OF 93 b. 4, f. Aug–Dec 1941.

10. *New York Amsterdam Star-News,* 25 October 1941; *Baltimore Afro-American,* 22 November 1941.
11. J. Edgar Hoover to L. W. C. Smith, 1 December 1941, FBI; Malcolm X, *The Autobiography of Malcolm X* (New York: Grove, 1964), 71.
12. *New York Age,* 20 December 1941.
13. *Pittsburgh Courier,* 31 January 1942.
14. *Baltimore Afro-American,* 20 December 1941.
15. Chester Himes, *If He Hollers Let Him Go* (1945; reprint, Chatham, NJ: Chatham Bookseller, 1973), 3; *Washington Afro-American,* 28 March 1942; Holcomb quoted in Sherie Mershon and Steven Schlossman, *Foxholes & Color Lines: Desegregating the U.S. Armed Forces* (Baltimore: The Johns Hopkins University Press, 1998), 47.
16. *Pittsburgh Courier,* 18 April 1942; *New York Amsterdam Star-News,* 10 January 1942.
17. *Chicago Defender,* 13 December 1941; *New York Amsterdam Star-News,* 17 January 1942.
18. *Chicago Defender,* 4 July 1942; *Philadelphia Tribune,* 6 June 1942; Davis quoted in Nat Brandt, *Harlem at War: The Black Experience in WWII* (Syracuse, NY: Syracuse University Press, 1996), 174; *Washington Afro-American,* 24 January 1942.
19. Robert A. Hill, ed., *The FBI's RACON: Racial Conditions in the United States During World War II* (Boston: Northeastern University Press, 1995), 9.
20. Quoted in Richard M. Dalfiume, *Desegregation of the U.S. Armed Forces: Fighting on Two Fronts, 1939–1953* (Columbia: University of Missouri Press, 1969), 59.
21. Dalfiume, *Desegregation of the U.S. Armed Forces,* 54, 55, 60–61.
22. *Philadelphia Tribune,* 11 April 1942. For his bravery at Pearl Harbor, Dorie Miller became the first African American to receive the Navy Cross. The Navy promoted him to Mess Attendant First Class. He died at the Battle of Tarawa in 1943.
23. *Pittsburgh Courier,* 18 April 1942; *New York Amsterdam Star-News,* 11 April 1942.
24. Address by Eugene Davidson to the Non-Sectarian Anti-Nazi League, 1 March 1942, FDRL OF 4245g OPM b. 3, f. FEPC; pamphlet quoted in Robert C. Weaver, *Negro Labor: A National Problem* (New York: Harcourt, Brace and Company, 1946), 16.
25. *Washington Afro-American,* 25 July 1942.
26. *New York Amsterdam Star-News,* 11 April 1942.

27. Randolph quoted in Herbert Garfinkel, *When Negroes March: The March on Washington Movement in the Organizational Politics for FEPC* (Glencoe, IL: Free Press, 1959), 85.

28. *New York Amsterdam Star-News*, 18 April 1942; MOWM Flyer [1942], APR reel 20; MOWM Flyer [1942], APR reel 22.

29. *Pittsburgh Courier*, 6 June 1942.

30. Garfinkel, *When Negroes March*, 93–94.

31. *New York Amsterdam Star-News*, 20 June 1942.

32. *New York Amsterdam Star-News*, 27 June 1942.

33. Waller died in the electric chair a few days later. See Richard B. Sherman, *The Case of Odell Waller and Virginia Justice, 1940–1942* (Knoxville: University of Tennessee Press, 1992).

34. *New York Amsterdam Star-News*, 20 June, 4 July 1942.

35. Milton P. Webster to A. Philip Randolph, 10 April 1942, APR reel 8.

36. "Wake Up Negro America" [flyer], [June 1942], APR reel 20.

37. "A. Philip Randolph address to MOWM, Chicago Coliseum," 26 June 1942, APR reel 28.

38. *Pittsburgh Courier*, 27 June 1942; *New York Amsterdam Star-News*, 1 August 1942.

39. Eardlie John to A. Philip Randolph, 1 August 1942, APR reel 20.

40. Roy Wilkins to Walter White, 24 June 1942, NAACP reel 23.

41. *Los Angeles Tribune*, 20 July 1942.

42. A. Philip Randolph to Walter White, 7 April 1942, NAACP reel 23.

43. "Proceedings of a Conference Held in Detroit," [September 1942], NAACP reel 23.

44. *St. Louis Post-Dispatch*, 29 August 1942; "Pamphlet Passed Out to the Public at March on Bell Telephone Co.," 12 June 1943, BSCP, Saint Louis Division Scrapbook, 1942–1944.

45. *St. Louis American*, 20 January 1944; "Announcement at Leading Churches," 6 June 1943, BSCP, Saint Louis Division Scrapbook, 1942–1944.

46. Eugenie Settles to A. Philip Randolph, 10 November 1942, APR reel 7.

Chapter 5: An Hour of Crisis

1. Roi Ottley, *New World a-Coming: Inside Black America* (Boston: Houghton Mifflin, 1943), 307; Malcolm X, *The Autobiography of Malcolm X* (New York: Grove, 1964), 105–6.

2. For this and the following paragraphs, see Milton Starr, "Report on Negro Morale," [Fall 1942], Nash b. 20, f. Minorities—Negro—Negro Morale.

3. Quoted in Jody Rosen, *White Christmas: The Story of an American Song* (New York: Scribner, 2002), 138.

4. Quoted in Rosen, *White Christmas*, 149–50.

5. Office of War Information, "Government Information Manual for the Motion Picture Industry," [1942], 1:7, 6, http://www.libraries.iub.edu/index.php?pageId=3301. Accessed 3 September 2012.

6. Clayton R. Koppes and Gregory D. Black, *Hollywood Goes to War: How Politics, Profits and Propaganda Shaped World War II Movies* (Berkeley: University of California Press, 1990), 84–90.

7. Quoted in Koppes and Black, *Hollywood Goes to War*, 88.

8. Office of War Information, "Negro Opinion Study," January 1943, Nash b. 20, f. Minorities-Negro-Negro Opinion Study.

9. Office of War Information, "Certain Characteristics of the Negro which Affect Command of Negro Troops," [1944], Papers of Philleo Nash, White House File b. 55, f. Minorities—Negro—Publications—Army Service Forces Manual no. 5, Harry S. Truman Presidential Library, Independence, Missouri.

10. *Pittsburgh Courier*, 13 September 1941.

11. *New York Amsterdam Star-News*, 14 March 1942; *Washington Afro-American*, 13 December 1941.

12. Mark Ethridge to Stephen Early, 23 December 1941, FDRL OF 4245g OPM b. 3, f. FEPC.

13. *Chicago Defender*, 14 March 1942.

14. *Gadsden (AL) Times*, 16 June 1942; Studs Terkel, *"The Good War": An Oral History of World War Two* (New York: Pantheon, 1984), 340; Merl E. Reed, *Seedtime for the Modern Civil Rights Movement: The President's Committee on Fair Employment Practice, 1941–1946* (Baton Rouge: Louisiana State University Press, 1991), 67.

15. *Louisville Courier-Journal*, 21 June 1942.

16. Mark Ethridge to Stephen Early, 22 June 1942, FDRL OF 4245g OPM b. 3, f. FEPC; Marvin McIntyre to Stephen Early, 26 June 1942, FDRL OF 4245g OPM b. 3, f. FEPC.

17. *Birmingham Age-Herald*, 24 June 1942; *Richmond Times-Dispatch*, 23 June 1942; *New York Amsterdam Star-News*, 11 July 1942; *Pittsburgh Courier*, 15 August 1942.

18. *Chicago Defender*, 25 July 1942.

19. E. G. Trimble to Lawrence Cramer, [1942], FDRL OF 4245g OPM b. 3, f. FEPC Jan–April 1943.

20. Sumner Welles to Franklin Roosevelt, 20 June 1942, FDRL OF 4245g OPM b. 3, f. FEPC.

21. *Chicago Defender,* 15 August 1942; Milton Webster to A. Philip Randolph, 25 August 1942, APR reel 8.
22. Franklin Roosevelt to Marvin McIntyre, 8 August 1942, FDRL OF 4245g OPM b. 3, f. FEPC Jan–July 1942; FDR Press Conference, 7 August 1942, in Jonathan Daniels, ed., *Complete Presidential Press Conferences of Franklin D. Roosevelt* (New York: DaCapo, 1972), 20:47.
23. A. Philip Randolph to Walter White, 5 August 1942, NAACP reel 11; A. Philip Randolph to Franklin Roosevelt, 5 August 1942, APR reel 14; *Pittsburgh Courier,* 15 August 1942.
24. *Washington Afro-American,* 5 September 1942.
25. *Pittsburgh Courier,* 3 October 1942; Webster quoted in Reed, *Seedtime for the Modern Civil Rights Movement,* 81; Dickerson quoted in Reed, *Seedtime for the Modern Civil Rights Movement,* 83.
26. *PM,* 22 January 1943.
27. Workers' Defense League Press Release, 18 January 1943, BSCP, Saint Louis Division Scrapbook, 1942–1944; BSCP Press Release, 12 January 1943, APR reel 22; MOWM St. Louis Chapter, "Memo to all local organizations," 14 January 1943, BSCP, Saint Louis Division Scrapbook, 1942–1944.
28. Verbatim Transcript, "Conference on Scope and Powers of FEPC," 19 February 1943, APR reel 14.
29. MOWM Press Release, 23 February 1943, BSCP, Saint Louis Division Scrapbook, 1942–1944.
30. Howard W. Odum, *Race and Rumors of Race: Challenge the American Crisis* (Chapel Hill: University of North Carolina Press, 1943), 68.
31. Philleo Nash to R. Keith Kane, 23 December 1942, Nash b. 22, f. Minorities—Negro—Negro Opinion Studies—Project Development.
32. Roy Wilkins and Tom Matthews, *Standing Fast: The Autobiography of Roy Wilkins* (New York: Viking, 1982), 182; Robert A. Hill, ed., *The FBI's RACON: Racial Conditions in the United States During World War II* (Boston: Northeastern University Press, 1996), 143.
33. "The Detroit Race Riot," 6 July 1943, Nash b. 29, f. Race Tension-States-Michigan, Detroit; Richard Deverall to Clarence Glick, 28 June 1943, Nash b. 29, f. Race Tension-States-Michigan, Detroit.
34. "The Detroit Race Riot," 6 July 1943, Nash b. 29, f. Race Tension-States-Michigan, Detroit.
35. Biddle quoted in Nat Brandt, *Harlem at War: The Black Experience in WWII* (Syracuse, NY: Syracuse University Press, 1996), 151; Stimson quoted in Richard M. Dalfiume, *Desegregation of the U.S. Armed Forces: Fighting on Two Fronts, 1939–1953* (Columbia: University of Missouri

Press, 1969), 131; Rankin quoted in Herbert Garfinkel, *When Negroes March: The March on Washington Movement in the Organizational Politics for FEPC* (Glencoe, IL: Free Press, 1959), 144.

36. Quoted in Brandt, *Harlem at War*, 6.
37. Poitier quoted in Aram Goudsouzian, *Sidney Poitier: Man, Actor, Icon* (Chapel Hill: University of North Carolina Press, 2004), 38.
38. Quoted in Malcolm X, *The Autobiography of Malcolm X*, 114.
39. Office of War Information Research Division, "The Harlem Race Riot," 21 August 1943, FDRL OF 4245g OPM b. 6, f. FEPC Harlem; Brandt, *Harlem at War*, 217–18.
40. Roosevelt quoted in Brandt, *Harlem at War*, 215; *New York Amsterdam Star-News*, 6 November 1943.
41. A. Philip Randolph to Reverend S. T. Eldridge, 21 January 1943, APR reel 20.

Chapter 6: Bad and Getting Worse

1. Thurgood Marshall to Leslie Perry, 14 October 1943, NAACP reel 23.
2. *Pittsburgh Courier*, 2 January 1943; "Bank Accounts of the March on Washington Movement," 11 September 1943, APR reel 21; A. Philip Randolph to William J. Bell, 22 January 1943, APR reel 20.
3. Dwight MacDonald, "Two Outsiders Look at the MOW," 20 June 1943, APR reel 20.
4. A. Philip Randolph to Dwight MacDonald, 20 July 1943, APR reel 20.
5. MOWM, "Call to 'We Are Americans Too Conference,'" [December 1942], APR reel 21.
6. MOWM Press Release, 24 December 1942, APR reel 22; *Kansas City Call*, 5 March 1943.
7. *PM*, 4 January 1943; *Pittsburgh Courier*, 23 January 1943.
8. A. Philip Randolph, "Randolph Answers Critics of MOWM," [May 1943?], APR reel 30.
9. "Extract from the Minutes of the Board," 8 February 1943, APR reel 21.
10. Roy Wilkins to Walter White, 7 July 1943, NAACP reel 23.
11. *Chicago Sun*, 5 July 1943.
12. *Kansas City Call*, 16 July 1943; *Chicago Defender*, 17 July 1943.
13. "March on Washington Movement Balance Sheet," 31 December 1944, APR reel 21; *The People's Voice*, 27 November 1943.
14. A. Philip Randolph to Paula Pfeffer, 13 July 1973, APR reel 33.
15. "Proceedings of the 'Save the FEPC Conference,'" 5 February 1943, APR reel 14.

16. A. Philip Randolph to Thurgood Marshall, 27 March 1943, NAACP reel 22.

17. "Memorandum for the President," 2 March 1943, FDRL OF 4245g OPM b. 3, f. FEPC Jan–April 1943; James Byrnes to Franklin Roosevelt, 15 March 1943, FDRL OF 4245g OPM b. 3, f. FEPC Jan–April 1943.

18. Jonathan Daniels to Marvin McIntyre, 26 January 1943, FDRL OF 4245g OPM b. 3, f. FEPC Jan–April 1943; *New York Times*, 29 May 1943.

19. Francis J. Haas, *Catholics, Race, and Labor* (New York: Paulist Press, 1947), 8. The citation comes from Galatians 3:28.

20. A. Philip Randolph to Halena Wilson, 17 December 1943, BSCP b. 6, f. Sept–Dec 1943; *Pittsburgh Courier*, 25 December 1943.

21. In late 1944 the Supreme Court upheld the FEPC's finding that the railroads' hiring and promotion practices were unconstitutional.

22. Eleanor Roosevelt to A. Philip Randolph, 24 November 1943, FDRL ER b. 790, f. Randolph, A. Philip.

23. Webster quoted in Haas, *Catholics, Race, and Law*, 19.

24. "Speech of John Rankin in the House of Representatives," 26 May 1944, APR reel 17; Bilbo and Eastland quoted in Merl E. Reed, *Seedtime for the Modern Civil Rights Movement: The President's Committee on Fair Employment Practices, 1941–1946* (Baton Rouge: Louisiana State University Press, 1991), 160.

25. Balance Sheet, [February 1944], APR reel 16.

26. Reed, *Seedtime for the Modern Civil Rights Movement*, 162.

27. Roosevelt quoted in Reed, *Seedtime for the Modern Civil Rights Movement*, 164.

28. *Pittsburgh Courier*, 4 November 1944.

29. *Pittsburgh Courier*, 10 July 1943. Hall became the first African American to earn the Distinguished Flying Cross. After the war he applied for pilot jobs with commercial airlines. None would hire him. He eventually found work managing a restaurant.

30. Studs Terkel, *"The Good War": An Oral History of World War Two* (New York: Pantheon, 1984), 370; "A disgusted Negro trooper to *Cleveland Call and Post*," 16 August 1944, in Phillip McGuire, *Taps for a Jim Crow Army: Letters from Black Soldiers in World War II* (Santa Barbara, CA: ABC-Clio, 1983), 197.

31. Quoted in Nat Brandt, *Harlem at War: The Black Experience in WWII* (Syracuse, NY: Syracuse University Press, 1996), 104.

32. NAACP mass mailing, [1943], APR reel 20.

33. Terkel, "*The Good War,*" 152.

34. Terkel, "*The Good War,*" 152–53.

35. Terkel, "*The Good War,*" 151.

36. MOWM Press Release, 8 September 1943, APR reel 22.

37. MOWM, "The War's Greatest Scandal: The Story of Jim Crow in Uniform," [1943], APR reel 13.

38. Jervis Anderson, *A. Philip Randolph: A Biographical Portrait* (New York: Harcourt Brace Jovanovich, 1972), 280–81. Lynn's suit wound its way to the Supreme Court, which in 1945 refused to hear his case, thereby accepting a lower court's decision that segregation did not necessarily constitute discrimination.

39. OWI, "The Negro Problem and Radio," [June 1944], Nash b. 22, f. Minorities—Negro—Negro Problems and Enemy Broadcasts.

40. *Pittsburgh Courier,* 26 February 1944; Joseph McBride, *Frank Capra: The Catastrophe of Success* (New York: Simon & Schuster, 1992), 494.

41. Clarence Lovejoy to Josephus Daniels, 11 April 1944, FDRL OF 4245g OPM b. 9, f. FEPC Minority–March 1944; United States Army, "Leadership and the Negro Soldier," October 1944: 33.

42. Memorandum for the Commanding General, Army Service Forces, 17 April 1944, FDRL OF 4245g OPM b. 9, f. FEPC Minority, March 1944.

43. Stimson quoted in Richard M. Dalfiume, *Desegregation of the U.S. Armed Forces: Fighting on Two Fronts, 1939–1953* (Columbia: University of Missouri Press, 1969), 94.

44. *Pittsburgh Courier,* 27 May 1944.

45. Dalfiume, *Desegregation of the U.S. Armed Forces,* 99–100.

46. Patton quoted in Terkel, "*The Good War,*" 266.

47. *Pittsburgh Courier,* 4 March 1944.

48. Arnold Rampersad, *Jackie Robinson: A Biography* (New York: Knopf, 1997), 105, 107, 109.

49. *Chicago Defender,* 30 December 1944.

Chapter 7: Let Us Win Another Victory

1. Doris Kearns Goodwin, *No Ordinary Time: Franklin & Eleanor Roosevelt: The Home Front in World War II* (New York: Simon & Schuster, 1994), 598.

2. Goodwin, *No Ordinary Time,* 598–603.

3. *Pittsburgh Courier,* 21 April 1945; www.examiner.com/article/farewell-to-a-president-old-time-listening-14-15-april. Accessed 28 May 2012.

4. www.examiner.com/article/farewell-to-a-president-old-time-listening-14-15-april. Accessed 28 May 2012.

5. Quoted in *Chicago Defender*, 14 April 1945.

6. Allan Morrison, "A. Philip Randolph: Dean of Negro Leaders," *Ebony* 14 (November 1958): 108.

7. Goodwin, *No Ordinary Time*, 604.

8. Truman quoted in David McCullough, *Truman* (New York: Simon & Schuster, 1992), 247.

9. Harry Truman to Rudolph Schwenger, 16 December 1942, Harry S. Truman Papers, Papers as U.S. Senator and Vice President b. 161, Harry S. Truman Presidential Library, Independence, Missouri.

10. *Pittsburgh Courier*, 5 August 1944.

11. *Chicago Defender*, 2 December 1945.

12. *Chicago Defender*, 24 February 1945.

13. *Chicago Defender*, 25 August 1945.

14. *Chicago Defender*, 8 September 1945.

15. *New York Amsterdam Star-News*, 6 October 1945.

16. *Baltimore Afro-American*, 3 November 1945; *New York World-Telegram*, 2 November 1945.

17. Unnamed woman quoted in Adam Clayton Powell, Jr., *Marching Blacks: An Interpretive History of the Rise of the Black Common Man* (New York: Dial, 1945), 7; Unnamed personnel request quoted in Merl E. Reed, *Seedtime for the Modern Civil Rights Movement: The President's Committee on Fair Employment Practice, 1941–1946* (Baton Rouge: Louisiana State University Press, 1991), 330.

18. Quoted in Richard M. Dalfiume, *Desegregation of the U.S. Armed Forces: Fighting on Two Fronts, 1939–1953* (Columbia: University of Missouri Press, 1969), 133.

19. "Report of Proceedings of the Fourth Biennial Convention of the BSCP, 17–22 September, 1944," [1944], 40, BSCP b. 105, f. 1944.

20. National Council for a Permanent FEPC Press Release, 18 October 1945, Nash b. 22, f. National Council for a Permanent FEPC.

21. *Atlanta Daily World*, 26 October 1945.

22. *Washington Post*, 17 January 1946.

23. *Washington Post*, 6 February 1946; *Washington Times-Herald*, 29 January 1946.

24. Quoted in Reed, *Seedtime for the Modern Civil Rights Movement*, 342.

25. A. Philip Randolph, "Address at Madison Square Garden Rally," 28 February 1946, APR reel 28.

26. Reed, *Seedtime for the Modern Civil Rights Movement*, 345–57.

27. A. Philip Randolph, "FEPC—Present and Future," [1948], APR reel 30.

28. A. Philip Randolph to J. B. Martin, 8 July 1947, APR reel 15.

29. Truman quoted in Dalfiume, *Desegregation of the U.S. Armed Forces*, 138.

30. *New York Herald-Tribune*, 16 January 1947.

31. *New York Times*, 30 October 1947; *Baltimore Sun*, 29 October 1947.

32. Sherie Mershon and Steven Schlossman, *Foxholes and Color Lines: Desegregating the U.S. Armed Forces* (Baltimore: The Johns Hopkins University Press, 1998), 156; Bradley quoted in Dalfiume, *Desegregation of the U.S. Armed Forces*, 162.

33. Committee Against Jim Crow in Military Service and Training Press Release, 23 November 1947, APR reel 12.

34. David Niles to Matthew Connally, 20 January 1948, Student Research File, Desegregation of the Armed Forces b. 1, f. 1, Harry S. Truman Presidential Library, Independence, Missouri.

35. Harry S. Truman, Special Message on Civil Rights, White House Press Release, 2 February 1948, President's Secretary's File: Historical File, f. Civil Rights-FEPC, Harry S. Truman Presidential Library, Independence, Missouri.

36. *Canton (OH) Repository*, 3 February 1948; *Jackson (MS) Daily News*, 3 February 1948; *Pittsburgh Courier*, 15 May 1948.

37. A. Philip Randolph interview with John Slawson, 20 April 1970, APR reel 33; Allan Morrison, "Dean of Negro Leaders," *Ebony* 14 (November 1958): 110.

38. "Testimony of A. Philip Randolph before the Senate Armed Services Committee," 31 March 1948, APR reel 12; *Congressional Record*, 80th Congress, 2nd Session, Senate, 12 April 1948, 4416–18.

39. Rankin quoted in T. Vincent Quinn to J. Edgar Hoover, 19 May 1948, FBI.

40. Quoted in Daniel S. Davis, *Mr. Black Labor: The Story of A. Philip Randolph, Father of the Civil Rights Movement* (New York: E. P. Dutton, 1972), 129.

41. Executive Order 9981, 26 July 1948, http://www.trumanlibrary.org/9981a.htm. Accessed 15 March 2012.

42. Randolph quoted in Dalfiume, *Desegregation of the U.S. Armed Forces*, 173; Randolph quoted in Paula Pfeffer, *A. Philip Randolph: Pioneer of the Civil Rights Movement* (Baton Rouge: Louisiana State University Press, 1990), 148.

43. Phyl Garland, "A. Philip Randolph: Labor's Grand Old Man," *Ebony* 24 (May 1969): 34.

44. "Statement by Grant Reynolds and A. Philip Randolph," 11 October 1948, APR reel 12.

45. Quoted in Dalfiume, *Desegregation of the U.S. Armed Forces*, 199; Mershon and Schlossman, *Foxholes & Color Lines*, 179, 184, 177.

46. Mershon and Schlossman, *Foxholes & Color Lines*, 224.

47. Mershon and Schlossman, *Foxholes & Color Lines*, 225–26.

Conclusion

1. *New York Times*, 18 May 1979.

2. Allan Morrison, "Dean of Negro Leaders," *Ebony* 14 (November 1958): 114.

3. "Convention Roars Welcome," *Steel Labor* 31 (October 1966): 2; *New York Times*, 14 October 1966.

4. Phyl Garland, "A. Philip Randolph: Labor's Grand Old Man," *Ebony* 24 (May 1969): 31; Charles Kenyatta Revolutionary Center Flyer [1968?], APR reel 33.

5. Garland, "A. Philip Randolph," 36.

6. *Congressional Record*, 91st Cong., 1st sess., 1969: 11436.

7. Quoted in Daniel S. Davis, *Mr. Black Labor: The Story of A. Philip Randolph, Father of the Civil Rights Movement* (New York: E. P. Dutton, 1972), 162–63.

INDEX

....

Page numbers in italics refer to figures.